C000321297

TO LOVE, HONOUR AND BETRAY

Also by Zelda West-Meads

The Trouble With You

To Love, Honour and Betray

Affairs and How to Survive Them

Zelda West-Meads

Hodder & Stoughton

Case Histories
All case histories in this book are based on real people.
However, all names and distinguishing details
have been changed so that the couples are unrecognisable.

Copyright © Zelda West-Meads 1997

The right of Zelda West-Meads to be identified as the Author
of the Work has been asserted by her in accordance with the
Copyright, Designs and Patents Act 1988.

First published in Great Britain in 1997
by Hodder & Stoughton
A division of Hodder Headline PLC

10 9 8 7 6 5 4 3 2 1

British Library Cataloguing in Publication Data

West-Meads, Zelda
To love, honour & betray
1. Man-woman relationships
I. Title
307.7

ISBN 0 340 65403 1

Typeset by Hewer Text Composition Services, Edinburgh
Printed and bound in Great Britain by
Cox & Wyman Ltd, Reading

Hodder and Stoughton Ltd
A Division of Hodder Headline PLC
338 Euston Road
London NW1 3BH

For my Mother

ACKNOWLEDGEMENTS

My grateful thanks go to the many men and women who agreed to be interviewed for this book, who bravely talked about their experiences, the good times and also the very painful ones. Also the many people I have counselled over the years who have helped me gain insight and understanding about why people have affairs and the effects they have on their lives.

I would like to thank my husband and my children, Tim and Caroline, for their loving support, and their belief in me. To my mother for all her love and encouragement. Also thank you to my father. To Sarah Litvinoff for her invaluable advice and friendship. To my many friends who are wonderfully encouraging and supportive: Alastair and Messie Stuart Henderson, Catherine Mack Smith, Harriet and John Cullis, Bill Carver, Martin and Ann Vessy, Louise Davies, Patricia and Sidde Shirman, Peter Gavan and to Charlie Crowther Smith who continues to sort out my computer when things go wrong. Also Diana Chilcott, Jo Young and everyone else at Elmbridge Relate. Finally, my thanks to Rowena Webb, my editor, whose enthusiasm, advice and judgement I deeply appreciate.

CONTENTS

Chapter One

FROM BETROTHAL TO BETRAYAL

> *Julia had honour, virtue, truth, and love*
> *For Don Alfonso, and she only swore*
> *By all the vows below to powers above,*
> *She never would disgrace the ring she wore*
> *Nor leave a wish which wisdom might reprove.*
> *And while she pondered this, besides much more,*
> *One hand on Juan's carelessly was thrown,*
> *Quite by mistake – she thought it was her own . . .*
>
> *And Julia's voice was lost, except in sighs,*
> *Until too late for useful conversation.*
> *The tears were gushing from her gentle eyes;*
> *I wish indeed they had not had occasion,*
> *But who, alas, can love and then be wise?*
> *Not that remorse did not oppose temptation;*
> *A little still she strove and much repented,*
> *And whispering, 'I will ne'er consent' – consented.*

> Lord Byron, *Don Juan*

When Rosie was eight years old, her father invited his mistress to stay for the weekend. Emma was tall, willowy and very blonde. Children sense when an adult is being nice to them just to make an impression with their parents, rather than because they like them, and Rosie instinctively knew Emma fell into this category. Rosie said, 'She used to give me lots of attention when my father was around, but the rest of the time she just ignored me. I remember very clearly that I didn't like her much.' Rosie's feelings were later confirmed when she heard her parents arguing about Emma. 'How could you bring her here,' sobbed her mother through her tears, 'it's obvious she's your mistress.' 'Oh, don't be so stupid,' her father replied crossly. Rosie said, 'I was too young to understand why my mother minded him inviting a girlfriend for the weekend, but what I did know was that it was hurting my mother.'

She remembered a particularly painful day: 'We lived in Surrey surrounded by wild rhododendrons and tall pine trees. I had been telling Emma how I loved to climb right up to the top of the fir trees. "Oh," she replied, "I'm terrified of heights. I would die of fright at the thought of climbing so high." That afternoon my father, mother, Emma and I went for a walk. I ran ahead as fast as I could and climbed up one of the tallest trees I could find. I waited silently for Emma and my parents to approach. Just as they reached the tree, I called to them all, shouting and waving, "Hello, look at me!" Much to my distress, nothing happened. I remember Emma stood looking at me in horror, but that was all. She did not die of fright, she didn't even fall over or faint with shock. She was still very much alive. I don't think I believed I could really frighten her to death, but I knew I wanted to hurt her. I knew I longed for her to leave and go far away because she was hurting my mother and causing arguments between my parents.'

For Rosie it was an early introduction to how much hurt and pain affairs can bring, not only to the adults involved but also to children caught up in the crossfire. Affairs are illicit, exciting, passionate and romantic relationships, and because of this the people involved can be so caught up in their own secret lives that they ignore, or fail to realise, how much they can hurt those who love and trust them. This is precisely what happened in the case of Charlotte, a wonderfully pretty and greatly loved friend of mine.

Charlotte was having a cup of coffee with me, before dashing off to collect her children from school, when she leaned across the kitchen table and said, 'Can I tell you something? It's terribly secret.' Before I had time to reply, she said, 'I'm having an affair. I never thought I could behave so badly, but it's blissful. He's great, I feel so alive.' Then she added, 'Do you think it's terribly wrong? Because I couldn't bear to hurt Simon. If he knew, I think he would kill me.' With that, she looked at the clock and cried, 'Look at the time! Have I shocked you? I must dash, otherwise I'll be late for the children.' A moment later she was gone. I wasn't shocked; she was too great a friend for that. I had always found her husband Simon rather insensitive, pompous and arrogant, and had often wondered why she had married him. Even so, I did feel sorry for him because I knew that, in his own way, he did love Charlotte. I was also afraid for her; if Simon ever found out I knew he would be totally unforgiving. Divorce petitions would come flying through the letter box, and there would be all the repercussions of an acrimonious, messy breakup for her and the children. Charlotte knew she was taking a huge risk but she did not want to hear me tell her so. She was so caught up by desire that she refused to contemplate what would happen if the affair were ever discovered.

Not every affair happens because the people involved are carried away on gossamer wings. Sophie, an intelligent and extremely successful woman in her early forties, discovered as much.

When Sophie resigned from her job I was sad to hear it, because I knew how much she had enjoyed her work. I was also aware that the man she worked for was an incredible bully who had made her life utterly unbearable for several years, so I was not really surprised that she had at last decided she had had enough. Sophie telephoned me a few weeks after she left the company. Julian, the group finance director of the company, had rung and invited her out to lunch. He said he was sorry she had left, but he was not asking her to change her mind and simply wanted to thank her for all she had contributed. He asked if perhaps it would help her to talk through the reasons why she had decided to leave.

She met Julian at a pretty French restaurant in Soho. She'd always liked him and they had enjoyed each other's company when they worked together. They talked a little about why she left, and though he listened kindly, Sophie felt he was not really all that interested. This hurt, but she tried not to mind too much. He was, after all, good fun and interested in what she was planning to do. As they were talking over coffee, he told her about his family house in Tuscany. He and his wife had bought it in a dilapidated state, and had spent the last few years doing it up. 'My wife is there now,' he said smiling, 'but I've a proposition I'd like to put to you. I love my wife and I'd never leave her, but we've been married for nearly twenty-five years. I've sometimes been unfaithful.' Here he paused, and smiled at her. 'I'd like to have an affair with you. I love being with you. I'm very fond of you and always found you incredibly attractive. I've wanted an affair with you for so long, so please think about it. I know we'd be good together.' As she sat there trying to assimilate what he was saying, he continued pressing her, 'While you worked for the same company I knew it was quite out of the question, but now it's different.' He put his hand across the table, gently brushing her arm, 'As we're both married we'd obviously need to be very discreet.' He went on to tell her that he had a flat in central London where there would be no chance of his wife turning up unexpectedly.

Sophie declined the proposal. Later she kicked herself for having been so naïve, and remembered the saying 'there's no such thing as a free lunch'. When she rang me to express her astonishment at Julian's proposal she asked, 'Is there really so much unfaithfulness around?' The simple answer is yes.

Forsaking all Others

As long as marriage exists I suspect there will always be affairs. When people fall in love and marry, or decide to live together in a committed relationship, the vast majority promise love and faithfulness. In the marriage service the priest asks the man, 'Wilt thou love her, comfort her, honour and keep her in sickness and in health, and, forsaking all others, keep thee only unto her, so long as ye both shall live?' The man answers, 'I will,' and the priest then asks the woman the same question. These are very solemn vows which the couple make to each other and believe they will keep.

The registrar's words at a civil marriage ceremony are also very solemn, and faithfulness is part of what couples promise each other. 'Before you are joined in matrimony I must remind you of the solemn and binding nature of the vows you are about to make. Marriage, according to the law of this country, is the union of one man and one woman, entered into freely, to the exclusion of all others, for life.' Those who decide to live together are also likely to promise to be faithful, though without the formality of the marriage service.

When men and women are asked what the key ingredients are for a happy relationship, fidelity is always near the top of the list. Yet the reality is that most people do not live up to their promises. The journey from betrothal to betrayal is a well trodden path. Millions of people, despite promising to be faithful, break their vows. In my experience most people who betray their partners also say they still love them. Yet when partners discover their spouse has been unfaithful they ask, 'How could he do that if he really loved me?' or, 'If my wife loved me she wouldn't be prepared to hurt me like this.'

Betrayal knocks at the very foundations of a marriage or relationship. It attacks our belief in our partner and ourselves. Enemies betray us, not our spouses and our partners who have promised to love and cherish us. Rosie sensed betrayal and felt there was something wrong. She saw that, 'Daddy was hurting Mummy,' and knew that somehow this other woman was involved. Charlotte's affair made her feel on top of the world; here was someone intelligent and attractive who made her feel good about herself. She knew she was betraying Simon but she told herself, 'He's a difficult man,' and she felt she had been submerged in the everyday life of bringing up their three children with little help from him. Julian was planning his betrayal very carefully, no doubt as he had planned previous affairs. They were secret, and as well organised as the company finances for which he was responsible. So, in his opinion, no one would get hurt. After all, he was committed to his wife, his children and his lifestyle; he did not want to rock any boats.

Understanding Affairs

I know from people I meet in everyday life, from research, from counselling, from the thousands of letters to my advice column, and from the huge number of telephone calls to my counselling line that affairs are very common. Affairs cause huge devastation and disruption to marriages and relationships. To some it is a problem which might occur only once in the lifetime of a marriage, to others affairs are like a drug which once experienced becomes irresistible. An affair is one of the most frequent reasons why couples and individuals turn to counselling, and that is one of the main reasons I decided to write this book. Why are so many men and women having affairs? What goes wrong? Why is real life so different from people's intentions and expectations? Why, despite the risks involved, are affairs on the increase?

In this book I will look at infidelity from all three perspectives: the husband's, the wife's, and the mistress's or lover's. I will explore why people are unfaithful, and the effect it then has on the lives of all those involved; how the secrecy of an affair can erode the intimacy of marriage; how trust is shattered when an affair is discovered. I will look at the different priorities men and women have when embarking on an affair, and how the different qualities men and women look for when they marry are mirrored in their affairs. How many men and women feel that infidelity can enhance and even sustain their marriage? For them their betrayal is a journey into creative adultery. I will also look at affairs from the other side of the marital bond, from the mistress's perspective. She may well be happily independent, or she may be reluctantly sharing the man in her life with his wife, often waiting years for him to leave and be with her. This book is not written to judge, nor for that matter to encourage infidelity. It is intended to give you some insight into why affairs happen and to guide you in what to do if it happens to you.

Statistics, Statistics and Damned Lies

It is notoriously difficult to be accurate about how many people have affairs because, of course, the majority are carried on in secret. If people are interviewed, or answer surveys, or take part in research, we can't know if they are being entirely truthful. Some fear their partner might find out, or wish to exaggerate or play down the true number of affairs they have had. Others have lost count or can't remember. But in the majority of random surveys the estimates are that between fifty and seventy-five percent of people have at some stage in their marriage been unfaithful. This can range from one-night stands to ongoing love affairs, some of which last almost as long as the marriage.

Studying the sexual behaviour of the nation statistically is likely to be a little unreliable. Nonetheless, all the evidence points to affairs being on the increase. The double standards that still exist between men and women may well add to this. Men want to be seen as sexually active and philandering and play up to the macho image that men and society still hold of them. When questioned about their sexual experiences they may well exaggerate or even brag about their performance. The opposite is true where women are concerned. They tend to play down how sexually experienced they are or how many sexual partners they've had prior to marriage, especially if it's in double figures.

What also seems to be true is that most people try to keep their affairs secret. I would suggest that the majority of affairs go undetected. A very high store is set on fidelity in modern marriage, and an affair seems such a huge betrayal that most people are reluctant, even if discovered, to admit to it. They know how much it is going to hurt their partner and also fear that it will be the end of the marriage. But an affair does not have to mean the marriage is over. Most surveys seem to show that the majority of marriages survive. A survey conducted by ICM in 1995 showed that as many as eighty percent of those who had an affair stayed with their long-term partner.

More Men than Women have Affairs?

The majority of surveys show that women are less likely than men to have affairs, but over the last fifty years or so the gap has narrowed rapidly. It is now estimated that over sixty percent of married men have affairs, as opposed to over forty percent of married women.

In 1953 Alfred Kinsey, in the second of the famous Kinsey reports, *Sexual Behaviour in the Human Female*, found that twenty-six percent of women admitted being unfaithful. At the other extreme Shere Hite, the American historian and researcher, published a new report in 1988, *Women and Love*, which showed that seventy percent of women married five years or longer had been unfaithful. If accurate this meant that women's rate of infidelity had almost trebled in thirty-five years, an enormous increase which, according to Hite's report, brought women almost level with men. Her research showed that after five years of marriage seventy-five percent of men had been unfaithful. Interestingly seventy-nine percent of the women said they believed their husbands were faithful, even if they themselves were unfaithful. Today, I frequently notice that unless a man has come for counselling because of his wife's affair, men tend to think much the same way. Even though a man may have been unfaithful, he rarely thinks that his wife has. So either there is a lot of self-delusion going on, or both sexes are determinedly turning a blind eye. If not, men and women are surprisingly good at deceiving each other.

Annette Lawson interviewed hundreds of men and women in Britain for her book *Adultery, An Analysis of Love and Betrayal*, and suggested that nowadays men and women are not only having more affairs, but that they are having them far sooner than previous generations. Her research showed that women who married before 1960 waited on average fourteen and a half years before their first liaison, whereas men who married before 1960 used to wait about eleven years before their first affair. However, women who married in the 1970s waited just over four years before embarking on their first liaison, while men waited a little over five years.

The fact that people are having more affairs, and embark on them sooner, does not surprise me. It is what I see reflected in the counselling room and what is apparent in the social behaviour and different moral attitudes around today. But what I do find surprising in Lawson's research – and I would challenge the findings – is that women are more likely than men to embark on an affair first. From my experience it is far more likely to be the other way around. Men not only have more affairs than women but also tend to take the lead sexually and initiate affairs. Until comparatively recently, women who had affairs were judged far more harshly than men. The effect of this double standard still lingers on. Even when many women, after only a few years of marriage, may well have become disillusioned and start to look elsewhere for the closeness and intimacy they are not getting from their partners, they often find that nature has a habit of getting in the way. Most couples embark on child rearing within the first five years of marriage, and though this is a time when men are notably unfaithful, most women are so involved in having babies and so exhausted by meeting their demands, that they often lose interest in sex altogether. Women frequently don't become active again sexually until the children are past babyhood.

Madeleine had been married six years and had been having an affair with Patrick for the last three of those years. The affair even continued throughout her pregnancy, though in the last three months she and her lover were not having sex. They still talked on the phone and had lunch together. But when her baby was six months old Madeleine ended the affair, much to her lover's distress. She said, 'Once Charlie was born I found that instead of longing to see Patrick, or looking forward to his calls, I was just no longer interested.

All my attention was on my new baby. I just loved being a mother, I didn't want to be apart from him for a moment, there was no time in my life for an affair. Also, I was now terrified of what would happen if my husband found out. I had new responsibilities. An affair for me was just too risky.'

To have an affair you have to be in a position to meet someone who attracts you, and those opportunities are severely restricted if you are at home with small children. Women are far more likely to start an affair when the children start school, or when the mother returns to work, or embarks on a career after several years of being at home.

When is an Affair an Affair?

An affair is where two people are involved in a sexual relationship and one of them is married or committed to someone else. It can range from one single act of infidelity, a one-night stand or a fling, to a relationship that may last several months or even years. Sexual penetration may not occur, though it usually does in the vast majority of affairs, but I would still describe two people as having an affair or being unfaithful if their relationship involved touching and kissing with relatively few or no clothes on, and where one or both were orgasmic. Not perhaps strictly defined as an affair, but I would suggest very close to it, is the situation where a man and woman feel very strongly attracted to each other emotionally and sexually and, though they have never been to bed, the possibility is always in the air. When they meet and talk they are very intimate with each other, they share thoughts and feelings they would normally reserve for their spouses and, because this relationship is very important to both, it is a secret from their partners. Affairs may be deeply loving and endure for many years, or they may just be a brief moment of shared lust. They do, it seems, come in all shapes and sizes.

The Pleasure and the Pain

An affair can be passionate, exciting, and wonderfully romantic. It can make you feel on top of the world, totally alive, like dancing on air. But an affair can also drive you to the depths of despair. How you are going to feel rather depends on the nature of your involvement in the affair: whether it's you who is having the affair or your partner; whether the affair is in those early, heady days; or whether you are at the stage where your lover is trying to dump you while you are still mad about him or her. Or maybe he has yet again promised to leave his wife for you, but somehow never seems to be able to get around to doing it? Whichever position you're in, you are bound to experience very different feelings. But one thing is certain, whether you wish to recognise it or not, affairs may be one of the world's most exciting activities but they are also one of the most dangerous. For most people it's the danger and the illicit nature of the affair that makes it so exciting.

Affairs may send the adrenalin soaring but they can also wreck relationships, shatter marriages, drive people to the edge of despair, and even to suicide or murder. Affairs are a form of sexual Russian roulette where you can never be sure that you won't be caught out. When you embark on it you may think you can conduct 'the perfect affair', but although you may be able to control your own behaviour there is no way you can be sure that your lover will be as predictable. However careful you think you are being there are no guarantees that your secret will be kept. Look at the number of politicians and men in high-powered jobs who thought they could trust the women for whom they risked their marriages, only to find that those women in the end were all too prepared to kiss and tell. As one man who is well known on the political scene said to me recently, 'If you are going to have an affair, you should always make sure it is with a married woman who, if the affair is ever discovered, has more to lose than you.' Cynical maybe, but not without truth. And even if your infidelity is not discovered, or you feel that your affair has enriched your marriage, people often deceive themselves about quite how much even a secret affair can affect their marriage. There is no doubt that undiscovered affairs do alter the degree of intimacy. A couple's original expectations are that they will share everything with each other and have an open, trusting and honest relationship. But the very nature of an affair involves lies and deception. The betrayer is no longer the person the partner thinks he or she is. So whether you are the one having the affair, the one who has discovered your partner's betrayal, or the one whose affair still remains your secret, the relationship with your partner has inevitably changed.

Maggie was married to a man twelve years her senior when she began an affair with an old boyfriend who came back onto the scene. She was just thirty, with two small children of five and seven. In the last year her relationship with her husband had come under a lot of strain. They were always arguing about money and his long working hours. She said, 'Since Phil and I started this affair my relationship with my husband has improved, I am less demanding, and we are arguing far less. Surprisingly our sex life has also improved. I think I'm putting more into my marriage, and being more tolerant of my husband because underneath I'm feeling really guilty. I do love my husband, but I'm having the best fun I have had in years.' Maggie felt her marriage improved as a result of her affair. I doubt if her husband would have agreed with her if he had known the real reason why his wife was more loving and understanding. Alongside the fun Maggie was having was the fear of being found out because she added, 'I keep panicking about what I could lose. I don't think he would ever forgive me.' Yet, like thousands of other women, Maggie was still prepared to take the risk. Her affair was not just a brief encounter but an intimate, loving relationship with a man whom she described as a close friend as well as an exciting lover. She also knew that her husband would be bitterly hurt if he ever discovered it.

A one-night stand or a brief fling, or even one act of unfaithfulness, can feel devastating to the betrayed party, as the actor Hugh Grant discovered when he was caught out with a prostitute in a hire-car on Sunset Boulevard. He accepted that he had deeply hurt and humiliated his girlfriend Elizabeth Hurley and said, 'If I was a single guy it would be hysterical. But I am not. I have a girlfriend. I have done an abominable thing. She has been amazing about it. We are trying to work it out. Time is of the essence.' But often a man will think that a brief sexual encounter is meaningless and will say to his wife or partner when she discovers that he has been unfaithful, 'Darling, it didn't mean a thing,' almost convincing himself, if not her, that it was no more than a foolish act of indiscretion. To his wife or partner, however, it usually means quite a lot more than that. She is unable to brush it aside so lightly.

John and Lucy had a fairly up-and-down sort of marriage, with quite a lot of good times, but some very difficult times as well. Since the birth of their son two years ago, Lucy was a lot less interested in sex than John, who described his sexual relationship with Lucy as, 'A sexual desert, with hardly an oasis in sight.' He went away for a two-day conference, and ended up in bed with a work colleague. He bitterly regretted it, and because he felt so guilty told Lucy. She was outraged, not so much because of the infidelity, but because of the betrayal of trust. For many years after that she found every excuse to blame John for everything that went wrong in the marriage. It was only when she was able to stop doing that, and see how much John loved her and the three boys that they were able to tackle the marital and sexual problems that led to the affair in the first place.

John was not as cavalier as many men are about his single act of unfaithfulness. But in my experience, if the boot is on the other foot and the wife has had a one-night stand, the man tends not to take such a laid back approach. One man summed up the perceived difference to me. Having brushed aside his indiscretion, even though his wife was deeply hurt by its discovery, he looked at her and said, 'Well, of course, she wouldn't have gone to bed with a man unless she felt something for him. It's different for women. My wife just would not behave like that.'

Even nowadays many men believe that it's all right for them to behave badly as long as they are not found out, but that it's not acceptable in their partner. This male viewpoint, though not held by all men, is heavily influenced by social attitudes which have been prevalent for many centuries. In the past, society judged women caught in adultery far more harshly than it judged men indulging in the same extramarital activity.

A Brief History of Adultery

Throughout history male adulterers have been viewed and treated differently to female adulterers. In biblical times, for example, women were stoned to death for such an act, but there was no such punishment for men caught in adultery. When Mary Magdalene was accused of adultery and was on the point of being stoned to death for her sins, the scribes and Pharisees asked Jesus what they should do. Jesus rescued her with the words, 'He that is without sin among you, let him first cast a stone at her.'

In England right up until the nineteenth century adultery was seen as commonplace for the man, particularly in the arranged marriages of the upper classes, yet it was not acceptable in women. The historian Professor Lawrence Stone has said of the Middle Ages that the taking of a mistress was what made arranged marriages tolerable. There are many famous cases among the kings and princes of Great Britain right up to the beginning of this century. In fact, the current Prince of Wales is the first to have his affair deemed unacceptable. Not only has he been much criticised for his affair with Mrs Parker Bowles, but he has also been divorced for it.

During most of the last century double standards abounded. Adultery by a woman was not acceptable. If she was discreet and got away with it, that was one thing, but discovery and exposure meant a fall from grace. She would often be divorced and denied access to her children and, if this happened, it was almost impossible for her to be accepted in society again. In her book written in 1988, *Myths of Sexuality*, Lynda Nead writes:

> Adultery by women was seen as sexually deviant behaviour. Women were seen as morally pure and their role was to maintain the home as a spiritual haven for her husband and children.

If a woman behaved wantonly by having an affair, it had very serious social consequences. She was then seen as irresponsible and possibly not fit to look after her home and children. Her suitability as a wife and mother was called into question and her social position as a married woman could be threatened. For a man, infidelity was seen as the indulgence of natural urges; sexual lapses were regarded as regrettable but unavoidable. For a woman in the patriarchal family, infidelity was seen as a betrayal of her father, her husband, her home and her family.

It was also a common belief in the nineteenth century that sexual enjoyment was different for men and women. It was thought that women's capacity for sexual pleasure was much more limited than men's, if indeed it existed at all. William Acton, a genito-urinary surgeon writing in 1857, certainly held these beliefs. He wrote:

> I should say that the majority of women (happily for them) are not very much troubled with sexual feelings of any kind. What men are habitually, women are exceptionally. It is true, I admit as the divorce courts show, there are some few women who have sexual desires so strong they surpass those of men ... there can be no doubt that sexual feeling in the female is in the majority of cases in abeyance ... and even if aroused (which in many instances it never can be) is very moderate compared with that of the male ... I admit, of course, the existence of sexual excitement terminating even in nymphomania, a form of insanity which those accustomed to visit lunatic asylums must be fully conversant with.

It seems that one way in which sexual behaviour in women outside marriage was controlled was to portray it as a form of medical abnormality. Behaviour that was seen as normal and healthy in men was seen as a form of madness in women, or something that was really only acceptable in mistresses and prostitutes but definitely not desirable in wives. So, was it understandable for men to be tempted, but not for women? We might ask whether it was in men's interest to believe this as well. For the many men who were inexperienced or indifferent lovers, who were only aware of how to take pleasure and knew little about giving it, it is not surprising that their wives should seem sexually unaware and unresponsive. How could the Victorian husband acknowledge to himself that his wife could possibly enjoy sex with someone else if she was not enjoying it with him?

Women were also far less aware of their own sexual potential. There was no open discussion of sex, and the usual maternal advice was to, 'Lie back and think of England.' Is it any wonder that women had little or no expectation of their own sexual capacity? As marriages were often more about convenience than romance, in many cases the vital sexual chemistry never existed in the first place. As Oscar Wilde said, 'Sex was the price women paid for marriage and marriage was the price men paid for sex.'

Nowadays nearly every women's magazine advises on how to satisfy a woman, and discusses the joys of the multiple orgasm. Twentieth-century man might well have the occasional pang of envy for his nineteenth-century counterpart who did not have to worry too much about whether he was making the earth move for his wife, or indeed his mistress, unlike Jeremy. He had a very demanding job, hectic lifestyle, pretty wife, and a lovely and even more demanding mistress. He told me, 'Sometimes I used to fake orgasm when making love to my wife, because I was saving myself for my mistress!'

Another key reason why Victorian man set a high store on his wife's fidelity was because an adulteress could be carrying another man's child. His inheritance was at stake; an act of adultery could not only undermine the marriage and family values but deprive a man's children of their rightful inheritance as well. Lord Cranworth, then Lord Chancellor, in a debate on divorce law reform in 1857 said:

> A wife might without any loss of caste, and possibly without reference to the interests of her children or even her husband, condone an act of adultery on the part of the husband; but a husband could not condone a similar act on the part of his wife. No one would venture to suggest that a husband could possibly do so, and for this, among other reasons . . . that the adultery of the wife might be the means of palming spurious offspring upon the husband, while adultery of the husband could have no such effect.

Today I receive many letters from women who do not know whether the child they are carrying is their husband's or their lover's, and most choose not to tell their husbands. There is the story of a woman who looks at a new baby in a pram and says to the mother, 'Oh! He looks just like his father.' The mother replies anxiously, 'I know. I do hope my husband doesn't realise that.'

The 1857 Matrimonial Causes Act highlights how men and women were treated differently when it came to adultery and divorce. The act permitted husbands to divorce their wives on the grounds of adultery alone. For wives, there was no such equality. Adultery on its own was not sufficient grounds for a woman to divorce her husband. She had to prove that there were additional grounds such as incest, or bestiality. Gladstone, the Prime Minister and grand old man of British politics, maintained that the public did not want the Act, and that there would be no more than twenty or thirty divorces a year but, in fact, in 1858 there were 326 divorces and by the year 1901 there were 848.

As we moved into the twentieth century, attitudes towards women and adultery eventually started to change. In the twentieth century, two world wars and women's suffrage had far-reaching effects on marriage and relationships. Both contributed to significant change in the role of men and women. During both world wars, owing to the labour shortage, millions of women joined the workforce. With their newly found freedom, economic independence and earning power these women were later reluctant to return to the home and hearth. Their horizons had been fundamentally changed. After World War II, the number of divorces soared too, from 7,000 in 1938 to nearly 30,000 in 1946 – an increase of 350 percent. In wartime many couples had married in haste because the man wanted to have a girl back home, someone of his own to love and be loved by. It represented the reality they'd lost in the awfulness of war; they could share their dreams and plan how their lives would be when the war was over. There was also the fear that, if they did not marry, one of them might be killed and they would miss their chance for ever. Sadly, for many these hasty marriages ended in divorce when the war was over. In the cold light of peacetime they all too frequently realised that they had little in common. Many men discovered on returning home that the woman they had left behind had been having an affair with someone else.

Economic historian Dr Peter Howlett, in his report *Fighting with Figures* for the Central Statistical Office wrote:

> Before the Second World War it was mostly women who filed for divorce, but that was reversed during the war with 56% of divorces being filed by men because of their wives' adultery . . . The wives were suddenly meeting men at work as more and more were required in the workplace. They enjoyed coming out from under the thumb of the traditional male, having some independence, and earnings of their own.

Now that women had the freedom to work for a living and at last had some financial independence, they began to have more power in relationships. So along with their developing ideas about what they wanted in marriage and in the workplace, they were also becoming far less sexually ignorant and less inhibited. It was inevitable that as more women realised their sexual potential within marriage, or at least were more aware of its existence, they would start to catch up with men when it came to affairs. What is more, marriage twentieth-century-style was increasingly based on love, equality, sexual attraction and friendship, rather than security, status and the opportunity to leave home and start your own family. Naturally women were going to expect more from marriage. And if their expectations were raised in what they wanted from marriage, so it would also mean that if they were not met, women would be more likely to look outside marriage for sexual or emotional fulfilment.

Attitudes to sex were also changing, particularly sex before marriage. It is estimated that in the 1950s two thirds of women and about a quarter of all men were virgins when they married. The majority of people still disapproved of sex before marriage. Only half of all men and one twelfth of women had had sex with someone other than their spouse when they married. Interestingly, it is a commonly held myth that if you sow your wild oats before marriage you are more likely to be faithful after marriage. In fact, the reverse is true: the more promiscuous you are prior to embarking on marriage or a committed relationship, the more likely you are to stray afterwards.

The 1960s and All That

The '60s were really the start of the sexual revolution. Sex before marriage started to become the norm and, by 1970, most couples had had sex before marriage and had done so with more than just one partner. If you had a serious relationship it was generally accepted that that also included a sexual relationship. This sexual revolution did not start in time for Philip Larkin, who wrote of his regrets in his well-known poem *Annus Mirabilis*:

> *Sexual intercourse began*
> *In nineteen sixty-three*
> *(Which was rather late for me)—*
> *Between the end of the* Chatterley *ban*
> *And the Beatles' first LP.*

Up till then there'd only been
A sort of bargaining,
A wrangle for a ring,
A shame that started at sixteen
And spread to everything . . .

                                    Philip Larkin, *Annus Mirabilis*

The 1960s, with the combination of the growing influence of the women's movement, the introduction of the pill, and total freedom from any fear of Aids, meant that for many, sexual liberation had arrived. This sexual freedom increased over the next thirty years. It is now quite usual for both sexes to have had a variety of sexual partners prior to marriage. But at the same time even greater expectations have been placed on marriage. The modern idea of marriage is that it is the formal underlining of an all-encompassing, loving relationship which supplies all, or nearly all, of each other's needs.

The Fashion for Faithfulness

Love, friendship, and sexual compatibility are the central themes of today's marriage. With such expectations has also come an increased emphasis on sexual exclusivity and fidelity. But here is the paradox: although in today's relationship people expect faithfulness from each other when they embark on marriage, adultery has actually increased among men, and especially so among women. The majority of people are unfaithful during the life of their marriage, and they are frequently unfaithful more than once. It does seem that the higher the expectations couples have of marriage, the more devastating the discovery of an affair.

In the more old-fashioned marriages, where couples were not looking to each other to fulfil nearly so many of their emotional and sexual needs, as long as their partner was discreet it was easier to turn a blind eye to their unfaithfulness. Unfaithfulness was very common, particularly among the upper classes and aristocracy, though it was usually done with discretion.

The Unfaithful Husband

Not all men were discreet when it came to affairs, even in the days of old-fashioned marriages. Some men liked to show off about their mistress, sometimes even to their wives.

Edward, a good-looking and arrogant man from a smart family, was not only in search of sexual excitement and the novelty of a new sexual encounter, but he also used his affairs to compensate for the constant rejection he had endured as a child. His mother died when he was three and he was then looked after by a succession of uninterested nannies and by a cruel stepmother who worshipped her own child from a previous marriage, and completely ignored Edward. Sibyl, Edward's wife who is now a lively, slim and attractive woman in her seventies, endured Edward's affairs throughout twenty years of marriage. This went on until he had one affair too many and she eventually divorced him. She said, 'I knew about his unfaithfulness from very early on in our marriage. But how could I divorce him, this highly decorated hero coming home from the war? A lot of our marriage was good. We had an interesting life together and we travelled a lot. Much of the time we had a good marriage and a great relationship in bed. I always knew when he was having an affair, I became accustomed to the signs. But I was Catholic and believed marriage was for life. In those days you didn't divorce as you do now, and I also had two small children.' She continued, 'Once, when I challenged him about his latest mistress, he turned to me and said; "You are much better in bed than she is, so why are you worried?" When I asked him why he told me that, he said, "I just thought you would like to know, she isn't any threat to you. It's you that I love." Most of his affairs were short-lived. I think it was the novelty factor that attracted him,' she said with a hint of long-forgotten resignation.

Edward had been so badly hurt as a child that it was almost impossible for him to trust a woman enough to really love her. With Sibyl who, in his way, he did love, he was continually sabotaging that relationship because he was so afraid of intimacy. To make up for the rejection he felt from the women who had littered his childhood, he was always in search of love and admiration from women in his adult life as a way of filling that deep empty well of insecurity. To feel desired and loved by women was all-important. At the beginning of many of his love affairs he often thought he had found 'the real thing' only to find that once the initial passion had worn off, so had his interest. Well, at least until the next time. Then another desirable woman would catch his attention, and once more he would set out to woo and seduce her. A positive response from the woman and her eventual surrender made him feel better about himself because here was another woman who had not rejected him, unlike the women in his childhood.

After his marriage broke up Edward, who was by then in his mid-forties, remarried. It turned out that his new wife was unable to have children, and she deeply resented Edward's only child, a shy, slight girl of fourteen. His second wife took every opportunity to undermine his relationship with his daughter, and Edward proved quite unable to stand up to his second wife on this matter, just as his father before him had been unable to stand up to Edward's stepmother. The result was that he hardly ever saw his daughter, much to his second wife's satisfaction. He also continued his affairs, much to her fury.

The Whys and Wherefores of Affairs

Most men and women who have affairs do not want their partner to know they are unfaithful. They take care to cover their tracks and often, if challenged, will deny the truth. But the reality is that affairs are on the increase, and for every affair discovered there are many more that continue in secret. Is ignorance less disturbing than discovering the truth? Is it better to confess, or remain silent? Why do so many people risk so much for the excitement of illicit sex? What makes marriages vulnerable to affairs and why having been caught out once, do some men and women betray their partner time and time again? When adultery is discovered, how does it affect the marriage, and what impact does it have on the children?

I will be looking at all these issues in the following chapters. I will also be exploring why men and women frequently have different expectations as well as a different order of priorities when they embark on an affair. Top of the list of men's priorities are:

- delighting in the novelty of new sexual experiences
- believing in their macho image
- the inability to resist temptation
- the enjoyment of the chase
- thinking that if they are not caught, no harm is done
- falling in love

Women's priorities are almost exactly in reverse order. They have affairs because:

- they fall in love
- all is not well within the marriage
- they are looking for the intimacy of a close relationship
- they want romance back in their lives
- they want exciting sex

There is no denying that affairs are very exciting but they can also bring in their wake an enormous amount of hurt and devastation. It is also important to remember that, even though it may be very painful, marriages can and do survive affairs.

Chapter Two

IS MONOGAMY A NATURAL STATE?

The Question

I am a young married woman of thirty. I have fallen in love
with the manager at the place where I work, and although he
has shown me a few attentions, I am afraid he is not serious.
You see he has a typist (also a married woman) who really
does throw herself at him. I think she has guessed my secret
and goes out of her way to be spiteful and to make me
jealous. Would you advise me what to do?

The Reply

Leave the job, my dear, if you possibly can and forget all this
nonsense. Why on earth should you fall in love with another
man when you have a' perfectly good man of your own?
Especially as your manager seems to be quite uninterested
in you. Let the other girl make a fool of herself if she likes
– there is no need for you to be so stupid.

Letter to an agony aunt, 1944, *Woman* magazine

The scene is a railway station, the day is overcast and windy.
A man and a woman are looking at each other with intensity
and longing. They are very much in love, but they are both
married to someone else. They met by chance on a railway
station when she got something in her eye. And, as a doctor,
he asked whether he could help. They started to talk, then
they shared a cup of tea in the little cafe on the station. It
is one of those relationships that seemed to be just perfect
right from the very beginning. They began to meet just briefly

each week, but as the weeks go by and their feelings deepen they both recognise that the relationship is running into deep waters. They have fallen in love.

Is this the start of an affair? He desperately wants to make love to her, and every part of her mind and body is telling her that this is what she wants most in all the world. She summons up all her courage and determination and says she can't do that to her husband, she cannot betray him. He too thinks about his wife. He is loving and gentle and reluctantly accepts what she says. They both know that their relationship cannot continue. Seconds later her train pulls into the station; they kiss goodbye. With tears streaming down her face she leans out of the carriage window and waves to him. He stands on the station platform holding his hat and looking after her and the departing train. Smoke swirls around him as the train draws even further away and they are parted for ever.

Later that day the woman is at home in the drawing room with her kind but very dull husband. She is sitting in a chair, thinking of that afternoon's meeting. Her husband gets up from his chair and comes across to her and says, 'You've been a long way away.' She smiles up at him and says thoughtfully, with her heart breaking, 'Yes, but I'm back now.'

The poignant and moving love scene on the station is from the 1945 film *Brief Encounter* with Trevor Howard and Celia Johnson. If the film was set in the 1990s they would probably have that affair, or even divorce their partners so that they could marry each other. But what the film does show, which is just as relevant today as it was then, is that being married does not mean that you will never fancy, or even fall in love with, someone else.

Is there a Monogamy Gene?

Woman wants monogamy;
Man delights in novelty.
Love is woman's moon and sun;
Man has other forms of fun.
Woman lives but in her lord;

Count to ten, and man is bored.
With this the gist and sum of it,
What earthly good can come of it?

'Dorothy Parker, *General Review of the Sex Situation*

I don't think we need to take Dorothy Parker too seriously here. She no more believed that women were programmed to be monogamous than men. Having had many love affairs herself, this poem is more likely to recall the fact that she had frequently been badly hurt by unfaithful men.

Lifelong monogamous devotion isn't necessarily natural but it is something that we can choose if we want to. Once we are married it does not mean that we only have eyes for our partner, however lovely or wonderful they are. We do not stop finding the opposite sex sexually attractive. When a woman says, 'I've never looked at another man since the day I married,' I wonder if she has just shut down all her sexual feelings and therefore has also ceased to look at her husband with any sexual interest as well. I do not believe that our genes programme us to fidelity. Sexual exclusivity is what the majority of couples promise each other when they marry, or chose to live together in a committed relationship. Yet, as research shows, the majority of men and women are unfaithful at some time during their marriage. However, they still place faithfulness very near the top of their list when asked what qualities are the most important in a good marriage.

It is generally accepted that a loving marriage or a committed relationship is the best place in which to bring up children. A secure and loving home is where children flourish best. That is not to deny what a good job many single parents make, frequently a lot better than two parents at war. Being a parent is a fairly demanding job, even when there are two of you. It is made all the more difficult if you are constantly at each other's throats, or trying to manage on your own.

The state and the church have realised for hundreds of years that encouraging marriage and stable family life is a sensible investment for the economic and moral welfare of their citizens and their flock. Marriage is expensive when it breaks down, with the state having to pick up the bill. Marriage is thus seen by both state and church as the best place in which to bring up children. The marriage service itself stresses the church's belief in the sanctity of marriage when a couple promise to love each other in sickness and in health, 'til death us do part'. They also promise to 'forsake all others'. So both church and state have a huge investment in controlling and legitimising sexual activity, rather than encouraging people to 'do what comes naturally'.

In some other cultures monogamy is not prized at all. Polygamy is favoured, where one man can have many wives, provided he can support them. This is because the number of wives a man has is linked with power, status and money. An Inca chief was allowed up to thirty wives, whereas a petty chief was only permitted seven. A Zulu king could have as many as a hundred wives. The kings of the Tikari tribes in the Cameroon grasslands claimed to have several hundred wives as late as the 1970s. This did not, however, mean that the wives all stayed faithful to their often elderly lords and masters. Itinerant salesmen of the Ibo tribe in Nigeria were banned from some neighbouring townships because they gained a reputation for adultery with the kings' wives, the problem being that the kings did not want to be cuckolded.

The fundamentalist element within the Mormon church still persists with polygamy, particularly in Manti in the USA. Mormon wife Joanne said she had nightmares when her thirty-five-year-old husband Jeffrey said he wanted to marry a pretty seventeen year old. 'But after lots of prayer, I knew it was the right thing,' she said. Her husband married his new bride and they went off for a three-day honeymoon in Colorado. Joanne said the pain had abated by then, 'It was not at all like he was off cheating with another woman, because she was his wife. You have to look at it totally differently.'

Elaine, another Mormon wife who had to learn to accept her husband taking several more wives, said the first time was the toughest, 'If you find your husband is having an affair, you feel jealousy, rage, betrayal. All those same feelings come into it, even in polygamy. You have to deal with all these feelings.'

*   *   *

There are far fewer examples of cultures where polyandry is the norm, that is where women are permitted to have several husbands. Perhaps this is because men are less able or indeed less willing to learn to deal with their jealous feelings, as Elaine had to do. Maybe men are also less easily influenced than women into accepting such an unfair distribution of sexual favours.

When Christianity and traditional tribal customs clash, a similar situation to the one experienced by Mormon wives can arise. In the Cameroon grasslands Christianity runs hand in hand with tribal beliefs. The two rub along happily until the subject of taking a second wife comes along.

When Vincent, secretary to the Fon (king) of Bali, decided in 1976 that he wanted a second wife, he faced many problems with his first wife. He eventually had his way by giving his first wife the right to veto his choice of a second partner. His dilemma exercised the minds of all his friends, who were also Christians but found that the inclination and the desire to go back to their roots was very strong. When Vincent, aged about thirty-five, finally got his wife to pick a new, fourteen-year-old bride for him, the effect on his friends was considerable. They were forced to examine their own marriages and found they wanted to be like him, even though they knew their wives would be very jealous. In Vincent's case, modern beliefs prevailed and he resigned his position with the local church after marrying his new bride. He was still allowed to go to church to worship, but it would have been seen as hypocritical to carry a senior position within it.

The African's attitude was no different to that of Europeans who want the added sexual spice of other partners. They simply had a traditional precedent on which they could call as justification. Whether those of Vincent's friends who couldn't overcome the effects of a modern education and Christian beliefs had affairs to compensate for not being able to discuss with their wives the possibility of taking a second wife, was never revealed. Most of them chose monogamy, mainly because they lived in a poor area and couldn't afford more than one wife, but also because their new found Christian religious beliefs kept them in a monogamous condition.

Is it Possible to Resist Temptation?

I would be a rich woman if I had a pound for every time a man or woman has said to me when talking about how their affair began, 'I just couldn't help it,' or, 'It just sort of happened, I was powerless to resist.' Or, as Oscar Wilde wrote in *Lady Windermere's Fan*:

I can resist everything except temptation.

Though monogamy may not be a natural state it does not mean that we cannot resist temptation. We do have a choice. If you really love your partner, and you know an affair would really hurt them, you can chose not to be unfaithful. The very nature of an affair is that it is kept secret from your partner, so an affair does mean that you are deceiving them. You are doing something behind their back that you know they would not like. The deceit is at odds with what you have said you wanted from marriage, which is an open and honest relationship. If you are ever discovered, the trust between you will be broken. It can be repaired, but that is not easy and the reality is that it may never be as good as it was before the affair.

I was once taking at a Christmas party to Adam, a delightful and extremely amusing man, and to Ben, an old friend of his from university. Adam was an international lawyer who constantly travelled through Europe and America. He said that on an eight-hour flight he had been sitting next to a really attractive woman. For the whole of the flight they had just talked and talked. 'It was almost like love at first sight,' he explained, 'but, though I was tempted, I thought of all I had back home: a beautiful wife whom I loved very much, two children I adored, a great life, apart from having to work too hard. And I thought, no, I'm being stupid to put all that at risk. After all, I love my wife,' he said, glancing across the room at her. 'So when we arrived at Heathrow, and the time came to say goodbye, we looked at each other with such intensity, but neither of us said anything. I leaned over and kissed her fleetingly, then I turned and walked away, I did not take her telephone number or anything. We were both happily married and we both knew that if we saw each other again it would only lead to trouble.' 'What would you have done,' enquired Ben, leaning forward in his chair with a slightly teasing air, 'if you had been flying the other way, from London to America, with several nights alone in a big city?' Adam smiled, 'I don't know, I hope I would have made the same decision. How about you?' Adam asked Ben. 'Oh, the same as you,' Ben replied quickly, though a little less convincingly!

Adam was disarmingly honest about how he felt. It's so easy at that stage to think, 'What's the harm? Just a telephone call or two to keep in touch, or maybe an occasional lunch, surely there's nothing wrong with that!' The time to say no is when you realise that this is what you desperately want to do. It's not easy to resist beginning an affair, to simply say no. It is all too easy to reason with yourself, to pretend that no harm will be done, or that it will just be a friendly and enjoyable meeting. But if we are honest with ourselves, that sort of self-deception is how so many affairs begin.

If you meet someone whom you find very attractive and you sense that the feeling is reciprocated, then resisting temptation can be incredibly difficult. This is particularly so if the marriage is going through a bad patch. Perhaps you are feeling taken for granted by your spouse, or you are so stressed out at work that you are putting all too little of yourself into the relationship. Sex may have become mundane because it has become a habit and only happens at the same time, the same place and in the same way. In other words, if your marriage is at a vulnerable point, then that makes an affair all the more attractive and all the more difficult to resist.

But make no bones about it, an affair always puts a marriage at risk. You can never be one hundred percent sure that it will not be discovered and, if you are caught out, you can never be one hundred percent sure that your marriage will survive. Furthermore, even if at the beginning you think you can handle both your marriage and an affair, you can never be absolutely sure. If the liaison is more than just a one-night stand, you never know whether you will become obsessed with the object of your desire, or even fall in love with the person concerned. Either of those two possibilities can really rock the boat in any marriage. In Adam's case, he resisted the temptation of an affair because he loved his wife very much, and he did not want to put his marriage on the line. For him the risks were just not worth it.

Is Pair Bonding Really for Life?

Robert Wright writes in his book *The Moral Animal*:

> The language of zoology used to be so reassuring. Human beings were called a 'pair-bonding' species. Lasting monogamy, it seemed, was natural for us, just as it was for geese, and swans. Family values, some experts said, were in our genes ... This picture has lately acquired some blemishes. To begin with, birds are no longer such uplifting role models. Using DNA testing, ornithologists can now check to see if a mother bird's mate really is the father of her offspring. It turns out that some female chickadees indulge in extramarital trysts with males that outrank their mates in the social hierarchy. For female barn swallows it's a male with a long tail that makes extracurriculars irresistible. (So perhaps it is a myth that size is not important.) The innocent looking indigo bunting has a cuckoldry rate of 40%.

Wright suggests that it is to a man's evolutionary advantage to sow his seeds far and wide. Women instead seek mates with the best genes and with the most to invest in the offspring. These strategies, he claims, put the sexes in conflict with each other and undermine love. He writes:

> The good news is that human beings are designed to fall in love. The bad news is that they aren't designed to stay there. According to evolutionary psychologists it is natural for both men and women, at some times, under some circumstances, to commit adultery or to sour on a mate, to suddenly find a spouse unattractive, irritating and wholly unreasonable. (It may even be natural to become irritating and wholly unreasonable and thus hasten the departure of a mate you have soured on.) It is similarly natural to find some attractive colleague superior on all counts to the sorry wreck of a spouse you're saddled with!

Wright does admit that what's natural isn't necessarily unchangeable. The whole basis of evolutionary biology is that all plant, animal and human life is designed for the purpose of transmitting their cells or genes to future generations. Feelings of lust exist in humans in order to make sure we procreate, but contraception of course exists nowadays to make sure that we don't have to procreate when we choose not to.

Jealousy, the Green-eyed Monster

A fundamental reason why such store is placed on monogamy in marriage is to avoid the dangerous and intense feelings of jealousy which a betrayed partner feels. It is hard to tell whether jealousy is something we are born with, or whether we are conditioned to feel jealous by the way we are brought up. I suspect it's a little of both. But more often than not jealousy does seem to coexist alongside love. Most of us experience some jealousy if we see our partner flirting with a very attractive member of the opposite sex, or if we are stuck at home while our partner is off at a conference with that incredibly attractive girl he met at the office Christmas party, who will of course be just the type to throw herself at him. Jealousy still occurs even in cultures where monogamy is not part of the social order and men are allowed more than one wife, as we have seen.

I know from counselling, and from the letters and calls I get to my advice column, that deep feelings of jealousy are ignited without fail if an affair is discovered. Even many years on when the affair is long since over, the thought of your partner making love to someone else still evokes those jealous feelings. David Buss, an evolutionary psychologist at the University of Michigan, undertook some interesting research to find out what type of affair would distress the betrayed partner the most. He placed electrodes on men and women and asked them to envisage their mates doing various things which disturbed them. When men imagined sexual infidelity in their partners, their heart rate took great leaps; they sweated and wrinkled their brows with worry and anxiety. When they imagined their partners involved in an emotional attachment they calmed down, though not quite to their normal level. However, with women the situation was reversed: when they imagined their partners' infidelity, emotional or redirected love caused them greater stress than pure sexual lust.

This difference, it is suggested, is based on human evolution. Men experience greater stress about women's sexual infidelity because of their fear of being cuckolded and the possibility of their partner conceiving another man's child. In purely evolutionary terms, a man seeks to perpetuate his own genes, not spend time and resources bringing up another man's child. A woman, on the other hand is more likely to panic at a man becoming emotionally involved, because he might leave her. In doing so he would take away from her not only love, but also the male parental investment of time and money that looking after her and the children involves.

Lord Mishcon speaking in the House of Lords in January 1996 in a parliamentary debate on divorce law reform said, 'An errant husband should not be allowed to simply abandon his wife in favour of a little floozy.' He seemed to be speaking up for family values – a popular theme in the '90s among politicians – but he was also speaking on behalf of the outraged and betrayed wife who, having been abandoned by her husband, was replaced by another and possibly much younger woman. Men of course would not agree that they leave their wives for a little floozy; they would say it's for 'the woman they love'. But the ditched wife is more likely to agree with Lord Mishcon's description of the 'other woman'. I have also frequently heard her described by ex-wives as 'my husband's whore', 'the bitch', 'that tart', and other such names.

In France, leaving your marriage for another woman is known as an English habit. It is not that the French are more monogamous than the British, rather that they seem able to get away with having a mistress, or mistresses, as well as a wife and are therefore less likely to leave the marriage for the mistress. President François Mitterrand, who died in February 1995, was married to his wife Danielle for fifty-one years but, according to her, he was unfaithful throughout his marriage. She said of him, 'I can see how my husband excelled in games of seduction with young women. He was François the Seducer. Over the years, I was more irritated by it than hurt.'

His long-time mistress Anne Pignut and Mazarine, his illegitimate daughter, attended the state funeral and stood alongside his wife. It seems that it was Danielle's belief in the quality of their marriage and the feelings they had for each other that made it possible to accept this unfaithful marriage. She said, 'As his wife and mother of his children I was faithful to my role. I was never bored in sharing his life, either in happiness or in pain. I never needed to lie, and what remained unsaid between us was sufficiently revealing for neither of us to be mistaken. There was never anything banal or mediocre. For those who loved us, François and Danielle are inseparable.' She continued, 'What woman can say, "I've never been cheated on," or that she never cheated in her own love life?' Mme Mitterrand was very open when she added, 'You have to admit that a person is capable of loving and loving passionately, and then as the years pass, he loves differently, perhaps even more deeply, and then he can fall in love with someone else.' Maybe that was how it was, or maybe it was her way of rationalising the situation and, in doing so, protecting herself from the pain that his affairs caused her.

It is not only men who may openly flout the concept of monogamous marriages. Dorothy Macmillan, the daughter of the Duke of Devonshire and wife of the former prime minister Harold Macmillan began a life-long and passionate affair with Robert Boothby (Lord Boothby) in the late 1920s. The relationship continued in one form or another until her death in 1966. The love affair between Dorothy Macmillan and Robert Boothby was obviously central to both their lives. Although Harold Macmillan accepted it, it is believed that it caused him considerable pain.

The Heredity Factor

Unfaithfulness does appear to run in families. That does not mean to say that if your mother and father were unfaithful to each other, you will also automatically be, but there are undoubtedly family patterns. Just as the person who has experienced divorce or violence in their family of origin is more likely to repeat that behaviour, so it is with adultery. In her book *Adultery*, family therapist Dr Bonnie Eaker Weil says she believes that adultery can be inherited. She suggests that adultery, like alcoholism and violence, can be a multi-generational trait. Her argument is that adult children of adulterous parents can react to philandering in one of two ways: they repeat or retreat. Repeaters have affairs themselves because they hope to rewrite the script or avenge the cuckolded parent. Retreaters shirk from intimacy, refusing to get hurt by a loved one ever again.

Adult daughters of adulterous fathers may try to recreate their father by marrying an adulterer, or imitate him by becoming unfaithful themselves. Alternatively, they may repudiate him by picking someone who will never stray. Adult daughters of adulterous mothers often fear close relationships and are attracted to adulterous, distant or married men. Some become predatory and promiscuous, identifying with or getting back at their mothers by stealing other women's husbands, while some retreat into frigidity.

Sons of adulterous women will often find it difficult to form relationships with women because of the way they have seen their mother behave to their father, causing subsequent lack or loss of trust. Adulterous fathers, because of their double standards, may boast of their exploits to their adult sons. Sons see that adultery is a way of life to their father, so they may come to believe that it is a woman's place to put up with male infidelity. This pattern is well established in royal and upper-class marriages, where there is frequently no intention to remain faithful.

The most seriously wounded children of adulterous parents are those who feel abandoned by their mothers and fathers through divorce or adultery. If, in addition, they are later betrayed by another loved one, the anguish may be almost unbearable. The emotional legacy is a gnawing sense of inadequacy and loneliness. Most will try to bury their fears with furious activity, phoney cheerfulness, alcohol, drugs or workaholism.

I am Faithful to you Darling in my Fashion

The composer William Walton told his wife when he married her that he would not be faithful, and that she would have to accept his affairs. She also had to agree that they would never have children; he did not wish to share her with children but wanted her all to himself. With a smile, she said of her husband, 'He married me because I was a South American woman and all women from South America were brought up to be slaves!' When they married she thought that she was coming over to lead a smart life in London, only to discover that her husband was taking her to somewhere near Naples. She had no say in the decision. He told her that he had been taken to Southern Italy by the Sitwells, had fallen in love with it, and that is where he intended to live. While William wrote and created his musical world around him, Lady Walton designed an exquisitely beautiful garden on which she worked for most of her married life. Perhaps it was a substitute for the children she never did have.

Angela Fox, the matriarch of the theatrical Fox dynasty, was aware that her husband Robin Fox was unfaithful to her for most of their married life. Angela, mother of actors James and Edward and theatre producer Robert, developed an equally accepting view of her husband's infidelities. She was told by her husband when she was pregnant with their first child that he could never be faithful. She said, 'I grew not to mind his physical infidelities at all. I don't think it's faintly important. He and I had such a marvellous mental rapport. I felt jealous when he would share things of the mind that he and I shared.' She felt that she was absolutely central to her husband, and that his dalliances were of no consequence. She said, 'We were very, very good friends. I don't know what the word love means but I know if he entered a big room where we would be with masses of other people, even if he had his latest mistress on his arm, he would look across the room and we would exchange a glance. We would know for better or worse what we meant. I never expect a man to be faithful, not if he's a real man.'

The Fox family are an interesting example of adultery running from generation to generation. Angela's mother had a long-term affair with a man by whom she had three daughters. She stayed with her husband who, even though he knew they were not his children, brought them up as his own. It would seem that in her mother's eyes the real man was her lover and father of her three children, whereas her husband merely brought them up. So perhaps Angela Fox learned at her mother's knee that men who don't stray are not real men. To those women real men are so sexually insatiable they are driven to go out and have affairs, so men are split into either safe, secure types, or exciting philanderers. In her sons' generation, the pattern of adultery continues.

Open Marriages

The reason why so few people settle for an open marriage is, I'm sure, because most people are not like Lady Walton or Angela Fox and cannot cope with the idea of sharing their husband or wife with someone else, even if it is only on a part-time basis. People in open marriages (where both agree it is all right to have a sexual relationship with other people) feel that the fact they are open about their sexual activity outside their relationship means that there is no betrayal, as they are not deceiving each other.

Open marriages do seem to work for some couples or, at least, they work for some couples for some of the time. The ones I see in my work are naturally the ones that are having difficulties or have come to grief. Couples who agree on an open marriage do so because they think it is unrealistic to think that either they or their partner can be expected to be faithful to each other. They also hope that by giving each other the freedom to have sexual liaisons outside the marriage, these relationships will run their natural course and therefore not threaten the marriage. They believe that this sexual freedom will refresh and keep their own relationship sexually alive, so having sexual relationships with other people is seen as cementing the open marriage rather than undermining it.

Open marriages or relationships inevitably run into difficulties if a spouse gets too emotionally involved with their lover. Sexual infidelity is bearable in an open marriage, but if love comes into the equation it usually feels too threatening. After all, a real love affair can be very absorbing – you only have eyes for each other, you want to share everything with that person – and this is bound to instil the fear of breakup in the partner you married. The extramarital relationship now becomes just as threatening as it would be to a more conventional marriage because, despite the agreement, the ground rules have changed. Either your partner is threatening to leave to be with their new love, or jealousy now rears its ugly head and you can no longer bear the fact that your partner feels so much love for someone else.

In open marriages, as in all marriages, couples draw up their own codes of behaviour. They might agree to tell their partner that they have embarked on a new affair, but they might not always tell them in advance. They may well agree not to bring the person to the family home, but it may be all right to talk about them to each other. They might agree not to go into detail about what they do sexually, but be happy to share with their partner the details of when and where they met. It does not surprise me, when such a delicate path has to be laid, that it so frequently seems to come to grief – but this is not always so.

Jean-Paul Sartre, the French philosopher, and Simone de Beauvoir, one of the major feminist writers of the twentieth century, had a relationship with each other that lasted for over fifty years. Both promised the other that their love affair was central to their lives (marriage in all but name) but both agreed that they could and would have sexual liaisons outside this central relationship. It seems that Sartre's infidelities did cause painful and jealous feelings in Simone de Beauvoir, which she describes in her autobiographical novel *A Woman Destroyed*. In the following letter to Sartre she describes quite graphically one of her own sexual liaisons with Sartre's close friend Bost.

> *Hôtel de la Gare*
> *Albertville (Savoie)*
> *Albertville, Wednesday [27 July 1938]*

Dear Little Being,

I'm not going to write you a long letter, though I've hundreds of things to tell you, because I prefer to tell you them in person on Saturday. You should know, however:

1. First, that I love you dearly – I'm quite overcome at the thought that I'll see you disembarking from the train on Saturday, carrying your suitcase and my red hat box – I can already picture us ensconced on our deck-chairs overlooking a lovely blue sea and talking nineteen to the dozen – and feel a great sense of wellbeing.

2. *You've been very sweet to write me such long letters. I'm hoping for another this evening at Annecy. You tell me countless pleasing little items of news, but the most pleasing of all is that you've found your subject. The big page looks extremely fine with that title, just the perverse kind you like: Lucifer – I can find no fault with it.*

3. *Something extremely agreeable has happened to me, which I didn't at all expect when I left – I slept with little Bost three days ago. It was I who propositioned him, of course. Both of us had been wanting it: we'd have serious conversations during the day, and the evenings would be unbearably oppressive. One rainy evening at Tignes, in a barn, lying face down only inches away from one another, we gazed at each other for an hour finding various pretexts to put off the moment of going to sleep, he babbling frantically, I racking my brains vainly for casual, appropriate words I couldn't manage to articulate – I'll tell you it all properly later. In the end I laughed foolishly and looked at him, so he said: 'Why are you laughing?' and I said: 'I'm trying to picture your face if I propositioned you to sleep with me.' And he said: 'I was thinking that you were thinking that I wanted to kiss you but didn't dare.' After that we floundered on for another quarter of an hour before he made up his mind to kiss me. He was tremendously astonished when I told him I'd always had a soft spot for him – and he ended up telling me yesterday evening that he'd loved me for ages. I'm very fond of him. We spent idyllic days and nights of passion. But have no fear of finding me sullen or disoriented or ill at ease on Saturday; it's something precious to me, something intense, but also light and easy and properly in its place in my life, simply a happy blossoming of relations that I'd always found very agreeable. It strikes me as funny, on the other hand, to think that I'm now going to spend two days with Vedrine.*

Goodbye, dear little being – I'll be on the platform on Saturday, or at the buffet if you don't see me on the platform. I'd like to spend long weeks alone with you. A big kiss.

Your Beaver.

What does Simone de Beauvoir's letter reveal? She starts by saying this will not be a long letter, that she has hundreds of things to tell him, but that she would rather tell him when they are together. Yet she chooses the letter to tell him about perhaps the most important thing of all, which is her latest affair. I suspect she had many conflicting reasons for writing about this affair in a letter. She clearly wanted the time she had with him to be wonderfully good, but they also had an agreement that they were to be totally honest with each other about their sexual liaisons. If she told him by letter, he would have more chance to adjust to her affair before their meeting.

Her letter starts by showing a longing to see Sartre, and describes with intimacy how much she wants to share with him all their news and what they have each been doing while apart. She also offers him much encouragement and an intellectual closeness when she praises him for his choice of subject – Lucifer. At the same time as she tells him of her seduction of Bost, she also shows that he is no threat to the intellectual closeness that she and Sartre share. She refers to Bost's frantic babbling, and her inability to be really articulate in her response. She understands that Sartre would not like her to find another man more intellectually stimulating than him; this would be far too intolerable and threatening to the relationship than just sleeping with another man.

De Beauvoir assures Sartre that she is not in love with Bost, but discloses that Bost is in love with her. Does she want to show Sartre that she does indeed inspire love in other men, and that he should not take her love for granted? She cannot resist also telling him how idyllic the days and nights had been. She probably wanted to make him feel a little jealous, as she so often felt over his affairs. She does not want to push this too far, however, so she ends by assuring him that this affair will not in any way come between her and her love for Sartre, nor will it affect her delight in being with him. So in her final words she expresses this when she says, 'I'd like to spend long weeks alone with you.'

It is a letter which portrays very sensitively many of the emotional and sexual issues that arise in an open marriage, and perhaps shows why they are only undertaken by a very small minority of couples.

Together but Separate

There is another central paradox to the modern marriage which I haven't yet touched on. At the same time as couples accept that when they marry they will be true friends and lovers who share everything with each other 'til death us do part', they also feel they have a right to a considerable degree of autonomy within the relationship. They want to develop themselves fully as individuals, but frequently get frustrated and resentful when they feel they are prevented from fulfilling these desires. We live in a society where people are encouraged to believe their dreams are attainable and that personal happiness is a right. The development of the individual, however, is often at odds with the shared goals or needs of the couple and their children.

Hannah's husband wanted both his marriage and his affair. For several months he managed to have both, but one evening he returned home late reeking of another woman's exotic scent. When Hannah confronted him he admitted he had been having an affair with the ex-wife of a friend of his. Hannah said, 'When I asked him if he loved me, he said yes, but the feelings he had for the other woman were also serious. He asked me just to leave things as they were for a few weeks. I did this, as I still loved him and did not want to lose him. But I was in agony.' She continued, 'Then he told me that he had explained to his mistress that he could not leave me. He said he told her that as we had been married for over twenty-five years there was too much history, too many family commitments, that if he left it would alienate our close friends, that I had always been loving and had worked hard, and had been a good mother to our now grown-up children, and that most of all he still loved me.'

Hannah said that his mistress had apparently agreed that, if she could not have him on a full-time basis, she was prepared to share him. 'He then asked me if I would do the same. He insisted on continuing to see her, saying she was a good friend, that she needed him, and that he couldn't just abandon her.' Hannah was devastated by this and asked her husband to leave several times. She was not prepared to share him. Eventually he did finish the affair.

The 'marriage is for everything' model sets unrealistically high expectations from the relationship. There is a romantic view of what marriage should be, but when dreams of happy coupledom fail they are pushed aside by the equally strong modern belief in the individual's right to find happiness. Previous generations of women settled for far less out of marriage than their modern-day sisters. Women, like men, now pursue their own individual happiness outside marriage if need be.

According to American writer Dalma Heyn in her book *The Erotic Silence of the Married Woman* many American women are breaking out of the perfect wife mould and seeking personal happiness by combining marriage with an affair. She describes it as women discovering a capacity for pleasure through their affair (which I will discuss at greater length in Chapter Seven, on creative adultery). One woman is quoted as saying:

> I'm happy in my marriage. And happy in my affair. It's supposed not to work, or I'm supposed to be deeply troubled, and here I am, feeling better than I ever have. I know intellectually something's got to give, but then I think, why? Who said that?

Barbara Ehrenreich, the American feminist, commented on Dalma Heyn's findings. She said:

> Women are sexual beings and for women as well as men sex is a fundamentally lawless creature, and not easily confined to a cage.

When I met Dalma Heyn she told me that when she was touring America to promote her book, she was viciously attacked by nearly all the male interviewers on radio and television from coast to coast. They felt she was not only not telling the truth but by writing about it was actively encouraging immorality in American women. She insisted, however, that she was only reporting what the thousands of women she interviewed had told her.

Affairs that Remain Secret

The majority of affairs probably do remain a secret although it may be touch and go, with the unfaithful partner nearly being found out. Their partner may suspect that there is an affair going on but decides not to confront the possibility, or they may have absolutely no idea at all that their partner is deceiving them. It is quite fashionable to believe that you can have an affair, and that it really doesn't affect your marriage. I do not subscribe to this view. You cannot, I believe, have an affair that does not in some way affect you as an individual and, if so, it will also have repercussions within your relationship. I am not suggesting that these will necessarily be negative. The repercussions might be positive, but the reality is that they will be there.

You may feel that you have been extremely successful at compartmentalising your marriage and your affair. You may be very sure that the one does not affect the other, but the very fact that you have been unfaithful (unless you have an open marriage and therefore have each other's consent to sex outside marriage) means quite simply that you have deceived your partner. Your partner may not know it, but you do. You know you have broken the promise you made to your partner when you married, a promise that both of you probably took very seriously at the time.

It is interesting to look at how people handle this deceit and breach of their own code of behaviour. I think there is a male–female difference here, though the gap is narrowing. Men have an easier time justifying their affairs to themselves than women do. Men tend not to sacrifice their own desires, needs and interests to those of their wife and children as much as women do with their husband and children. Men are more used to achieving their need for self-fulfilment at the expense of others than women are. Women still tend to put their needs and the demands of their children and partners before their own. The women's movement and the trend in the 1980s towards 'the right to be me' has closed the gap to some extent between men and women, but the majority of women still see adultery as more of a breach of their commitment to marriage than men do.

The Moral Maze

Darwin believed the human species to be a moral one, in fact the only moral animal species. He wrote:

> A moral being is one who is capable of comparing his past and future actions or motives, and approving or disapproving of them.

Robert Wright, author of the book *The Moral Animal*, writes:

> In this sense, yes, we are moral. We have at least the technical capacity to lead an examined life: self-awareness, memory, foresight and judgement. Still, subjecting ourselves to moral scrutiny and adjusting our behaviour accordingly is hardly a reflex. We are potentially moral animals which is more than any other animal can say, but we are not naturally moral animals. The first step to being moral is to realise how thoroughly we aren't.

It is perhaps by accepting how very difficult it is to be monogamous throughout the life of a marriage that we can then be more honest with ourselves about the choices we make. It is tempting to say to ourselves, 'The affair just happened,' or, 'I couldn't help myself,' or even, 'My marriage was going through a very difficult time, so it's not surprising that I became involved with someone else.' Socialite Dai Llewellyn said, 'We're just not naturally monogamous.

We all occasionally like to go like a rat up a drainpipe and have a bit of a lark.' Judge Pickles would seem to agree with him when he said, 'What normal man can resist the thought of going off for a weekend with a lusting, busting, thrusting young woman?'

Perhaps one wronged wife, Frances, in the BBC programme on mistresses put the case for the defence rather poignantly when she said, 'I got silk underwear, silk pyjamas, anything I knew he liked. I worked hard at it. And thinking about it now, he must have had a rotten few months, busy sleeping with her and then coming back and sleeping with me.' Unless her husband was deeply troubled by his conscience, I rather doubt that he suffered much. We are free to make our own choices about whether we are going to be faithful or not, but we also need to accept responsibility for what those choices are. Or perhaps, as George Bernard Shaw wrote in *Man and Superman*:

> Self-denial is not a virtue, it is only the effect of prudence on rascality.

Chapter Three

DANGEROUS LIAISONS –
WHY MEN AND WOMEN HAVE AFFAIRS

Had we but world enough, and time,
This coyness, Lady, were no crime.
We would sit down and think which way
To walk and pass our long love's day.
Thou by the Indian Ganges' side
Shouldst rubies find: I by the tide
Of Humber would complain. I would
Love you ten years before the Flood,
And you should, if you please, refuse
Till the conversion of the Jews.
My vegetable love should grow
Vaster than empires, and more slow;
An hundred years should go to praise
Thine eyes and on thy forehead gaze;
Two hundred to adore each breast;
But thirty thousand to the rest;
An age at least to every part,
And the last age should show your heart;
For, Lady, you deserve this state,
Nor would I love you at lower rate.
  But at my back I always hear
Time's wingèd chariot hurrying near;
And yonder all before us lie
Deserts of vast eternity.
Thy beauty shall no more be found,
Nor, in thy marble vault, shall sound
My echoing song: then worms shall try
That long preserved virginity,
And your quaint honour turn to dust,
And into ashes all my lust:
The grave's a fine and private place,
But none, I think, do there embrace . . .

Andrew Marvell, *To His Coy Mistress*

I had been speaking at a conference on marriage and relationships, when one man came up to talk to me afterwards. He said he did not agree with my description of affairs. 'A brief fling,' he said, 'does not constitute an affair.' I looked at him questioningly. He continued, 'I don't consider that I have been unfaithful as none of my flings has lasted more than six weeks, and there has never been any commitment on my part to any of the women. So as long as there was no commitment, and they were only brief, they weren't really affairs.' He did not see his acts of infidelity as important or even as being truly unfaithful, and he seemed to relieve himself of any feelings of guilt by always ending the affair before his self-imposed deadline of six weeks.

When I asked if the same freedom applied to his wife, he said, 'Of course not,' and added that his wife had no knowledge of his dalliances. He smiled confidently, and said, 'She wouldn't really be interested in brief relationships like that.' I wondered why he thought this about his wife, when fortunately for him he was able to find so many women around who apparently did not share his wife's opinion. Perhaps this man would have agreed with the French writer Honoré de Balzac who said, 'There is no infidelity when there has been no love.'

What's Sauce for the Gander is Sauce for the Goose

Apart from a good deal of arrogance and a high degree of self-deception, which allowed the man at the conference to not only deceive his wife but also himself about what he was doing, he was also falling into the trap of believing that his behaviour did not affect his marriage. As his wife did not know, how could it possibly do any harm or affect their relationship? This is a mistake many people unfortunately make. He was also making the assumption that what was sauce for the gander was definitely not sauce for the goose. This isn't necessarily so. Though many more men than women engage in no-strings sex, it is not exclusively a male trait by any means. But so often when it comes to men's views of their own wives' sexual desires, they think that what's OK for other women to feel or do is not likely, and certainly not desirable, in their wives.

I watched a Kilroy programme on television about sexual addiction. Sitting in the front row was Jan, a young woman who the previous year had been prosecuted and lost her job because of her sexual harassment of an engine driver. She said that she was in a fourteen-year relationship with her boyfriend and had two children. She then explained, 'All year, I had been just lusting after this man who, as it happened, worked in the same company. Then I couldn't stand it any longer. I knew I just had to have him, that was all there was to it. So when I discovered him alone in one of the carriages, I just went for it. I wanted him so much that I made it very obvious what I had in mind. The trouble was that halfway through, for some reason, I changed my mind. Then I think he started to worry that his wife might find out what we had been up to. So despite the fact that he had been an extremely willing participant, he did me for sexual harassment.' She continued, 'I don't see anything wrong with what I did. Men see girls in the street with a short skirt, or large breasts and they think, "I'd like to give her one." Well, I think just the same way. I'm not looking for a relationship, I've got that back home. I just fancied him rotten.'

I have not come across this behaviour or attitude so much in the older generation, but I am increasingly seeing it among the twenty-somethings. It's still true, through, that men more than women seem able to enjoy a single act of unfaithfulness, a brief fling or even an ongoing affair at a purely sexual level. Although women can also enjoy this sort of sexual experience, they usually want a little bit more than just sex.

Woman as Carer

There are other ways in which men and women differ when it comes to affairs. Women see themselves, and are seen by the world around them, as the nurturers and carers. Even in this age of emancipation it is still women who have the main responsibility for looking after their husband, the children and the home. This nurturing role is frequently at odds with their longings for sexual excitement and experimentation outside the home and family. Men are not influenced nearly as deeply by domestic conventions.

These sort of 'ought' and 'should' messages of how women should behave have operated for hundreds of years. They have been perpetuated by previous generations of men but by women as well. So women have had drummed into them from the cradle to the grave that certain behaviour is not acceptable from them, but double standards are more accepted or natural in the case of the male. Old beliefs and expectations die hard when it comes to the changing face of women's sexuality.

Men and Women's Different Reasons for Having Affairs

When a woman embarks on an affair she is usually looking for more than just a good sexual relationship. The attraction of the affair is heightened if she really likes the man and if, in return, she feels he cares for her. Unfaithfulness for a woman more often occurs when she is emotionally as well as sexually attracted to a man. She is usually looking for more commitment from the man than he would want from the affair. This is born out by the writer and researcher Annette Lawson in her book *Adultery*. Her research shows that men and women have very different priorities when it comes to the reasons most frequently given for starting an affair.

Women's Reasons

1. 'I felt compelled by my emotions to have an affair.'

2. 'My spouse and I had grown apart.'

3. 'I had sexual needs which were not being met at the time.'

4. 'Life felt very empty.'

5. 'Life is for living.'

Men's Reasons

1. 'With care, the affair would not harm my marriage.'

2. 'I was curious to know what sex would be like with someone else.'

3. 'Life is for living.'

4. 'I had sexual needs which were not being met at the time.'

5. 'I felt compelled by my emotions to have an affair.'

Sexual Pleasure and Emotional Pleasure

In my experience of counselling, the differences between what motivates men and women to have affairs are borne out. Men are generally more able to separate out their sexual desires from their emotional needs. Infidelity for men is often, though not always, just about wanting variety, good sex, or an affirmation that they are great in the sack.

The difference with women is that they are more likely when unfaithful to be seeking a combination of sexual and emotional pleasure. For a woman to enjoy really good sex with a man, she is usually not only looking for good sex but also for a reassurance of her desirability as a whole woman.

Sexual fulfilment is entwined with the need to be loved, or at least cared for. A woman seeks in the man the possibility of friendship, of feeling understood and being valued. The old cliché of, 'Will you still respect me in the morning?' may be very dated, and may seem inappropriate to present-day sexual equality, but inside most women there is still a desire that if they are going to be unfaithful, it should be with someone to whom they mean something.

Zoe's description of her lover is typical of how many women feel at the start of an affair, 'He is wonderfully romantic, unlike my husband. He will tell me that a book he read or a film he saw made him think of me. Whereas with my husband, when he leaves the house in the morning I don't think he gives me a second thought until he returns at the end of the day. If my lover buys me flowers, they are the sort I like. Not as my husband does, which is to pick up a bunch of multi-coloured blooms at the local station or garage because he can't be bothered to get anything else.' In affairs, most women are looking for a combination of a good sexual relationship and an emotionally pleasurable one as well. Lovemaking for most women really is a mind and body experience, and though this can also be what many men want, they tend to be less demanding in this department than women.

Men tend to be rather better than women at separating their emotions from their sexual desires. Most men, if they are really honest with themselves, have at least once in their lives told a woman that they love her, or that she is beautiful or the most exciting woman they have ever met, simply as a ploy to get her into bed. Women rarely sink so low, or are men perhaps just easier to seduce?

If, as Lawson's research shows, women embark on an affair because they 'felt compelled by their emotions', it perhaps explains why more women than men are so distraught at the ending of an affair, and why many men find it so devastating when they discover that their partner has had an affair. Women frequently say, 'If my husband thought I was having an affair, he'd kill me.' I'm not saying that men would actually do this (though a significant proportion of domestic violence towards women happens when an affair is discovered), but the anticipation, real or imagined, is high in women regarding their partners' violent reaction to unfaithfulness. A man knows that for the woman in his life, the affair meant more than just sex, and so he is more likely to sue for divorce on the grounds of unfaithfulness than a woman is. Nor does he really believe her if she says reassuringly, 'Don't worry darling, it didn't mean a thing.'

The Different Types of Affairs

Just as there are a variety of reasons why people have an affair, so there are also a number of different types of affairs:

- the way-out-of-the-marriage affair
- the avoidance-of-intimacy affair
- the retaliatory affair
- the sexually compulsive affair
- the creative-adultery affair
- the marriage-in-trouble affair

The Way-Out-of-the-Marriage Affair

I believe that the reason most affairs are never discovered is because the majority of those who have affairs don't want to break up their marriage with all the upset, pain, turmoil and expense that entails. What they do want is to have their cake and eat it. There is, however, another category of people who, consciously or unconsciously, use the affair to sound the death knell of their marriage. Frequently, affairs that are open to discovery are the ones where the unfaithful partner wants the marriage to be over or, at the very least, they want their partner to recognise that the marriage is in serious trouble unless some fundamental changes are made within the relationship. Quite often, the person they are having the affair with is someone with whom they have fallen deeply in love, someone for whom they want to leave the marriage so they can settle down with their new partner.

Vivienne was married to a man who was becoming increasingly violent towards her. Despite her strong Catholic beliefs she eventually left her husband and took her ten-year-old daughter with her to live with Peter. Vivienne had begun an affair with Peter a few years earlier because she was finding her marriage more and more unsatisfactory. Peter seemed such a kind and gentle man in contrast to her husband. As a Catholic, Vivienne felt that divorce was not really an option, so she embarked on a very long and gruelling annulment.

Seven years on, despite the fact she desperately wanted marriage, Peter continued to avoid the question. If she tried talking to him about it, he would withdraw into silence until she felt she could push him no more without even more loss of dignity. 'He says he loves me, so why won't he marry me?' she asked herself continually. They had bought a house together, shared a life together, got on well, but despite her pleas he would never discuss marriage. For Vivienne this became increasingly difficult. Not just because of her Catholicism, which added to the problem – as far as she was concerned, she was living in sin – but because it seemed to her that if Peter really loved her he would want her to be his wife. She felt increasingly rejected and became clinically depressed. Peter would still not commit himself to marriage, and he also refused to see any link between this and Vivienne's depression.

Peter's parents had been unhappily married as far back as he could remember. His father was a quiet, withdrawn man and his mother had a very volatile and quick temper. She was always shouting, mainly at his father. Peter and his father had a good relationship. He was loving and kind and would spend a lot of time taking Peter fishing, and playing with him. But one evening, shortly after Peter's twelfth birthday, his father said he was going out to get a packet of cigarettes after yet another blistering verbal attack from his wife. Several hours later when he had not returned, Peter's mother called the police. They found his father. He was dead; he had quietly and silently committed suicide. He had gone to their lock-up garage at the end of the road and run some rubber piping from the car exhaust into the car, and had died of carbon monoxide poisoning. At the funeral Peter heard a neighbour say, 'She drove him to it, poor chap. He just couldn't take any more.' They were talking about his mother.

His mother never really recovered from the shock, and she never talked to Peter about his father again. Peter had to bury all his feelings of devastation, loss and anger as no one wanted to know. It was nearly thirty years later, when Vivienne became clinically depressed and the psychiatrist was talking to Peter about Vivienne's depression and the possibility of a suicide attempt, that Peter broke down. With tears pouring down his face, for the first time he talked about the devastating trauma of his father's suicide. He had never talked about the unimaginable pain he had experienced over the loss of the father he loved so much and who, he now realised, had probably been very depressed in an unhappy marriage. He also talked about how he, like the women he overheard talking at his father's funeral, thought his mother was responsible for his father's suicide. Peter felt that marriage only made a couple unhappy, so unhappy that death was the only escape, although all of this was deeply buried within him. Every time Vivienne had wanted to talk about getting married he had experienced feelings of intense pain and panic, but the only way he knew how to cope was to do what he had learned at the age of twelve, to withdraw into silence. It was not safe to talk about it. This was just what his mother had done after the death of his father. As it could not be talked about, nothing could be dealt with or confronted.

It was only when Peter was able to understand why he was so afraid of marriage that he was able to see quite what these irrational but understandable fears were doing to his relationship with Vivienne. One frosty April morning, a year later, they were married in a little country church surrounded by a few close and loving friends who had stood by them both, and who were delighted to see that Peter had at last made Vivienne his wife.

There are those, too, who abandon their marriages for their lover or their mistress, and then discover that the other man or woman is only transitional for them. In this case it is usually because the marriage is in such a bad state that the unfaithful partner has sought, and seemed to find, some of the things missing in the marriage. Closeness, understanding and desire are powerful feelings which can make the unhappily married partner feel that the person with whom they are having the affair is very important to them. But when the separation and divorce are over, they often find that they have rather less in common with this person than they thought. The reality is that the mistress or lover fulfilled a need at the time, but it was no more than that. It's pretty tough if you were that transitional person, especially if for you it was an affair of the heart.

When someone in this position really wants to end the marriage, they are not necessarily traumatised by their partner discovering their affair. It's an opportunity to confront them with the fact that they want out. Their partner, on the other hand, may have been trying to avoid this reality. Or they may have buried the facts so deeply that they say when confronted, 'I had no idea, I thought we had a happy marriage.' Either way it is pretty devastating for the betrayed partner, who is then forced to look at the real issues.

It is at this point that many couples come for counselling. As a counsellor I find this a very painful situation, not only because the couple have different agendas, but because the unfaithful partner is at a different stage too. He or she has been gradually moving out of the marriage emotionally, whereas the faithful partner is only just at the beginning of that journey. When one person really wants to end the marriage, it's more a question of how to do it, not whether to do it. The person who has not had the affair often still loves their partner, still desperately wants the marriage and continues to hope that things can be resolved, only to see their world falling apart around them.

'We had such a Perfect Marriage'

When I first met Beth, she was in a dreadful state. She could not believe that her husband had been unfaithful. 'We had such a perfect marriage', she said with tears streaming down her face. Derrick, her husband, shifted uncomfortably in his chair. 'Come on Beth,' he said rather too cheerfully, 'you know that's not true.' As they argued over this point, with Beth becoming increasingly weepy and Derrick more and more irritated, it became painfully obvious to them that they both saw their marriage quite differently. Beth could not accept that everything in the garden had not always been rosy whereas Derrick, because there was a new woman in his life, wanted to diminish a lot that had been good between them. What they were trying to work out was what they wanted to do. Beth wanted the marriage to continue, but Derrick was pretty certain that for him it was all over. But he had agreed after much pleading from Beth to try and work things out between them. To start with Beth was immensely angry – how could Derrick have done this to her? But the more angry she became, the more Derrick withdrew from her. He promised her the affair was finished, but she found it hard to believe him and watched his every move.

As they started to look at the marriage it became increasingly clear that Derrick was fond of Beth but did not love her. The more Beth felt this, understandably the more frightened she became. He was the only man for her, and she felt she could not live without him. Unknown to Beth, Derrick soon restarted his affair. Beth insisted that they go away for the weekend, just the two of them, and arranged for her mother to look after the children. Derrick did not want to go, he said it was too soon. When they got to the hotel and checked into their room, Derrick left Beth to change and said he would meet her in the bar. She changed quickly and went down to join him. As she stepped out of the lift, she glanced sideways and saw Derrick using one of the pay phones in the hotel lobby. She walked toward him, but when he saw her he hurriedly put the receiver down.

They had a telephone in their room, and Beth knew there

was only one reason why he was in a public phone box. Beth asked him if it was a call to his mistress, and he admitted it was. They went back to their room as it was too late to drive home, but most of the night was spent with Beth in tears. She begged him to give the other woman up, but he refused. Derrick was adamant he wanted a divorce. He told her that he had not been happy in the marriage for many years, he was not sure whether he loved the other woman, but he wanted to end the marriage.

Shortly after they returned home Derrick leased a flat and Beth reluctantly agreed that he should move out. He was not prepared to work on the marriage so there was nothing she could do. For the next year she wavered between hoping he would come back and trying to rebuild her life. She had a very loving family and many loyal and close friends that she had made over the years. They took her under their wing, and little by little life improved. After a year she filed for divorce.

Three years later Beth, much to her surprise, met and fell in love with someone else. He loved her, he was very companionable, and they loved doing things together. It was only then that Beth realised how very little she and Derrick had shared together, particularly in the final years of their marriage. She blossomed with the new man in her life and settled into a happy second marriage.

The Avoidance-of-Intimacy Affair

Intimacy in marriage is something most women seek. When men embark on marriage and relationships they, like women, want to love and be loved but their need for independence and separateness is top of their list of priorities. With women, intimacy and closeness are at the top of their list.

Many men, and indeed many women, are quite nervous of too much intimacy in their relationships. People are often cautious about getting too close to their partner, because it makes them feel too vulnerable. Being really close to someone also opens up the possibility of getting hurt: you might lose the loved one through death, divorce, or because they fall in love with someone else and out of love with you. Whichever it is, it involves a lot of pain. So a person who is afraid of intimacy avoids getting too close to their spouse by having affairs. An affair, even if undiscovered, undoubtedly, puts some emotional distance between the partners in a marriage. The unfaithful partner is frequently unaware of the real reason why they are seeking an affair. They are not operating at a conscious level, and are not in touch with their inner feelings. I am not offering this as an excuse, purely as an explanation.

These sort of fears are frequently rooted in childhood, and stem particularly from the relationship a person had with one or other of their parents. They may have experienced a closeness to their mother or father which they experienced as being overpowering or suffocating, and they fear that if they allow themselves to get too close to their partner that pattern might repeat itself. Alternatively they may have had a very loving relationship with their mother or father, but this closeness was broken or disrupted by death or divorce. They then lost contact with a much loved parent and the pain has gone unresolved.

The long-term effect of this is that a person is afraid to love too much in case it entails loss all over again. So when they feel in danger of loving too much, they sabotage the marriage or their committed relationship by having an affair. They take the initiative and reject their partner because they fear their partner might reject them. It is a sort of emotional damage limitation exercise. The sad thing is that their partner was probably never intending to abandon or reject them.

For Piers, promiscuity was like a drug. As soon as his affairs were discovered, Piers would beg and plead with his long-suffering wife not to leave him. He told her she was the only one he loved, that he would never leave her as she was the one he wanted to be with. He would add reassuringly that the affair did not really mean very much anyway, and he promised never to be unfaithful again. But it was like an addiction – as soon as he felt he had wooed her into staying, and the marriage was feeling loving and secure again, he would begin to get withdrawal symptoms. The adrenalin, the excitement, the secrecy, the chase, the conquest – how could he give it all up?

Piers wanted a secure base and a wife who loved him, but he was frightened of getting too close to her and of needing her too much. He wanted constant reassurance that he was desirable, and affairs provided him with proof that he was worth loving. They also provided him with an illusion of intimacy, a safety blanket in case his wife abandoned him.

Rosalind, Piers' wife, minded deeply when she discovered his first affair. She had suspected there had been others as he worked abroad a lot, but she had chosen to turn a blind eye. However, on this occasion she had gone to his desk to look for something and by mistake had opened the wrong drawer. She found a love letter from an unknown woman and was reading it as Piers came into the room. Finding the letter meant she had to confront her fears. She was deeply hurt, but she loved her husband and did not want the marriage to be over. They talked into the night; Piers promised the affair was over, that it was Rosalind he loved, and that he would never hurt her again. She believed that they both wanted the marriage to work and that they were happy together, so the marriage continued. However, a year later Piers was embarking on yet another affair. Each time an affair was discovered Rosalind was devastated, and Piers always promised it would never happen again. She loved him and, as much as Piers was capable of really loving any woman, he loved her. Sexually the marriage was very fulfilling and very good.

Piers' parents had split up when he was ten. It was a very bitter and acrimonious divorce. Piers loved both his parents, but he was closer to his mother. His mother was given custody of both him and his fourteen-year-old sister, to whom he was also very close. After a year, his mother met and fell in love with someone else, and his father applied for custody of both children. There were endless court battles and the result was that he went to live with his father, while his sister stayed with his mother.

It really was the worst of all solutions. From then on Piers, who by now had been sent to boarding school, only saw his mother and sister for an occasional weekend, and two weeks during each of the school holidays. He changed from being a confident, outgoing and rather clever child, and became withdrawn one moment, then very naughty the next. His behaviour was unpredictable because underneath he was deeply unhappy. This went almost unrecognised because after a year or two he threw himself into his school work as a way of blotting out the pain. He achieved very good exam results and everyone thought he was fine. Inwardly, however, he felt rejected and unloved, and used his achievement as a way of getting attention and praise.

Piers was attractive and clever, and he had no difficulty attracting plenty of girlfriends when he went to university. He would often be dating two or three at a time, with each of them being kept in the dark about the others. This was a pattern he carried on into his marriage. It was only many years later, when Rosalind threatened divorce and meant it, that he was able to make some changes. He was so afraid of loosing her that he agreed in desperation to go for counselling. After many months he started to understand what he was doing and why. It was very painful for him to look at his childhood and to acknowledge how it had affected his present behaviour, but he did. As he learned to trust the counsellor and to understand himself better, he was able to learn to trust Rosalind. He saw how much she loved him, and it was only then that he was able to give up his affairs and form the loving and close relationship he longed for with her.

The Retaliatory Affair

If you have been badly hurt, you often feel that you want to hit back. The desire to try and hurt the person who has betrayed you as much as you feel they have hurt you can be a very powerful emotion. It becomes a matter of, 'See how it feels', or, 'I too can have an affair,' or, 'You're not the only one the opposite sex finds attractive.' The problem is that this approach usually makes things worse in the end. The original unfaithful partner may not be able to accept and forgive the reasons for their partner's subsequent unfaithfulness as an act of retaliation.

Len, a very jovial publican, had a brief affair with one of the barmaids he employed. When Carol, his wife, found out, the affair ended along with the barmaid's job; just one of the hazards of mixing work and pleasure.

At first Carol was so angry that she locked Len out of the pub, and he had to spend the next few days with friends. The following six months were fairly difficult, but Len very much regretted the affair. He was trying hard to repair the marriage, although Carol was still very hurt and angry. She started a brief relationship with one of the customers, and another customer promptly told Len what was going on. Len was devastated and shouted at Carol, 'How could you do this just as we were trying to patch things up? How could you go off and do it with one of the customers? You made me look such a fool! How could you?' 'Easy!' Carol replied triumphantly, 'How could you humiliate me by having an affair with one of the barmaids? Half the pub knew, so now you know how I felt about that.'

It took a long time for Len and Carol to learn to trust each other enough to let go of some of their anger, but only then were they able to look at what had led to their affairs. It took an even longer time to repair the damage that they had caused. It's one thing to understand something intellectually, like the reasons for a retaliatory affair, but it's quite another matter to accept it emotionally.

The Sexually Compulsive Affair

Martin and Jennifer had been married for fifteen years. Even when they were engaged Martin, unknown to Jennifer, had been unfaithful. Since their marriage Jennifer had occasionally caught him out, and there had been tears and upset. She had once or twice threatened to leave him, but each time he'd talked her round.

Martin constantly brags to his friends about his latest sexual conquests and feels sure that Jennifer does not know quite how unfaithful he actually is. He lives life in the fast lane, always looking for new thrills at work and in his leisure time. He drives flashy, fast cars and is a member of several flying clubs, many of whom have terminated his membership as he takes such risks with the planes he flies. His friends are reluctant to fly with him – they can just about stomach the aerobatics, but when he cuts off the engine and only restarts it minutes before hitting the ground, that's more adrenalin than they want coursing round their veins. Once he was flying so low that he only narrowly missed the washing lines in the gardens, and on another occasion he put the aeroplane into such a sharp spin that the wings bent with the force of the wind pressure.

Martin impressed his many girlfriends by taking them out in his fast cars, and taking them flying. He even managed to become a member of the 'mile high' club. He would persuade his girlfriends to take off their shirt and bra while he looped the loop so he could enjoy the added excitement of seeing their breasts from all angles, or he would put their bras over his ears like earphones and pretend to call control.

Why so many women fell for his line of chat was hard to see, but they did, only to find themselves soon discarded for the next one. He always told them that he loved Jennifer, and he had no desire at all to leave his marriage. She was desperately hurt by the few affairs she discovered, but she adored him, found him amusing and stimulating, and they had a good and busy life together.

Martin's father had been a very successful international businessman. He had been a fairly distant, though charismatic, figure in the background as he was always away working somewhere. On the few occasions when Martin remembers him being around, he would show Martin off to his friends, bragging about his clever son, and what he was going to achieve in the world. Martin was aware as he grew older that his father had a series of mistresses, because he heard his parents arguing about them. His mother was fairly devoid of maternal feelings, and seemed to regard her son as an obstacle to leading the busy social life she so loved. She was constantly leaving him with long-suffering relatives or friends while she pursued her own interests. He remembered, when he was very small, protesting with tears and begging her not to leave him, or trying to be charming and entertaining so that she would want to be with him, but to no avail.

In Jennifer he had found someone quite different from his mother. His wife did love him, and he desperately needed her, but he was constantly afraid that if he loved her too much and she did leave him, all that terrible pain of his unsatisfactory relationship with his mother would come bubbling to the surface. He was not as successful as his father in his work, and he transferred his lack of success into trying to gain his father's interest and approval by his daredevil aerobatics. However, his father constantly made clear to Martin how disappointed he was over his son's missed career opportunities. So Martin moved from one conquest to the next, constantly trying to prove to himself that he was at least as successful with women as his father was. He was always trying to prove that he could pull more women than his father had.

Martin, like so many men and indeed some women, was so hurt by his mother's lack of love and interest in him that the only way he could relate to women was as objects of sexual desire. He was deeply angry with his mother and projected this onto women by using them for his own pleasure. In Jennifer, he looked for the mother he never had, but then he sabotaged that love by being constantly unfaithful to her. Deep down he was so needy of her love, but quite unable to trust her in case she abandoned him as his mother frequently used to do. In the end, what he feared most did happen – Jennifer could take no more and she ended the marriage, which devastated Martin.

The person who seems to need a constant supply of affairs or sexual liaisons may indeed find sexual variety extremely enjoyable, but there is more to it than that. They are also motivated by the constant need for approval, or the need to feel sexually desirable. Often, the chase and the power of the conquest is as much a sexual turn-on as the sex itself. Men and women who fall into this category are able to achieve such success with the opposite sex because they are charming, good looking, and skilled communicators. At a superficial level, the men know how to make the women feel good, yet when they are discovered they will go to endless lengths to persuade their partner that their latest affair was not an important relationship. It is their wife that they really love; they beg her not to leave and swear it will not happen again.

The addiction is like a drug – they need constant doses or they get withdrawal symptoms – and as they rarely analyse their behaviour they see little need to change it. The Casanova who is out to prove his sexual powers wants to collect as many scalps as possible, quantity being the name of the game. Yet another conquest proves that he is more attractive than the next man, that he still has that pulling power. This promiscuity is often masking fears of inadequacy, a constant need for reassurance, or even latent fears of homosexuality. This behaviour is not confined to the male of the species, but it does tend to be a more common male than female trait.

There is, too, the man or woman who is continually looking for perfect love, for their soul mate. So they sally forth from the safety of marriage and all too easily find their idealised lover or mistress. Everything is wonderful, they dance about on cloud nine, all their energies are focused on the new love object. Daily life and their long-suffering spouse take a back seat. Their motivation is unrealistic as they are trying to satisfy an infantile need for perfect, unconditional love, which is of course unattainable. A time will come, and it always does, when the new love in their life does something that makes them fall from grace. After all, they are human but have been invested with totally unrealistic qualities. The philanderer then feels let down, and discovers that their soul mate is no better than their spouse. So the prodigal now returns home, promises his or her spouse that they really love them, and that they will never stray again. But it is not long before they set forth once more in search of their ideal partner. If their marriage does split up, they are soon up to their old tricks again when they remarry.

Some spouses behave so badly that they drive their partners to extremes of rage. One such example was newly widowed

Stella Serth, who was convicted of a public order offence in Tasmania. Mrs Serth was fined £200 for dancing on her husband's grave and singing, 'Who's Sorry Now?'

The Creative-Adultery Affair

This sort of affair has a tremendous appeal for men and for women. The women I have spoken to who indulge in this behaviour have told me that they love their husbands, are committed to their children, and are not planning to leave their marriage. On the contrary, they feel that they have a happy marriage. For them, their affair brings great excitement and joy. It makes them feel alive again and they claim it enhances their capacity for pleasure.

Francis is by no means unique in saying, 'Because of my affair I feel more sensual and sexy. I often fantasise about Joshua when I am just going about the normal tasks of family life, thinking about how we made love when we were last together, or the brief meeting we hope to have in a couple of weeks' time. I do feel guilty. If I stand back and look at what I am doing I can't believe it's me behaving badly. But on the other hand, I feel so alive again, I'm sure I am happier and easier to live with.' She adds with a smile, 'It's not that I don't love Tony, my husband. I do. He is kind and dependable, but this affair is just something that I never expected to happen. But now it has, I have no regrets. I want my marriage, but I also want Joshua as well. In different ways both men are important to me.'

Many women as well as men are happy with their secret affairs. As therapists we tend to say, 'Ah yes! But there is something missing within the marriage, which explains why they are looking outside as a way of compensating for the problems within the marriage'. The vast majority of affairs probably come into that category, but these women do not appear to be saying this. Nor are they wanting to leave their marriage for the affair. However, neither are they just seeking sexual variety. Though some of these affairs are purely sexual, the majority of women want more than that. The relationship they have with the other man in their life is exciting emotionally as well as sexually. I will be looking at this in more depth in Chapter Seven. This type of affair is not of course exclusive to the fairer sex, just as the opportunist affair or fling is not exclusively a male prerogative.

The Marriage-in-Trouble Affair

I believe that by far the most common reason why people have affairs is because of unresolved problems in their marriage, such as lack of communication, constant rows and arguments, or a marriage where each of you is undermining the other, where put-downs and criticism are the order of the day, rather than support and affirmation. In these sorts of situations the resentments grow, you spend less and less time with each other and, when you are together, you are both too busy putting your own point of view to listen to what your partner is really saying, so nothing ever gets resolved. Eventually you may calm down and peace is restored, but if this pattern continues the resentment lingers on. The problem may be put on hold for a day or two, or a month or more, but then it rears its ugly head all over again because it was never sorted out. Within no time you have once again embarked on full-scale war or long embittered silences.

If you are constantly making each other feel rejected and unloved, it is a great killer of a relationship. You spend less and less time in each other's company because the times when you are together feel so bad. This frequently leads to more arguments because one of you resents the other for always being somewhere else. It may not always be rows, it can equally well be long, withdrawn silences – either way, nothing is resolved. You then stop talking things through together and begin to feel that you can no longer trust one another. If you start feeling pretty unloving towards your partner, you will soon find that you are making love less and less often. These things are indicators that all is far from well with the relationship. It is hardly surprising that people in vulnerable marriages are also vulnerable to affairs.

At last, along comes someone who you feel understands you, to whom you can talk, who listens with a sympathetic ear, who finds you very attractive. You tell yourself they are just a friend, someone to talk to. Maybe that's as far as it goes, but it is undoubtedly very easy to look to someone else for love and support, intimacy and friendship, sexual excitement and passion if you are missing out on these things within your marriage.

Lucinda was a woman waiting for an affair to happen, though she did not realise this for some time. She was in her late thirties, pretty, very lively and intelligent, and was taking a career break to bring up her four children. The trouble was that she felt her husband was taking a break from their marriage to build his career. It was very important to him to climb to the top of his profession. Even his parents said when she complained to them, 'You must try not to make things difficult for him by burdening him with your demands. It's natural he wants to make a success of his career. You should be prepared to take a back seat. And look at the lifestyle you have. What are you complaining about?'

Harry, her husband, was a couple of years older than Lucinda and seemed to share much the same view as his parents. For the past four years of their fifteen-year marriage he had spent more and more time at work, leaving before seven in the morning, and rarely arriving home before ten o'clock at night. He hardly ever called her from work, unless he wanted a lift from the station, or to tell her that he would be having dinner in town with the other guys from work, so she needn't wait up for him. Yes, he knew there was a parent-teachers' meeting that evening at his daughter's school, but he just was not going to be able to make it. There were a lot of things he wasn't able to make: his eldest son playing in the school concert; an important football match that his second son really wanted him to be at; not to mention countless dinner parties where he would show up two or three hours late, not only to the annoyance of his wife but also his hosts.

All Lucinda's pleading came to nothing. Harry either got cross and told her she did not understand, or claimed it would be different when he had finished this particular piece of work he was involved in. Sometimes he would make an effort for a couple of weeks, but it was never maintained.

Lucinda felt more and more that she could not compete with his work, which always seemed to take priority over her and the children. As time went on she was becoming very unsure about what she felt and whether she still loved him any more. She spent so much time resenting him and his treatment of her, that at times she was very angry with him and felt she just hated him. There was hardly any sex in the relationship because she did not feel close enough to him and he was often too tired. She admitted to herself that she was now so disillusioned, and felt so rejected by him that she had cut herself off from him emotionally as well. So even if he wanted to show her some affection when he was at home, she found herself rejecting him.

Harry said he loved her, but she felt it was too easy to just say that, whereas he never really followed it through with any action. All she experienced was that he needed her as a wife and mother, but she did not feel he really wanted to be with her, which she found very painful and rejecting. Her dilemma was that though she increasingly felt she wanted to end the marriage, she could not reconcile this with depriving the children of their father. He was an absent father much of the time, but he loved his children and gave them a lot of time and attention at weekends. So though they were often hurt by his failure to show up, he was fun when he was around, he was supportive and loving, and they adored him.

They also had a very good lifestyle, with a lovely house, expensive holidays and fee-paying schools at which the children were very happy. A divorce would mean the children would see even less of their father, the family home would have to be sold, they would maybe have to go to less expensive schools, and this would affect their network of friends. Lucinda felt the children, who ranged in age from eight to thirteen, would be deeply distressed by a divorce. She knew they would miss their father being around, and she feared that they would resent her for divorcing their father.

Her difficulty was that she felt pulled in two directions: if she did what increasingly she felt she wanted to do, which was to end the marriage, she felt this might be at the expense of the children's happiness. It was only when her husband realised he might be on the verge of losing her, that he was able to make some changes. However, Lucinda felt he was acting more out of fear of what he stood to lose, rather than because he loved her in the way she wanted to be loved.

Lucinda did not want the sort marriage her parents had. They had stayed together, but the bickering and resentments were rife throughout her childhood and she knew it was not a loving marriage. She did not want hers to go the same way, whereas Harry was not unhappy with the way things were. 'Yes', he said, 'I would like to be at home with Lucinda and the children more, but with my job that is just not possible.' He said irritatedly, 'If only Lucinda could be happy, then things would be fine.'

But Lucinda was not happy; she felt very neglected and ignored by Harry. There were several fathers at her son's school, and she used to meet them when she took her sons to cricket matches, or when she stood on the touch line shouting encouragement to her sons on a windswept rugby field. One father in particular really caught her attention, and he increasingly made a point of seeking her out and talking to her. One day while they were talking, he asked her if she would have lunch with him. It made her feel great, but she also had very strong views about openness and fidelity. She knew Harry would not approve, but she also knew she wanted to accept. At first she refused, but Matt continued to ask her and she did eventually say yes. Over the next three months, they met frequently. She tried hard to keep it purely platonic, but he tried equally hard to persuade her otherwise.

What happens in the period preceding an affair is the establishment of intimacy. If you have a spouse who does not give you much time or attention, when you meet someone who does, the whole thing can be explosive. This is what happened with Lucinda. Matt was attentive, caring, sensitive and interested in her. He was also very attractive. He was so easy to talk to, and talk they did. They talked over lunch, they talked when walking together in the country, and for hours on the telephone, either when the children were at school, or in the long lonely evenings when Harry was still in the office and the children had gone to bed.

Matt of course could not fail to notice that Harry was hardly ever around and would remark on this, fuelling Lucinda's feelings of being neglected. When you share a lot of yourself with another person, as Matt and Lucinda did, it creates a bond and it makes you feel close to each other. If you create such intimacy with someone whom you find attractive, it frequently does not stop there. So it was with Lucinda and Matt, and after several months they began an affair.

After many years of rather dull and infrequent sex within her marriage, Lucinda found Matt quite devastating. He seemed to understand her body as wonderfully as he did her mind. She could not get enough of him. They would meet once or twice a week, whenever children and work allowed. Matt had a house of his own as he had been divorced for about two years. Lucinda ceased to mind what time Harry got back from work, and even found herself looking forward to his business trips abroad so she could see more of Matt.

She took much more care over how she looked and what she wore, she lost a little weight, and looked even prettier. Her confidence took off, and she was offered and accepted a new job. She felt as if she was walking on cloud nine. For the first time in years she felt she was with a man who really wanted to be with her. Lucinda said, 'Matt made me feel interesting, desirable, pretty, and fun to be with. He said all the things I had wanted to hear and did all the things I wanted him to do. They were all the things I wanted Harry to do and say, but Harry never did. I felt I was at the bottom of Harry's list of priorities, but with Matt I was at the top.'

About a year after the beginning of the affair Harry, who had noticed how much happier Lucinda was, started coming home earlier. He would ring her from work and suggest she come up to town to have dinner with colleagues from work, or to go to the theatre. He was less tired and wanted to make love more often, and was more adventurous in his lovemaking. At the same time, things came to a head with Matt. He had fallen very much in love with Lucinda. One day, just after they had made love and she was lying in his arms, he told her how much he loved her, and asked her to leave Harry and to marry him. Over the next few months Lucinda was torn in two. One day she thought she could leave her marriage and be with Matt, but the next day she felt she could not hurt Harry, or the children. As the months passed, Matt upped the pressure. He told Lucinda that he just could not cope with loving her, and couldn't bear to think of her living and sleeping with another man. As Lucinda still could not make up her mind, Matt ended the affair.

He completely refused to have any contact with Lucinda. He said, 'If I can't have you, the only way I can live without you is to have nothing to do with you. I love you too much to be just friends.' Lucinda was heartbroken. She begged him to give her more time, but he was adamant. From then on, if she saw Matt at the school when she was collecting her son from games, he would avoid her as much as possible. He refused to talk on the telephone or answer her letters. A year later, his son moved on to another school and she lost touch with him, but she did hear on the school grapevine that he had been seen around with another woman.

At first, the affair increased Lucinda's dissatisfaction with her marriage. Although she was aware that Harry was trying harder, she still felt resentful about all those years of being left on her own. But after several more months she also started to recognise that her anger with Harry meant that whatever he did, he could never get it right in her eyes. The next year was a struggle, and at times it seemed to her that the marriage might end, but Harry started to be around more, and they spent more time together. Her parents looked after the children quite a bit, which meant that she could meet him in town after work, which she enjoyed because she felt he wanted her to be there. As she started to feel more secure about his love for her, she was slowly able to let go of her anger and they became much closer. Her job flourished, which gave her a lot more confidence. She never told Harry about the affair. Although she thought he rather suspected that something had happened, he never asked her directly, and she was never tempted to tell him the truth.

An Escape from an Unhappy Marriage

It is very easy for people to condemn those who have affairs. Although affairs can, as I have said, cause tremendous hurt and pain, they can also at times be very understandable. The picture people have of men or women who have affairs is often very different from the reality. They are not all Casanovas and Jezebels, far from it. They are ordinary people frequently trying to cope with difficult circumstances, or very stressful relationships.

James found that an affair compensated for, or at least gave him a break from an extraordinarily difficult marriage. He is now sixty-five, aristocratic, tall, good looking, and well educated. He has held a number of top jobs in a wide range of companies around the world, and he has been married for nearly fifty years. When he married at twenty-four, Elizabeth his wife was two years younger. Her mother had told her nothing about sex, and she had absolutely no idea how babies were conceived. She had never seen a man naked and on her wedding night, when she saw her husband for the first time with no clothes on, she was so horrified that she fainted. Despite the gentleness, love and patience that James showed her over the next weeks and months she utterly refused to have sex with him. Probably nowadays they would have divorced, but Elizabeth did not want a divorce. She desperately wanted children, and after they had been married for five years with still no sexual relationship, James agreed to her pleas to adopt children. Over the next four years they adopted two little girls – Elizabeth did not want boys!

For the next ten years James had several affairs, but with little or no commitment. Elizabeth did not know about them, and seemed to think there was no reason why he should not accept a marriage devoid of sex. When James was nearly fifty, he met and fell deeply in love with Phyllida, a woman who was also married and had three young children. He felt that he could not leave his wife and their two daughters, whom he loved dearly and to whom he felt deeply committed. Phyllida felt the same way. Her husband was a good and devoted father, and cared for her deeply. The fact that she no longer loved him did not, she felt, entitle her to leave him for James. So for the last twenty years they have been having an affair, and they both really feel that neither of their partners knows.

James, who is still working part-time, has now evolved a life where he is away from home quite a lot. Phyllida's husband, who is quite a solitary man, is happy for her to spend time travelling for her painting, which is her main interest outside her children and grandchildren. But over twenty years they have managed to spend an increasing amount of time together, one way or another. About ten years ago James bought a little cottage in the west country, of which his wife knows nothing, and that is where they frequently meet. Since the children have left home, James has made suggestions to Elizabeth regarding separation or divorce, but they are always flatly refused by his wife. If he tries to force the issue, she says she will take her own life if he leaves her. James feels he could not take that risk, partly because of the children and partly because he feels he could not live with himself if she carried out her threat. So after all these years, this gentle and very loveable man still feels unable to leave.

Affairs don't Just Happen

Men say affairs just happen, while women say they happen because they are bored.

ICM poll, September 1995

When asked about why they embarked on an affair, people frequently say, 'Oh! it just sort of happened,' or, 'I couldn't help it.' This is often said because the sexual desire, the longing and lusting after the person you want to have an affair with, is explosive. Being in love, bowled over, immensely attracted to someone can of course make your emotions run away with you. You feel out of control, but in fact you are not. As Angelo says to Escalus in Shakespeare's *Measure for Measure*, ''Tis one thing to be tempted, Escalus, another thing to fall.'

It may be extremely difficult to resist temptation, and you may not even want to. But whether you struggle with it over several months, or for just a few moments, you still take a decision to be unfaithful. No one else takes that decision for you. It might be that you say you were seduced, that you were powerless to resist, but it's not true. You are only kidding yourself. Not taking responsibility for your own behaviour is a particular feature among people who are persistently unfaithful. When people say that 'it just happened', or they 'couldn't help it', they are opting out of the responsibility for having taken that decision. If they can convince themselves that they were not responsible for their actions, or not in control of their feelings, they can tell themselves that what they did was not quite so bad. Maybe that helps a little in coming to terms with their own behaviour. When they are under scrutiny from the offended partner it is also a way of playing down what they did. They are hoping that their partner will collude with them and so be more forgiving.

Unprotected Sex is not an Option

Almost half of those who have had an affair did not use a condom.

ICM poll, 1995

Colin was deeply shocked when Lucille, his mistress, told him she was pregnant. She said that the baby could be his, but it could equally well be her husband's. She had told him that she was on the pill, but she now admitted that she wasn't. She had in fact been having unprotected sex with both her lover and her husband. Not only was there uncertainty over who was the father of the child, but this situation also shows a total disregard for the fact that we live in the age of Aids. Just imagine that Lucille's husband was having his own affair or affairs. Maybe he, too, was practising unprotected sex. Colin's wife could also be having an affair, and maybe so was Colin's wife's lover, and so on and so on. It's so easy to see how people in heterosexual society can contract Aids or other sexually transmitted diseases. Time and again, however, this fact is ignored or seen as something that happens only to homosexuals, which is of course entirely untrue.

As this chapter has shown, there is a whole spectrum of reasons why people have affairs. All marriages are at times vulnerable, particularly if the marriage is deteriorating, if you are growing apart as a couple, experiencing disappointment in each other, or if the marriage is turning out to be very different from what you expected.

Chapter Four

CRITICAL TIMES – PRESSURE POINTS

The problem lay buried, unspoken, for many years in the minds of American women. It was a strange stirring, a sense of dissatisfaction, a yearning that women suffered in the middle of the twentieth century in the United States. Each suburban wife struggled with it alone. As she made the beds, shopped for groceries, matched slipcover material, ate peanut butter sandwiches with her children, chauffeured cub scouts and brownies, lay beside her husband at night, she was afraid to ask even of herself the silent question – 'Is this all?'

Betty Friedan, *The Feminine Mystique*

When Affairs are Most Likely to Happen

Infidelity is one of the most common ways of trying to evade the severe emotional pain we feel when we face the emptiness inside ourselves. All marriages go through highs and lows, ups and downs, and it is when a marriage is experiencing difficulties that people are more likely to be tempted into an affair, or even actively to seek one. It can be seen as an escape, an attempt to plaster over the pain of an unhappy marriage, to make up for disappointing sex or lack of sex in the relationship. An affair may offer relief from boredom, from the feeling of being rejected and ignored, or may boost flagging self-esteem. It can be a way of seeking personal or sexual validation, or even used as retaliation after a partner's affair.

Marriages become most vulnerable to affairs when there are major changes happening in a relationship. How a couple adapt to these changes is crucial to their long-term happiness and stability. Over many years of counselling it does seem to me that there are critical times in the life of a marriage or relationship when an affair is more likely to happen. These are:

- the early years of a marriage
- the arrival of a new baby
- the in-between years
- coping with the teenage years
- when the children leave home
- in mid-life
- facing retirement

All of these periods of change in people's lives can make them more susceptible to an affair. Violence is also a wrecker of marriages, as well as a partner's addiction to drugs, alcohol or gambling. If any of these problems are an ongoing factor in a marriage, the spouse can turn to an affair as a way of blotting out the pain. Outside pressures, such as redundancy, money problems, and excessively long working hours are all problems that can lead to affairs.

When a couple first marry they usually have high expectations of how their marriage will be. If the reality turns out to be very different, if adjusting to each other and learning to live together as a couple is fraught with disagreement and rows, they are more likely to be tempted to look outside the marriage for what they feel they are not getting from their partner.

The arrival of a new baby, and the need to adjust from being the two of you to being a threesome, is never easy. Many relationships come under enormous stress when trying to adapt, and that is frequently the point at which a couple feels things starting to go wrong. Just as a couple has to adjust to the arrival of children so, too, there are considerable changes that have to be made when the children leave the nest for the first time to go to school, or when the children eventually leave home. If a woman has not already returned to work she often does so when the children go to school. This may be with the support of her partner, or he may resent the extra demands made on him by his wife and children now that she is out at work. She may be enjoying her new found confidence and independence so, if there are lots of pressures at home, an affair can seem an attractive option.

For some couples the relationship is thrown into turmoil and confusion when they find that after twenty years or more it is just the two of them again, especially if they find that they have grown so far apart that the only thing they still have in common is the children. At about this time, people also have to face the fact that they are no longer young. They are not old, but the truth is that dreaded middle age has arrived – the sort of thing that happens to other people, but surely not to you! All these problems can precipitate affairs.

Those Early Years – Different Expectations

Prince Charles and Lady Diana's marriage seemed vulnerable from the start. Charles's choice of a bride owed much to his sense of duty towards his mother and his subjects, who expected him to marry and produce an heir. In order for his bride to be suitable she had to be, if not a princess, at least from the aristocracy. She also had to be pure and virginal. If she had a past, that would somehow contaminate the marriage. The fear that one day someone might sell their story about 'how I slept with the future Queen of England' seemed to haunt him. She had to be young and, most importantly, she had to be a suitable future queen and mother of the heirs to the throne. So, for Charles, all the traditional royal expectations about marriage were uppermost in his search for a bride. When he and Lady Diana posed for the world's press on their engagement, Prince Charles was asked, 'Are you in love?' by the press, who were eager to report a fairytale romance. 'Whatever love is,' he replied. I wonder, did the newly engaged Diana experience any foreboding at his words?

For Diana, he was her prince, her knight in shining armour, who was going to love her and protect her and be hers for the rest of her life. It was the romantic love of a nineteen year old. She would have embarked on marriage expecting to be faithful, and for her husband to be faithful to her in return. It is unlikely Charles thought the same way. After all, fidelity is not a royal tradition. His predecessors were rarely faithful to their spouses. If the spouses didn't like it, it was just too bad. But Princess Diana, unlike the royal wives of the past, was not prepared to tolerate her husband's long-standing affair with Camilla. So her friends, with her agreement it is alleged, fought her cause through the pages of Andrew Morton's book, *Diana, Her True Story*, which put her side of the story, with all its growing unhappiness, in graphic detail. She was the little girl who felt devastated by the acrimonious breakup of her parent's marriage. She had felt overwhelmed by rejection and loss when her mother ran off with another man. Certainly, it would be very easy for a little girl of Diana's age to feel that she had been abandoned by her mother. After all, through her young eyes her mother left to go and live with another man rather than stay with her and her brother and sister. She might even have thought, as children do at that age, that she had contributed to her mother's decision to leave because she had been behaving badly. She experienced at first hand how destructive affairs can be to marriages, and especially to children.

When Diana discovered once again that she was being displaced, because her husband loved someone else more than her, it would have felt absolutely devastating. Not only would she have been coping with the pain any wife has to endure when she discovers her husband has been unfaithful, but it would have also raised extremely painful, and probably unresolved, memories from the past. Maybe to keep quiet about this was just too much for her to bear.

When Prince Charles and Lady Diana married, it is unlikely that their very different expectations of the marriage and of faithfulness within that marriage were ever openly expressed between the two of them. So it was perhaps almost inevitable that the marriage would run into troubled waters. What Diana saw as a love match was, for Charles, more likely a marriage of convenience.

Marriages that run into difficulties fairly soon can be particularly vulnerable to breakdown. If the fantasy and the reality are too far apart, these sorts of marriage will run into trouble once the heady first stage is past. The partners' discover that they have little in common, and the deeper more enduring love does not emerge. Unfortunately, this is an all too common pattern.

Harriet's Affair

Harriet married when she was in her early twenties. She was very pretty, and had lots of boyfriends, but no one really serious. She had known Ralph since she was about sixteen, as he had been at school with her brother. They met up again when she was nearly twenty, at a family wedding. Ralph was six years older than her, and he appeared very sophisticated and attractive to this rather naïve twenty year old. Six months later they were married.

The marriage was not easy from the start. His job meant that Ralph was away for most of the week, only returning at the weekends. It was lovely when he was there, and they had a very busy social life, but when he was away Harriet felt incredibly lonely. She had been brought up in a close-knit family, but with a very dominant mother and grandmother who both felt that once you were married, you made the best of it and did not complain about things such as loneliness.

When she had been married nearly two and a half years, Harriet became pregnant. She was delighted, even though it was a little sooner than they had planned, and money was very tight. But at thirteen weeks she miscarried; she was devastated and became deeply depressed. Her mother and older sister told her to pull herself together, that she could always have another one, so why so much fuss? Her husband could not cope at all. He, too, was of the 'pull yourself together' school, so prevalent in the upper classes. Harriet felt he did not really mind that she had lost the baby, in fact she even felt in some ways he was quite relieved as he had wanted to wait a little longer before starting a family.

Ralph just opted out of her life. He did not want to talk about what had happened, he threw himself into work, and he was absent more and more. All of this increased Harriet's sense of loss and isolation. She felt she had not only lost a baby, but a husband as well.

An old friend of her husband's called Charley was having marriage problems. Charley was very good looking, tall, slim, self-assured and outward going, with masses of charm, and always much sought after by women. He started to spend a lot of time at Harriet and Ralph's house, talking to her about the breakup of his marriage. Ralph did not seem to mind, or even be very interested. As she and Charley talked, she also found he was quite a good listener as well, and he never told her to 'snap out of it'. He wanted to know how she was feeling, and this was a new experience for Harriet.

She found herself becoming more and more attracted to him, and this was very natural. He was always there for her, and was giving her all the emotional support that her husband was unable to give. Two vulnerable people, it was a potentially explosive situation. Over the next few months Harriet slowly started to emerge from her depression. As she did so, she fell a little in love with Charley. She started to long for his visits, which became more and more frequent. Charley wanted them to have an affair, which she desperately wanted as well. But despite every encouragement from him, and with great difficulty, she refused and asked Charley to stop coming round.

A girlfriend of Harriet's saw how miserable and depressed she was, and knew she had been going through a bad patch with Ralph. She suggested that Harriet and Ralph should come and stay with her and her husband for a week or so in their house in Italy. Ralph was much too busy with his job to go, but was very happy for Harriet to get away for a couple of weeks.

When Harriet arrived at Matilda's house in Italy she discovered that Peter, an old boyfriend of hers, was staying there as well. Peter soon made it very clear that he still fancied Harriet. Harriet had been very hurt that Ralph could not find time to come on holiday, even for a few days, and she was missing Charley dreadfully. She also felt worn out from the months of depression, and very frustrated at having said no so often to Charley's invitation to make love. She was far from home, unhappy and frustrated. One evening, after a little too much Italian wine, she went to bed with Peter. He was a very good lover and she felt great to be so desired after so much rejection from her husband. But Harriet was also aware that, even while making love with Peter, she knew she was really wanting it to be Charley. So it did not happen again.

Several months later Peter, who also knew Harriet's husband, invited himself round for dinner. After dinner, when Ralph left the room to get some liqueurs, Peter tried to take Harriet in his arms. He told her that he wanted to continue the affair but Harriet refused as she knew that she was not in love with him. She was feeling very guilty about what had happened in Italy, and she did not want to get into any deeper trouble than she already felt she was in. That night Ralph made love to Harriet, and it was almost as if he suspected that there was something going on between her and Peter. It was also the first time that they had made love since her miscarriage eight months earlier, and their first daughter was conceived.

Charley came back into Harriet's life and they continued their friendship, but did not become lovers. He was around when she needed to talk, and he brought her flowers when her baby daughter was born. When his divorce came through he remarried rather quickly and not very happily. His friendship with Harriet continued for the next ten years. During this time they never went to bed with each other, despite the fact that they both wanted it.

Harriet's depression was now behind her, she was emotionally stronger, motherhood suited her, and there was another baby on the way. But her marriage was not very happy. Ralph continued to be an uninvolved husband and father. She understood why she had had the brief affair, but she was having great difficulty learning to accept her own 'fall from grace', as she put it. Her family was a very strict Roman Catholic one, and Harriet herself was deeply religious. It was made quite clear to her that good Catholic girls just put up and shut up.

One summer weekend, ten years after the birth of her first daughter, Harriet walked out on to the terrace of their house and stood for a moment behind Ralph's chair. As she did so, she saw he was writing a letter. It began, 'My darling Susie, I'm missing you so much . . .' Ralph had not heard her coming out onto the terrace, so she quickly walked back into the drawing room and leant against the wall, feeling sick and dizzy. She then gathered herself up and returned. Ralph quickly put the letter away under some papers, but Harriet confronted him immediately. She asked who he was writing to. Ralph replied, after a moment's silence, that he was writing to his mother. Harriet shouted at him, 'I don't believe you,' and she grabbed the letter. After a quick glance at it she threw it in his face. The evidence was there before them, he could no longer deny it.

Ralph then announced that he wanted to leave. He said the other woman was not particularly important but that he needed time and space on his own. He added that he 'wanted to find himself', and that this was not possible while he was married to her. Harriet thought this was ridiculous. He was away so much anyway, surely they had enough separateness in their marriage for him not to need more? Harriet begged him to stay as they were just coming up to their family holiday with the children, but Ralph was determined to leave. It was only because of Harriet's endless pleading with him that he did not go then and there. He very reluctantly agree to go on holiday with her and the children.

Harriet wanted to try and sort their marriage out, but Ralph was not interested. As soon as they got back from holiday, Ralph packed his bags. He walked out of the house leaving Harriet and the children crying in the bedroom. She could not bear to watch as he drove away in his car. Harriet subsequently discovered that Ralph had been unfaithful right from the beginning of the marriage. 'His life was littered with affairs,' she said. He had frequently managed this by telling

Harriet that he was away at a conference when he wasn't. At other times he had come home from working abroad a day or two early so that he was able to spend time with the other women in his life.

In the following year, with her marriage breaking down and Charley still on the scene, Harriet did go to bed with him, just once. But their relationship was now more one of a friendship than one of potential lovers. Perhaps they had waited too long, and sexually it was disappointing.

Her mother and her sister continued to put pressure on Harriet to try and keep the marriage together, but there was nothing she could do. Ralph was adamant that the marriage was over. He refused to talk, as he had throughout their marriage, so Harriet had no choice but to accept his decision. This was a situation, when she thought about it, that had been familiar to her throughout their married life together.

Harriet was one of the last people that you would imagine would have an affair. She was undoubtedly pretty, very lively and did not lack plenty of opportunities, but she also had very high standards about how she felt she ought to behave. These high standards were constantly being reinforced by her family and by her religion. She could have rebelled but, in the main, she tried hard to live up to everyone's expectations of her. She was brought up to believe that life was all about how you 'should' and 'ought to' conduct yourself, and she was continually struggling to live up to those standards. All of this left her with a large amount of guilt, which she had to do a lot of work on in counselling.

When trying to help couples rebuild their marriages after the discovery of an affair, I always look to see what the early days were like. In my experience, if they were never very good or it became a difficult or disappointing marriage, then the foundations for rebuilding that marriage are often just too insubstantial and the marriage does not survive an affair. Alternatively, it survives for a while only to break down several years later.

The Arrival of Children

The man is more likely than the woman to stray just before or after the birth of a child. This is not really surprising because pregnant women do not exactly feel in the best shape to pursue an affair. After the birth, for several months or more, they are usually too tired and not exactly overloaded with free time. Also, it is depressing enough coming to terms with the fact that it's taking longer than you would like to get back into shape, without displaying this to anyone other than the father of the baby.

Why do men stray at a time when, I think most women would agree, their partners need them most? Many men, even though they want children, find they start to panic when the birth is imminent. Suddenly, something that has always been in the future is about to happen, and they are knocked for six by the full extent of the responsibility that a new baby entails. This can be emotional or financial responsibility, or both. Men who are particularly likely to feel like this are the ones who have difficulty with responsibility generally. Perhaps they have moved rather haphazardly from job to job, and now they fear they will have to think much more seriously about this area of their lives, which can make them feel quite trapped. Also, their wife or partner will be taking a career break, giving up work, or only doing part-time work. So the financial responsibility really can feel very arduous and quite scary. On top of that, there is a new mouth to feed and a whole load of new expenses, such as cots, prams and all the other baby paraphernalia. So, for them, an affair is often an escape from responsibility, a sort of regression in the hope of recapturing their carefree bachelor days. It may not be a very emotionally important affair for the man, but of course for the woman it is emotionally devastating because it has happened at a time when they are a new family, which is something they may have longed for and set such store by. Also, from the woman's point of view, it comes at a time when she feels she needs a massive injection of love and extra support from her husband or partner, but suddenly he is not there for her.

A man may also be tempted to have an affair for reasons

he does not fully understand because they are deeply buried within him. Suddenly he fears a new baby is going to replace him in his wife's affections. He starts to panic at the thought of having to share her with someone else. This is usually because, as a child, a new baby appeared on the scene and the arrival was badly handled by his parents. He may have been sent away to stay with relatives, only to return to find a new baby installed in the house, taking up everyone's time and attention. His underlying and unresolved fear is that this displacement will happen all over again. To prevent this pain, he looks elsewhere for someone who will make him feel special and be there for him. He therefore seeks comfort in the arms of another woman.

It is so important to talk these feelings through together, and for the man to understand that although his wife is bound to be very preoccupied and involved with the baby, she does not want to exclude him. What she needs and wants most of all is lots of love and support herself. If she gets this, she is far more able to give love in return. If a woman feels let down by the man in her life after the birth of their baby, resentment sets in. If the man refuses to acknowledge how she feels and to make some changes, this deep resentment can take root only to re-emerge years later, particularly if the marriage runs into further problems.

The first time that Peter was unfaithful was when his wife was in hospital for the birth of their first child. Peter had always worked long hours and this had caused many arguments, but never more so than in the last few weeks of Lara's pregnancy. Lara went into labour two weeks earlier than expected, right in the middle of an important work project that Peter was hoping to get finished before the birth. He took her into hospital, but when he realised that the birth was not likely to happen for many more hours, he left a protesting Lara and went back to the office to do some further work on the contract. Nicola, one of the women working on the contract, offered to stay late that Friday and help him on the project. Peter thought that, with Lara being in hospital, he could also work over the weekend to try and get it finished. He had taken the phone off the hook as he did not want any interruptions, and they both became completely absorbed in the work. Much later, when he looked at his watch, he realised he had been there a lot longer than he thought. He jumped in his car, only to find it was at the height of the London rush hour, with nothing moving. What seemed like hours later he finally arrived back at the hospital, but he was too late. His son had been born ten minutes earlier. Lara refused to see him, and when he tried to insist on seeing her she became completely hysterical and the doctor said he had better come back in the morning, Lara must get some sleep now.

He drove back to the office, feeling dreadful. To his surprise Nicola was still there. He told her what had happened. She seemed very understanding and suggested that, as it was so late, it would be more productive if they worked on the contract together over the weekend. She said that as neither of them had eaten all day, why didn't he come back to her flat? They could have a drink and she would cook him a quick meal before he went home – and that was the start of their affair.

Two children and ten years later, Lara discovered that Peter was involved with yet another affair. She turned to him with tears streaming down her face, 'Where were you when Paul was born? How could you not be there for me? I felt so totally alone in the hospital, constantly expecting you to turn up. How could you have let me down like that?' Peter stuttered, 'I thought I would make it in time for the birth. But that's years ago, why bring that up again?' 'But don't you understand, I wanted you there,' she sobbed uncontrollably. 'But you never said,' he responded, crossing his arms and shifting uncomfortably in his chair. 'I did,' she said, her voice full of misery, 'but the trouble was, you never heard.'

Peter and Lara's marriage had worked all right until the children came along. They had both worked long hours, enjoyed their jobs and travelled whenever they could. It was not until they started a family, and Lara needed more of Peter's time and attention than he was prepared or able to give, that the real conflict started. When the children were ill, when her mother died, when she needed emotional support, Peter always seemed more preoccupied with work than with her and the children. She just got on with things, but her resentment grew.

Perhaps if they had been able to tackle Peter's fear of intimacy in relationships and Lara's difficulty in communicating in a way that he could hear, things might have been different.

The marriage did not survive. There had been too much damage done over their years together. Time after time when Lara needed Peter, he was never there for her. It's so important to try and catch relationship difficulties when they first occur, rather than years later, by which time they have frequently become too entrenched.

Keeping Love Alive

Lizzie, a pretty woman in her mid-thirties, had a good and close circle of friends. They had become friends four or five years ago when they were embarking on the fairly bonding experience of having their first babies. They had not only become friends with each other, but there had also developed good couple friendships among their set. They were now about seven or eight years into their marriages, and were at the stage of recently having had their second or third child. Suddenly in this group, it seemed that several of them were having affairs and some of the marriages were breaking up.

Lizzie's new baby was the sort that could make you want to go on and have at least four – beautiful, happy, smiley, loved everyone, and slept all night. However, she was aware of the pressures a baby and a toddler or two can put on a marriage, of how easy it is for the woman to feel worn out and resentful if she finds she is the one 'doing it all', and how tempting it is for the man to have an affair if he feels that he is left out in the cold in terms of love and affection while small children and babies seem to be taking over his wife. She acknowledged that what was happening to the group was not only very sad but also fairly scary, even though she felt she had a good marriage. She said with a smile, 'I felt it was definitely time to try to look a little more alluring for my husband.'

* * *

Most women with new babies can at times identify with the woman who feels so overwhelmed by the arrival of a new baby that she never seems to quite make it out of her dressing-gown or, if she does, the baby is promptly sick all over her clean shirt.

The Mid-life Marriage

Mid-life crises often coincide with the children leaving home, not just because they both happen around the forties or early fifties, but because they are frequently connected. The responsibility that you have had for all those years starts to fade. The children have left the nest and are establishing their own independent lives. Their departure frequently means that, as a couple, you have more time and more opportunity to look at each other and ask yourselves whether you want to spend the rest of your lives together. I am not suggesting that it is as cold and calculating as this sounds, far from it, but it is not unusual for these sorts of questions to occur around this time: 'Have the intervening years brought us closer together?' 'Do you still love me?' 'Has our relationship survived the ups and downs of family life, or are we emotional strangers living under the same roof?'

If the reality of the situation is that now you and your partner are no longer engaged in the task of bringing up the children and discover you have little else in common, then that is a marriage that is vulnerable to affairs. This is why it's so vital at this stage of life to really take a fresh look at what is happening in your relationship. It is a time for assessment and evaluation of each other and the quality and durability of the relationship.

An affair at this point in the life of a marriage often prompts couples to seek counselling. It is not unusual for the person who has not had the affair to say, 'But I thought we had a happy marriage,' while the other is saying, 'But you know we have been growing apart over the years.' As a counsellor, it is not difficult to see how differently they view their marriage. An affair at this point can be quite devastating, especially if it happens at a time when one partner is looking forward to spending more time together, only to discover that their partner is planning to do this with someone else. They then feel the past has been devalued, and that they have been cheated out of a future together. The mid-life crisis is often joked about, but it is no joke if it is happening in your marriage.

Rosemary had been married to Geoffrey for twenty-five years. Geoffrey had always been a loving husband and devoted father, and they had three children. The oldest daughter had recently married; their son, much to his father's disappointment, was not interested in following his father into the company, but had gone to drama school and was trying to establish himself as an actor; and Ann, the younger daughter, had just started at university.

Rosemary and Geoffrey lived in a pretty house on the outskirts of a busy market town. They had a wide group of friends, and Geoffrey ran his own successful business. One cold and wet December, he left her in the middle of the night and went to live in a tiny flat they owned in Cambridge, about forty miles from where they lived. Geoffrey refused all her entreaties to return to the family home, but also said he did not want a divorce. He just wanted to live on his own; he wanted some space and denied that there was anyone else involved.

Rosemary soon discovered through various friends that it wasn't one other person, as she had feared, but a whole stream of them. When she confronted Geoffrey, he admitted that over the past three years he had been having brief relationships with a variety of much younger women. He said that Cambridge was a good place to do this because it was full of attractive young women. Rosemary was distraught, but she still loved him and wanted him back. When she was able to look back over the year or two before Geoffrey walked out, she realised that a lot of changes had been happening. Geoffrey had become increasingly less interested in his job. Instead of it being a driving force in his life, he had rather let it tick over. This seemed to run alongside their son's lack of interest in the family firm. He had become less and less interested in their mutual friends, and had increasingly complained when Rosemary wanted to entertain. Golf and tennis, to which he had once been passionately devoted, no longer interested him. Even his rather right-of-centre political views seemed to have been turned upside down.

Rosemary felt that everything he once valued he now rejected. What made it so awful was that Geoffrey, this formerly loving and totally devoted father, now did not even seem to care that his behaviour was alienating him from her and from his own children. Geoffrey wanted time to try and decide what to do, so they agreed that he would come home about once a week to pick up some clothes, or occasionally have a meal with her. They got on well unless Rosemary tried to talk to him about the future. On that subject, she just could not make any headway. If she asked him what he wanted to do, or whether he would come home, he would change the conversation to how attractive the younger women found him, or sound off about something happening in the world of politics. Geoffrey did indeed seem to be having a mid-life crisis, and it nearly wrecked his relationship with Rosemary.

The turning point came when Geoffrey announced he had signed up to try bungee jumping. It was the final straw. Rosemary felt she couldn't take any more, she no longer wanted to live with someone she felt she hardly knew, who was behaving more like an adolescent than a husband. She filed for divorce on the grounds of separation and attended counselling to help her come to terms with the end of the marriage. She still met Geoffrey most weeks when he came to the house. They talked together about the forthcoming separation and divorce, which Geoffrey increasingly found very painful and which he still insisted he did not want. What was also getting through to Geoffrey was that Rosemary was talking about how she was going to build herself a new life. Even though Geoffrey never came to counselling, he also started to look at what he wanted for the future. The more they talked, the more they both began to realise that it wasn't the relationship that was over, it was much more about the life they had shared over the past twenty-five years.

Geoffrey had thought that Rosemary was perfectly happy with their lifestyle and that she did not want any changes. By comparison, he had felt increasingly stuck and dissatisfied. As they met and talked over the course of the next year, they decided that they wanted to make the changes together. They sold the family home and bought a much smaller house in Cambridge. Geoffrey brought a partner into the firm, which gave him much more time to travel and write as he had always longed to do, just as his son longed to act. Rosemary and a friend set up a small business catering for weddings and parties. She very much enjoyed running this as she now no longer had the children to occupy her time and attention. In addition, she was also able to contribute to the family income, which became necessary as Geoffrey was bringing in a lot less. Geoffrey was able to advise on the financial side of things, which made it feel like a joint venture. The need for Geoffrey's extramarital activities became a thing of the past.

A mid-life crisis does not necessarily mean the person is rejecting you, though that's what it feels like. What is often happening is that they are reassessing the whole of their life, comparing the reality with what they had expected would be happening to them when they reached this stage in their lives. Mid life is a time when you want to reassess where you are and to see how you want live for the next thirty years or more.

Mid life is also a time when you become increasingly aware of your own mortality. This is often precipitated by the death of a parent. You suddenly find yourself the older generation, with youth slipping away, and that feels quite scary. The attractions of an affair with someone much younger, or throwing out the old lifestyle, are often ways of clinging onto your passing youth. So an affair, the rejection of a partner, or the loss of interest in all the things you have previously valued are very typical symptoms of a mid-life crisis. Many couples like Geoffrey and Rosemary, given time and a lot of hard work, are able to come through and rebuild a happy marriage.

Major Crises that Precipitate Affairs

Major crises can also make marriages vulnerable to affairs. These might include the death of a child, redundancy, having your house repossessed or having an elderly relative coming to live with you. People can embark on affairs at times like this because they provide escape routes from situations they find difficult to cope with. Sometimes affairs happen because, rather than feeling that the trauma they are experiencing is drawing them closer together, couples find that the pressures are driving them apart. An affair at this point naturally intensifies the problems in the marriage, because you have less time for your partner. When he or she discovers the affair, they feel doubly outraged and demand, 'How could you do that at a time when we needed each other most?'

Being made redundant can, in the end, turn out quite well, with new opportunities and a new or different job. However, at the beginning it is a huge shock to the system, especially nowadays when you fear that you will never find another job, or that you may have to settle for something well below your ability. In the early months of redundancy you often have to come to terms with fundamental losses of status and identity which men, in particular, gain through the work they do. It can mean the loss of a home, and certainly the loss of a lifestyle. It's much more difficult to go out to see friends, or to entertain at home, so isolation can creep in. You may find it difficult with children, as you have to cut down on what you want to do for them, whether that's a family holiday, a new bike or a pair of trainers like all the other kids have. Your partner may be very fearful about the future, or may find that they were not prepared for you to be around at home all day, which only increases your feelings of rejection and loss.

If someone makes a play for you in this situation, or you are attracted to someone who makes you feel worthwhile and desirable, it can be very heady stuff. If you embark on an affair it might give you back some self-esteem, but it might also stop you trying to sort out the original problem. That could drive an even bigger wedge between you both, and you may then find that you are not only having to cope with redundancy, but with the possible loss of the marriage as well.

Of course it's not only the person who has been made redundant who can be tempted by an affair. Supporting someone when they have been made redundant can be an uphill task. You may give too little thought to how your partner might be feeling or how difficult it is for them to cope with your redundancy, because you are so engrossed with your own problem.

When Elaine's husband was made redundant, she found it very hard to cope. Jim was naturally rather laid back, and in many ways Elaine would have found it easier if Jim had minded rather more about being made redundant. He settled, she felt, all too easily into not working and, as she only had a part-time job, money was really tight. They rowed a lot because she felt that Jim was not trying hard enough to get another job. His attitude was, 'I'm trying but there's no need to be constantly worrying about it. That just gets you nowhere, so stop nagging.' He also tended to go off fishing when she thought he should be helping her out with their three children and doing more round the house. One day, six months after he had been made redundant, Jim came home unexpectedly from a day out fishing. He had planned to spend the whole day fishing but had caught very little. He had become bored and had returned home earlier than expected. He discovered Elaine in bed with their next-door neighbour. Jim was outraged and, despite his usual mild manner, he suddenly flipped. He threw the man out of the house and flung his clothes after him. He grabbed his wife and forced her upstairs and pushed her onto the bed. Then suddenly all his anger was gone, he sat on the edge of the bed and wept and wept.

Many months later, when they were able to talk over this time, Jim said, 'Elaine is the only woman I have ever truly loved. I just can't believe that this has happened. I've always trusted her.' Elaine, who had been very shaken by what had happened, said, 'I've never seen Jim so angry or so hurt. I don't think I realised quite how special I was to him'. This was particularly reinforced for her when she discovered that the man she had had the affair with, who seemed to have all the get-up-and-go that she wanted in Jim, had rather too much get-up-and-go where women were concerned. She soon discovered that she was not the first in the area to fall for his charms and that there was quite a trail of women with whom he had also played around. Shortly after this episode, the neighbour and his long-suffering wife split up and they moved away.

For Jim and Elaine it was touch and go for some time, but they managed it. They talked a lot about how they had got into a rut, how they were taking each other for granted, and how neither felt very supported by the other. They also reviewed what they would really like to do as well as how to bring in more money. Elaine got a good job and Jim looked after the children, which he discovered he loved. He even learned to cook, much to Elaine's surprise. After a little while, he also found some part-time work, which he enjoyed and found he could fit it in around the children. They both enjoyed their changed role, and both were surprisingly good at it.

Sometimes affairs can precipitate a couple into really rescuing their relationship, painful though it is. If love is still there and they are both prepared to make changes, they can come out the other side with a stronger relationship or marriage than before the affair, but it takes a lot of time and hard work.

No Marriage is One Hundred Percent Safe

The fact that there seem to be certain times in a marriage when people are particularly vulnerable to an affair does not mean to say that this does not occur at other times as well. In marriage nowadays we want the combination of a companionable marriage where we are the best of friends, but also romantic love, and a passionate and satisfying sexual relationship. It is a lot to look for in any relationship, let alone in one that lasts many decades.

It is unrealistic to think that all of these things can exist at a totally satisfying level throughout the marriage. There will be times in all marriages when things are either better or worse than at other times. There will be highs and lows, ups and downs. There will be times when we feel very happy and satisfied with our partner and our life, and other times when we experience disappointment in them, or frustration and worry about what is happening in the rest of our lives. Sometimes the very sameness, or an 'Is this all there is?' feeling, seems to matter much more than at other times. If we are experiencing one of the less satisfying or disappointing times in our relationship, and this coincides with the opportunity or possibility of an affair, we are naturally going to be more vulnerable to temptation.

This does not mean that I am suggesting that an affair happens because, to use an age-old excuse, 'I just couldn't help it.' No, what I am saying is that at times it may all be that much harder to resist, but you can always say no. You do have a choice, unless you want to fool yourself.

How to Resist Temptation

First try and identify whether your relationship is at a critical point:

- Is your marriage or relationship at a low point or going through a difficult time?

- Is your partner taking you for granted?

- Do you feel that work is your partner's priority, rather than you?

- Are you spending enough time together?

- Is your partner unromantic, or has romance died?

- Are there sexual problems? Are you only making love infrequently, and has sex become mundane and predictable?

- Are you pulling in opposite directions because there are some major changes happening in your life, like the arrival of a new baby or the children leaving home?

If you are experiencing some or a combination of these problems, your resistance is likely to be low. It may feel easier and more fun to look elsewhere, or to respond to one of your colleagues at work who has suggested that it might be rather nice to have dinner together sometime. On the other hand, you may want to try and tackle the issues that are driving a wedge between you and your partner. If this is so, try some of the following tactics.

- **Start by identifying what you think your reasons are**.
  Talk to your partner about your dissatisfactions within the relationship, and see if you can do something about it. Work towards the changes you and your partner can make.

- **Own up!**
  It may sound crazy, but if you are very attracted to someone and genuinely want to resist temptation, tell your partner in a fairly light-hearted sort of way that you quite fancy this particular person. That way, if you are tempted to take things further, your partner will be alerted. They will be much more difficult to deceive, so you may not try. Also, your partner may well become more eager to meet your needs.

- **Introduce them to your partner**.
  It's more difficult to deceive your partner with someone they know.

- **Are you wearing rose-coloured glasses?**
  Ask yourself what a lover or mistress could provide that your partner can't. And if so, why not?

- **Is someone making a great play for you?**
  Are they offering love, friendship, great sex, excitement and novelty? Are they making you feel totally desirable, or madly in love? If so, you may well be sending out available messages or taking every opportunity to spend time alone with them, which is creating all this intimacy. People who play with fire often get their figures burnt. It could happen to you.

- **Has your sex life got a little boring?**
If it does need some spicing up, introduce more variety into how, when, where and how often you make love. Or, if the problem is deeper than that and you have lost all sexual desire and just shut down sexually, ask yourself if you are being realistic or fair to think that either you or your partner won't be tempted to look elsewhere. Isn't it better to try to sort out what is wrong, rather than imagining the grass is greener somewhere else?

- **Why not have an affair with your partner?**
People who embark on affairs tend to take more time making themselves look good. They spend extra time in the bathroom, working out at the gym, or losing weight. Buy some silky or sexy underwear, throw away those threadbare underpants and invest in something more stylish. As a man, don't walk around in just your socks – it's a real passion killer. As a woman, don't go to bed covered in face cream or with rollers in your hair – it's not exactly the *femme fatale* look. Buy some new scent, aftershave, or bath oils. Instead of taking all that trouble for someone else, take the time and trouble to make yourself look good for each other.

Finally, try to analyse why you are tempted by the idea of an affair. Is your marriage in such a bad state that you are no longer in love with your partner and an affair is a way out of the marriage? If so, embarking on an affair as an exit route is an extremely messy and painful method. If you think the writing really is on the wall, you may need to do some serious talking with your partner, and even consider counselling, to see if the problems can be resolved.

Chapter Five

CAUGHT IN THE ACT

I made him swear he'd always tell me nothing but the truth.
I promised him I never would resent it.
No matter how unbearable, how harsh, how cruel.
How come
He thought I meant it?

Judith Viorst, *Nothing but the Truth*

Andrew was searching through one of the drawers in the bedroom, which was full of old letters, bills and general paraphernalia, when right at the back of the drawer he came across a make-up bag that he had not noticed before. He was just about to put it back in the drawer when something made him open it. Inside were two packets of condoms of which one had a few missing, a bottle of expensive scent, and a couple of pairs of very pretty silk bras and pants. He put the bag back in the drawer in exactly the same place, but over the next week he found himself wondering why it was there. He loved his wife deeply and felt that they had a very good marriage, so why the condoms? After all, he had had a vasectomy five years ago, and before that his wife had been on the pill.

During the next few weeks he returned to the drawer, and felt sure that there were fewer condoms than when he had originally found the bag. However, the bag was always in the same place, so perhaps he was mistaken. His wife Polly had spent every Tuesday for the last couple of years with an old school friend. She would drop the children at school in the morning, then drive the thirty or so miles to her friend's house, and return in time to collect the children again. Andrew kept on checking the bag to see if there were any condoms missing. He thought that maybe there seemed to be fewer on the day after Polly had spent time with her old school friend. But despite the fact that there seemed to be enough evidence to make him pretty suspicious that Polly was being unfaithful, he did not confront her directly. Part of him could not face the fact that Polly might be being unfaithful, and he just could not bear to voice his suspicions. He said, 'I just wanted the affair to stop.'

The marriage was good; they had a satisfying sex life and two children they both adored. They both liked their jobs and had a good lifestyle with lots of friends. Andrew said, 'Sometimes I think I'm imagining everything, and at other times I'm fairly convinced that Polly is having an affair. But then I tell myself that, if I say nothing, she might just get this man out of her system. I want the affair to end, but I feel if I confront it, I might not be able to cope, because I love her so much.' He thought about checking up on Polly to see if she did spend the day with her friend, or perhaps telephoning her school friend and confronting her, but he could not bring himself to do this.

Andrew knew that above everything else he wanted the affair to stop. He decided that each week he would move the bag a little so that it was always in a slightly different place from where she had left it. He hoped that Polly would start to see some warning signs and realise that he knew what was happening. After a few weeks, he noticed the number of condoms remained the same and the scent was now standing on her dressing-table.

One evening they were watching a film on television in which a woman had been unfaithful to her husband. Andrew turned to Polly and talked about how unbearably painful he would find it if that happened to them. Polly was very quiet, and said she was tired and wanted an early night. As the weeks went by Andrew felt fairly sure that the affair had ended. He might have been deluding himself, but he had made the choice not to tackle Polly openly. Some might think he never tackled it at all. If Polly was having an affair, she never confessed it. Maybe she just became more careful, or perhaps she realised how much she was hurting Andrew and so decided to end the affair. It's now two years on, the marriage has survived, and Andrew says they are happy.

Jim handled things very differently from Andrew. During the eight years of his marriage to Holly, Jim had had several 'flings', as he described them. But when he discovered that his wife was having an affair, he threatened to end the marriage.

He remembers that gut-churning feeling that perhaps Holly was being unfaithful. His anxiety increased when he came home from work one day and heard his wife putting the telephone down rather too quickly. His suspicions were instantly aroused. He wasted no time in getting in touch with the telephone company and asking for an itemised bill. When the bill arrived he found lots of calls to a number he did not recognise. He immediately rang the number, and when a man's voice answered Jim hung up. That was proof enough for him. He got into his car and drove to where Holly worked, waiting for her to come out for her lunch-time break. She was surprised to see him there, but at his request she got into the car. As soon as she had shut the car door, Jim drove off at speed and they arrived home in record time. Jim screamed at her that he knew about the other man and that the marriage was over. Holly confessed that she had had an affair. She told Jim that it was not an important relationship, which was true, but was a reflection of the fact that she had felt very neglected by him over the last year. Holly finished the affair immediately.

The marriage did survive, but for over a year it hovered on the brink of divorce. When Jim's anger subsided a little, he admitted that he loved his wife. He had been taking her for granted, and had not been very involved with his children. But for a long time, try as he might and despite his own indiscretions, he found it impossible to forgive Holly for the brief, and as far as she was concerned not very important relationship, with another man. Once Jim became more loving and more involved with the family, Holly was able to forgive him for his 'flings', though she could not forget the fact that Jim had been unfaithful.

Andrew and Jim are perhaps at opposite ends of the spectrum in their reaction to their suspicions about their wives' affairs. Whether you choose to see the tell-tale signs or to ignore them is something everyone has to deal with in their own way. In this chapter I will be looking at what you can do if you suspect your partner of having an affair. Some people choose to remain silent, while others are determined to confront their partner with their suspicions. Some people choose to confess their affair, and yet others keep their affair secret. If you are going to disclose the affair, to whom should you confess? There are no hard and fast rules about the right or wrong way to behave in such circumstances, but there are usually tell-tale signs if you choose to notice them.

Tell-Tale Signs that can Indicate your Partner is Having an Affair

- Coming home later and later from the office or the pub, sudden weekend conferences, or an increase in meetings out of town which entail spending nights away.

- Being emotionally unavailable, reluctant to spend time with you, and constantly being too busy to talk.

- A change in behaviour, such as spending longer in the bathroom, new scent or liberally applied aftershave.

- A lack of interest in sex, or a sudden renewed energy, introducing little things into your lovemaking that they have never done before.

- Lipstick on their collar (corny, but true!) or the lingering smell of a scent or an aftershave that you do not use.

- Rushing downstairs to be the first one to get to the post in the morning.

- An increase in the telephone calls which go dead when you answer, or if they take the call when you're in the room, somehow it's another wrong number.

- Constantly including another couple in all your social engagements, supper parties, trips to the cinema, even holidays. Sometimes the person you thought was your best friend is closer to your partner than you realised.

- A sudden interest in working out at the gym, along with standing in front of the mirror to see if their tummy is a little bit flatter, or their legs are in better shape.

- An air of preoccupation, as if they are somewhere else in a world of their own, enjoying a secret you cannot share.

- Suddenly finding fault with you, criticising everything you do, say or wear; a feeling that you can never get it right, and that somehow everything is all your fault.

- Dragging a reluctant dog out for a late-night walk, when the dog would much rather be left to sleep in his warm basket. On the otherhand, if they had previously seen this particular thing as a chore, they are now the first to offer their services.

- When your partner frequently dials 141 before making phone calls so that you cannot check to whom the last call was made.

- When beautiful silky underwear starts replacing the rather more functional variety, or they are worrying about which pair of pants or which particular shirt is washed and ready to wear.

- When you find an unexplained hotel bill, theatre tickets, or credit card receipts for flowers, jewellery, or a cashmere jumper that you never received.

- If he is over forty and suddenly starts listening to Radio One, he could be trying to get on the same musical wavelength as a much younger woman.

- If your partner starts to dress like a man or woman twenty years younger.

Having read this list, it's important not to jump to conclusions and assume that your partner is having an affair. If you discover just one or two of these things, they may be harmless enough. If you can identify several from this list, there may still be a perfectly acceptable explanation, but you may also be right to be suspicious. A lot will depend on just how significant these changes are, whether it's just a case of a one-off incident, or whether these changes persist, like constantly being away from home or being deliberately vague about where they are.

Forbidden Fruits

Secrecy is an essential part of an affair, which is at odds with the honesty which most people say they expect in a good marriage. The illicit factor, or the secrecy aspect, may be one of the excitements of an affair for many people – only being able to see each other in snatched moments, a few delicious stolen hours in the afternoon, an occasional blissful night together, or an idyllic weekend where you seem to exist only for each other. Sometimes this seems impossibly frustrating, and much time may be spent in telling each other how fervently you wish it could be otherwise.

For most people the secrecy is part of what makes it so exciting, an aphrodisiac even. As you do not really spend much time together it certainly does not allow time for boredom to creep in or for you to start taking each other for granted, the reasons that drive so many people into affairs in the first place. If these aspects do start to emerge, an affair is much easier to end than a marriage.

Basically, if two people have a good relationship it is usually because they share all the important aspects of their lives with each other. An affair is, by its very nature, conducted in secrecy, unless a couple have agreed on an open marriage.

Therefore, once an affair is embarked on, one of the partners is being deceived, and honesty is no longer applicable in that marriage. By introducing deception into a relationship, the ground rules are altered. The open and honest relationship that is part of a trusting and loving marriage has gone. The reason is that there is now an important part of your life that is not shared with your partner.

To Confront or not to Confront?

In most other aspects of relationships people benefit by being open and honest with each other, but when it comes to disclosing an affair, the waters are already muddied by dishonesty. A decision is more likely to be influenced by whether you think you can get away with it, irrespective of whether your partner is confronting you with some pretty damaging evidence. If your guilt is weighing you down, you may long to confess all. You will also be influenced by what you think the outcome of telling all is likely to be.

A realisation that your partner is having an affair usually starts with what can only be described as a gut feeling. Some people at this stage choose to ignore the feeling altogether. They try and rationalise their partner's suspicious behaviour, and deny the little signs that might be around, rather than confront the truth.

Rachel's husband Bob had a new secretary. For the first six months, whenever Rachel phoned Bob at the office Leslie, the secretary, was polite but distinctly cool. When Rachel wanted to speak to her husband, Leslie would often say she could not interrupt Bob as he was tied up with meetings, but she would get Bob to call her back.

Rachel eventually complained to Bob, and he said he would speak to Leslie about it. Leslie completely changed. When Rachel called she would engage her in conversation, ask about the children, and get Bob to the telephone with no problem. Rachel was delighted. If Rachel found she was short of milk or bread, Leslie offered to buy some for Bob to bring home. She even wrote Rachel and the children's birthdays into his desk diary. At the same time Bob was coming home later and later, and he seemed very preoccupied with work. He also frequently said he was too tired for sex. Rachel's reaction to these changes was to involve herself more and more with the children, and to throw herself into the work she did for a local charity.

One day Rachel was in town and had been a lot longer than she anticipated, so she called in at Bob's office thinking she could get a lift home in the car. Neither Bob nor his secretary were there. When Bob arrived home three hours later, complaining about his work schedule and how worn out he was, Rachel knew he was lying. But it was three months later before she actually confronted him, because part of her still wanted to avoid the truth. She was worried that if she did confront Bob, he might leave her.

Just as the person who is not having the affair will rationalise their partner's behaviour to avoid confronting the truth, so the person having the affair will also rationalise and justify their own behaviour, usually because they want to continue the affair and still have their marriage. They will say to themselves, 'What she/he doesn't know can't harm them,' or, 'No one is getting hurt, so what's the problem?' When this is happening the couple are caught in a collusive relationship.

A collusive relationship is one where both people are consciously or unconsciously agreeing to ignore what is happening. They are choosing to deny their own or their partner's behaviour. This collusive behaviour is usually only broken when there is just too much evidence of unfaithfulness, making it almost impossible to continue to deny the facts which are now staring them in the face. It can also be broken if circumstances change. For example, if the intensity of the affair begins to diminish the unfaithful partner is then more likely to realise how much they might lose if the affair were discovered. Even though their partner might not know or have said anything, they are able to see more clearly that they are hurting their partner by their affair. They may have been very critical of their partner, quite unfairly, to justify their entitlement to an affair. Alternatively, they may be finding the guilt about the affair too difficult to cope with.

If people are going to confront their partners with their suspicions, they can only do so in their own time and at their own pace. Some will rush in when the first doubts emerge, but the majority, once their suspicions are aroused, start to look for evidence.

Annie began to suspect her husband Steve was having an affair with Susan, her best friend. Her suspicions were aroused when it started to occur to her that Susan's visits always seemed to coincide with the times when Steve was around. Annie said, 'Every time Steve came into the room there was this incredible sexual tension around. Although Susan was talking to me, her eyes just followed Steve everywhere. One evening after I had gone to bed, I thought I heard Steve on the telephone. I crept to the top of the stairs, and I heard him arranging to meet someone. Then he said, "I miss you, I'm just counting the minutes until we can be together." My heart just stopped. He put the phone down and walked into the kitchen, and I ran back into the bedroom and dialled 1471, which tells you the number of the last incoming call. It was Susan's number. I knew it had to be.' A few minutes later, when Steve came upstairs to bed, Annie confronted him with the evidence.

Most people find it difficult to know the right time to confront their partner. One indication is that, even though they are afraid of confronting their partner with the truth, trying to avoid doing so feels even worse. The reason many people avoid confrontation is because, by not saying, anything, they are desperately trying to hang on to the hope that it might not be true. Or they are afraid of the repercussions if they do confront their partner. They are concerned that it will mean the end of the marriage, either because they think that is the only way forward for them, or because they fear that their partner will choose to leave them for the other person rather than opt to finish the affair. Sometimes the unfaithful partner still expects to continue with both the marriage and the affair.

How to Confront your Unfaithful Partner

Confronting a partner who you think is being unfaithful is not easy. It's not very helpful to charge in like a bull in a china shop at the first tiny sign that there may be something wrong. There could be a lot of other explanations for their changed behaviour, their apparent break from routine, or their preoccupations. So some gentle questioning about whether there is anything wrong, whether they are worried about something, whether it would help to talk about it may well uncover the reason for their changed behaviour and show you that your suspicions are unfounded. If there is total denial that anything is wrong, or if you get an aggressive response to a gentle question, then that is a warning sign. If they express complete surprise that you could possibly need to question them about anything, or if they are very indignant about the fact that you are expressing a slight lack of trust, then your suspicions may be well founded.

The reality is, if someone has nothing to hide they will be fairly relaxed in their response. It is usually the guilty who protest too much. However, if you are married to a polished deceiver, or someone who is an accomplished liar, then they will be unlikely to lose their cool at this stage. If your doubts are not allayed then it's usually a question of collecting more evidence. Sadly, if you are going to continue your investigations, it is rather like being a private detective within your own marriage, and it does not feel good. But if the evidence does accumulate and you are feeling pretty certain that your suspicions are well founded, then it is best to think carefully about when and where to confront your partner, rather than just blurting everything out.

Sara discovered her husband Larry's affair after finding a letter in his briefcase from a girl, describing in every intimate detail what they had done in bed together. She was trembling with fury and rang him at work, only to get his office answerphone. She screamed down the line that she knew he had been screwing another woman and that if he came anywhere near her she would chop his f-----g penis off with a carving knife. Larry was at the time sitting in his office having a meeting with a couple of his colleagues, and was so taken by surprise that he was too late to turn the answerphone off.

If possible, it is better to arrange a time and place where you know you can have some time on your own, away from the public gaze. A restaurant is not a good idea, because one of you is likely to be angry and there will probably also be tears. It is equally important to be out of earshot of the children. Pick a time when you are hopefully not going to get any interruptions. Take the telephone off the hook, to avoid a call coming at the wrong moment and giving your unfaithful partner the chance to try and get off the hook by insisting that they must take the call.

It is best to start with the simple question, 'Are you having an affair?' After your partner's response, follow this up with the reasons and, if possible, the evidence that has convinced you that this is what is happening. Eventually, when confronted with enough evidence combined with their awareness of the sheer cruelty of prolonging the deception, most people will own up, though you might have to go through this process several times. There are some people who, despite all the evidence apart from an actual photo of them having sex with someone else, will continue to swear blind that they are telling the truth.

However much you think you have prepared for the moment when your partner does confess to the truth, you are never really ever fully prepared. To start with, having your worst fears confirmed is always an enormous shock. There may be some relief in knowing the truth, in realising that you are not going mad, and that you are not just imagining things as you have been constantly told, but that usually comes later.

To Tell, or not to Tell: that is the Question

Dear, they said that woman resembled you.
Was that why I went with her, flirted with her,

raised my right hand to her left breast
till I heard the still sad music of humanity?
I complimented you! Why do you object?

Still you shrill, discover everything untrue:
your doppelgänger does not own your birthmarks,
cannot know our blurred nights together.
That music was cheap – a tune on a comb at best,
harsh and grating. Yes, you chasten me

and subdue. Well, that woman was contraband
and compared with you mere counterfeit.
Snow on the apple tree is not apple blossom—
all her colours wrong, approximate,
as in a reproduction of a masterpiece.

Dannie Abse, *In My Fashion*

Birmingham divorce solicitor Diane Benussi believes that women are much better at sussing out their men's affairs, and that men are nothing like as clever at doing this. She claims that, 'Women are just like the Mounties; they always get their man.' This is borne out by a poll undertaken by ICM in 1995, which states that women are more likely than men to discover their partner has been unfaithful: men do not find out about sixty percent of their partners' affairs, whereas women do not find out about forty percent of their partners' affairs.

The same poll shows that almost a quarter of those interviewed said that they would not forgive their partners if they found that they had been unfaithful. Both men and women experience enormous pain when they discover their partner has been unfaithful, but most men seem to find it harder to forgive than women. If you look at the divorce statistics, men are more likely to divorce their wives on grounds of adultery, and women are more likely to divorce their husbands for unreasonable behaviour.

It is up to each individual to make up their own mind whether or not to tell. In my opinion, there are times when honesty is undoubtedly the best policy and other times when to tell all is quite frankly an act of utter selfishness.

Kathy became suspicious about her husband's behaviour when a neighbour mentioned seeing Leonard, Kathy's husband, on the previous Saturday with a woman in another part of the town. This was some distance from where Kathy lived, and also a different district from his place of work. The next Saturday afternoon when Leonard said he was off to watch his usual team play football, Kathy followed him in her car. He did not drive to the football ground, but to the part of town where Kathy's neighbour had seen him with another woman. He stopped his car outside a house, rang the doorbell and was let in. Kathy waited for about half an hour, and then went and rang the bell herself. To start with no one came, so Kathy kept on ringing. Eventually the door was opened by a woman in a dressing-gown. Kathy pushed her way into the house and demanded to see her husband. Leonard had literally been caught in the act, and he could not deny it. He finished the affair immediately, and begged Kathy to forgive him. Then he dropped his bombshell.

He told her that, during their twenty-year marriage, he had had a seven-year affair with another woman who had died of cancer two years ago. He thought that, as Kathy had discovered this latest affair, it was better to admit to the other one as well. He said, 'That will give us a chance to be really open with each other, to start again with a clean slate.' He did not want a divorce, and he insisted that he loved Kathy and wanted to make a go of the marriage. Kathy said, despairingly, 'Why did he have to tell me? I think I could have coped with his brief three-month affair with a woman he said meant little to him. But not with a seven-year affair. I didn't believe him when he said it was just about sex. If it went on for that length of time, there had to be more to it than that. I was haunted with things like the anniversaries we had celebrated, knowing now that this other woman had also been part of his life.'

Leonard seemed to be using the discovery of his brief affair in several ways. Firstly, as a confessional box, where he offloaded all his sins in the hope of being forgiven. As he was having to deal with the guilt he felt over one affair, he thought that he could use this opportunity to lessen or get rid of the guilt about his seven-year affair, which up till now he had had to contain on his own. It may have helped him with his guilt, but it crucified Kathy. She said that she really had no idea that he had been unfaithful for all those years.

It also seemed that Leonard was fairly angry with Kathy for following him and catching him out. His response was to punish her for behaving badly by then telling her about his other affair. His attitude seemed to be one of, 'If you really want to know what I'm doing, then you can know the lot.' By doing this, he was also unconsciously projecting his own bad behaviour on to Kathy, then punishing her for it as a way of abdicating some of his responsibility for his own bad behaviour.

In the past, husbands were less likely to tell their wives about their affairs than they are nowadays. That was largely due to the fact that they felt more entitled to have affairs. This was the accepted, though unspoken, agreement of many middle-class and, in particular, upper-class marriages. Marriages were not usually based on the 'marriage is for everything' concept, but rather on finances, property, the right place to have children, and a man's desire to look after, protect and provide for his wife and the mother of his children.

In Annette Lawson's research into adultery she reveals that two-thirds of wives nowadays are told by their husbands of their affair. This is not because husbands are confessing in droves but more, I suspect, because their wives are a lot less accepting of affairs than wives in previous generations. In the second half of the twentieth century, if a wife suspects an affair, she is less likely to turn a blind eye and is far more likely to confront her husband.

Lawson's research also shows that women are more likely than men to confess to an affair. Men are more able to compartmentalise their relationships, so they tend to be more able to conduct a marriage and an affair without allowing one to affect the other. In addition, men tend to invest less of their emotions in affairs than women do, because men are often looking for sexual variety, rather than emotional intimacy. Just as women seek intimacy in marriage more often than men do, they are also more likely than men to look for it in affairs as well. Another reason why women are more likely to disclose an affair than men, is because they are usually more guilt-ridden than men. Women, in the main, still see themselves as the carers and the emotional protectors of husbands and children, and therefore they tend to judge themselves more harshly than men if they stray.

The Great Pretender

Lawrence had been having an affair with Chloe for two years. His wife suspected that this was so. She was continually confronting him about this, and constantly trying to check up on where he was and what he was doing, even driving past the house of the woman in question to see if her husband's car was parked nearby. When she was eventually able to intercept his car phone telephone bill, she discovered he was making up to eight or nine calls a day to Chloe. She confronted him with the evidence, shrieking at him that he was a liar. He calmly denied it and when she challenged him about why he was calling Chloe so much, Lawrence said that he was only trying to help her out as she was having problems with her business and needed some good financial advice.

The affair continued and so did the deceit, with his wife becoming even more distraught. His reason for not admitting to it was that he had no intention of finishing the affair. In the end, his wife got her evidence. She arranged to visit her mother for the weekend, but at about midnight on the Friday she returned to the family house and discovered Lawrence and Chloe in bed together. She gave Lawrence an ultimatum:

either he had to end the affair, or she would end the marriage. Lawrence chose his mistress.

To continue the deception, as Lawrence did, when all the evidence points to an affair is frankly cruel. It is probably also an indication that so much harm and damage has been done in the marriage that you no longer care whether more harm is being inflicted. The affair is then a way out of the marriage. If you are caught in the act, or confronted with mounting evidence of the affair, it is kinder to confess, or end the affair. To continue lying, when you can see the enormous hurt you are causing, is not fair to your partner.

In counselling I have frequently seen people whose partner is denying that there is any affair, despite all the evidence to the contrary. They often accuse their partner of being quite unjustly suspicious, or of having an over-active imagination. The person doing the accusing is almost driven to the point of breakdown, as their mind switches from knowing there is something going on, to wondering if they are going mad and imagining the whole thing. When they do discover the truth, that there is indeed an affair, it does not become any less painful, but it does restore their sanity, because they are not constantly being told that they have got it all wrong. In these circumstances, not to disclose can be very destructive to the wronged husband or wife. The pain of disclosure will be enormous, but it does at least give the marriage a chance to end, or to begin the lengthy process of rebuilding.

If You don't Tell them, Someone Else Might

Ian, a writer and saxophone player, had been having an affair without his wife's knowledge for five years. One night he and his mistress went to Ronnie Scott's Jazz Club. They met Ken, a musician and acquaintance of Ian's, whom he knew from playing in various bands. They chatted briefly, and Ian said he was setting up a new band. Ken expressed an interest in working with him on gigs.

About a week later, Ken rang Ian at his home to see if there was any chance of playing with his band. Ian was out, but his wife answered the telephone. Ken, in his friendly outgoing mood, said without thinking, 'Oh, hello. Do you remember meeting me last week at Ronnie's?' 'Oh, yes!' she said, then added, 'Just remind me. We met several of Ian's friends that evening. When did we meet you?' She paused. Ken offered helpfully, 'In the bar, in the interval. Ian was telling me about the new band he was forming, and I said I'd be interested in playing with him. We talked about how you loved coming to Ronnie's because they always played such good jazz.' 'Oh, I remember!' his wife said, 'I'll give Ian your message,' and she put the phone down.

When Ian returned a few hours later, his wife was shaking with fury and confronted him. Ian had wanted to leave the marriage for some time. There were no children, so he packed his bags and left.

Ian was caught in the act through the unintentional, careless talk of a friend. He had not intended things to come into the open that way. He had not given Ken his home number, but Ken had obtained it through a mutual friend who had also been at the club.

It is well recognised that if someone wants out of a marriage, they are sometimes not as careful as they should be over maintaining secrecy. For example, they leave a hotel bill in their jacket pocket, or the receipt for gifts not received. It can be an unconscious act of carelessness which results in forcing things into the open, precipitating the end of the marriage.

If you are pretty sure that someone else is going to spill the beans to your partner, it is usually better to get in first. It is painful enough for them to be told, but even worse if they hear through a third party. If your child has caught you out, it is not fair to ask them to keep the secret, especially if the affair is still continuing. They will feel very uncomfortable at being drawn into the deception, particularly if they are very close to the other parent.

The Kindest Ways to Confess

- **Never confess in anger**.
  It is unkind and very shocking if you blurt out in the middle of an argument that you are having, or have had, an affair. The shock is bound to be a major one. The news may be totally unexpected, or you may be confirming something that your partner has suspected. Either way, it should be done gently, when you are alone together, and when you have time to talk it through.

- **Realise that your partner is probably going to show extremes of emotion**.
  Your partner may express shock, anger, hurt and rage. Be prepared for them to shout and scream, threaten to leave, or tell you to leave home immediately. Recognise that is how they feel at that precise moment. They may or may not mean it in the long run.

- **Never defend the person you have had an affair with**.
  It is understandable that to your partner, they are the bitch from hell, the whore, the slag, the bounder, the creep, the scum of the earth. You know that is not how you feel about them, but that is the last thing your partner wants to hear.

- **Confession is not an end in itself**.
  Do not feel that once you have confessed all, that is it and you can now get on with the rest of your life. You will have to do much more talking than you will probably want to. The faithful partner's way of coming to terms with what has happened is to go over it again and again. If you withdraw into silence, that will only hurt them even more.

- **Tell your partner everything that has happened**.
  Admit with whom you were having the affair, when it started, when and where you met. If you don't, your partner will go on and on trying to extract

the information from you, driving themselves, and eventually you, mad.

- **Do not go into explicit sexual details**.
  These images will live on in the mind of your partner long after the affair is over.

- **Do not lie to your partner**.
  Try and look for positive things to tell them, and if possible to reassure them. If it was an unimportant fling, say so. If it was disappointing sexually, say so. If you bitterly regret it, say so.

- **If you love your spouse, tell them so**.
  Your partner may not believe you, because they will probably wonder how you could have treated them so badly. As time goes by, try to show them that you do find them attractive and desirable, because the chances are they will think you don't.

- **A confession should not be a prelude to sex**.
  The unfaithful partner might still find they are very involved with the loss of their mistress or lover. They may not be able to make love, which will feel to their partner like further rejection. The faithful spouse may think sex is a way of getting close to their partner again, or getting back at the other man or women, but it's too soon, feelings are running too high, and the regrets will be many.

- **Put an end to the affair**.
  If you care about your spouse and the marriage or relationship, the affair has to come to an end. It is difficult enough rebuilding a marriage after the discovery or disclosure of an affair, but if the affair is still continuing, love and trust cannot flourish or be re-established. If the affair was an important one, the loss will not be easy, but do not expect your partner to be able to support you with that. They may understand, but it is unrealistic to expect more than that.

When it is not a Good Idea to Tell

I can't Handle the Guilt

Perhaps your partner does not suspect, or perhaps the affair is drawing to a close or may even be over, and you are now weighed down by this terrible guilt. Maybe your partner does have a few suspicions, which worried you enough to end the affair, because you could see how it could threaten your marriage. Or perhaps you are growing tired of the affair, which is no longer important to you, and you want to end it. But what do you do with this awful guilt?

Many people confess to an affair not because their partner suspects anything, or has challenged them, but because they think that if they get it out in the open they will be forgiven, and then the feelings of guilt will disperse because they have made a clean breast of things. Furthermore, they tell themselves that honesty is what good marriages are based on, and they long to recapture that state. Unfortunately, human nature does not really work like that. In these circumstances it is often best to avoid the temptation to confess.

It is naïve to think that your partner will hand out forgiveness like a priest in a confessional. It is foolish to imagine that they will be upset, but would prefer it out in the open. Your motives are likely to be entirely selfish. You are perhaps hoping for absolution, but what you are likely to get is anger and fury, and you will cause tremendous pain. This is particularly so if your partner had no idea you were having an affair, or if they had a few niggling doubts but had very carefully chosen to ignore them.

If your partner does not want to know, it is unfair to tell them just so that you can feel better about what you have done. The reality is that your partner is not like a loving parent, who will give you unconditional love. They are unlikely to tell you that they know you are sorry, that it should not have happened, but try and behave better next time. They are a betrayed spouse with all the heartache and pain that entails. If you do tell them or you are caught out, hopefully they will eventually forgive, but there is a very long road to travel down before they reach that stage. And of course they will never forget.

It's all Over Now

It is usually pointless to confess to an affair that has finished some years ago. You may think that, well, maybe it's a long way in the past and won't hurt any more. It may be a long way in the past to you, but to your partner it is entirely new. They are more than likely to be hurt, angry and outraged. All the lengthy processes that the discovery of an affair causes will have to be gone through.

On a late-night radio phone-in on London Talk Radio, a woman called Jean rang in. She said, in a voice shaking with emotion, that she wanted a posthumous divorce. Even the over-jolly presenter was silent for a moment. Jean's husband had died three years earlier, and on the eve of his funeral she discovered that he had had a mistress for many years. The mistress turned up for the funeral. 'She was in full mistress regalia,' Jean said 'wearing a hat, dark glasses and dressed all in black.'

Further horrors were to follow. Jean also discovered her husband had left debts of £300,000. To start with, Jean said, she was totally shocked, but after the funeral was over and she began to face the facts, she also started to feel very angry. But the person she wanted to scream and shout at, to ask the when, the where, the how, and the why, was dead. She had thought she had a reasonably happy marriage, and she may well have done. It's not only people in unhappy marriages who have affairs. But what was so sad for Jean was not just the deceit and the debts, but the fact that she was now left with the feeling that her marriage had been a sham, and her husband was not around to tell her otherwise.

Thoughts of a posthumous divorce were Jean's way of expressing her anger, of rejecting a man who she felt had rejected her. She was, in effect, saying to the world, 'If he didn't want me, then I don't want him.' Jean was expressing how hurt she was because the picture she had had of her marriage was now shattered into little pieces. I hope in time she will be able to remember the good times that she had with her husband.

The Transitional Person

Most people know that their partner would be hurt by their unfaithfulness, so they choose to keep their affairs secret. Some affairs, as I have said earlier, are embarked upon because the marriage is in a very bad state, in which case they offer an escape route. Alternatively, a marriage can end because someone has fallen out of love with their partner, and are deeply in love with someone new. If you have a bad marriage and you are having an affair, it is often very difficult to be able to identify whether it is the real thing or an infatuation, because almost any relationship is going to seem so much better than the one you have got. Many people leave their marriage only to find that things do not work out with their lover or their mistress. An affair is very different from sharing your life with someone on a full-time basis.

During his sixteen years of marriage, Simon had had countless brief encounters despite a very good sex life within his marriage. He had also had three love affairs. Each time, when the relationship was new, he was quite convinced the woman in question was 'the love of his life'.

His third affair was with a woman in her mid-forties, a couple of years younger than him. Moira had never been married and, perhaps motivated by the passing years, was definitely on the look out for a husband. The fact that Simon was someone else's husband did not get in her way, and she struck when Simon's infatuation was at its height. Simon left his wife and two children, and after a quick divorce on grounds of adultery, he married Moira.

Too late, he realised she was not the love of his life, and

worse was to follow. Simon had a very high sex drive but, once married, he discovered that Moira had little interest in sex, other than as a means of capturing a husband. Sex was of little interest to her, now that she had got her man. Within a year of the marriage he had embarked on a further series of affairs which continued, much to Moira's fury, over the next twenty years. He even propositioned his ex-wife once. She was almost tempted, but admitted it was more to get back at the woman who had stolen her husband than because she still fancied Simon.

Why does Adultery Tear us Apart?

> *Do not adultery commit;*
> *Advantage rarely comes of it.*

> A.C. Clough, *The Latest Decalogue*

Why does infidelity feel for most people like an act of betrayal? Why is it so personally devastating and why, even though the relationship may well survive, does it rock most marriages to their very foundations?

It is, I believe, because we invest so much of ourselves, our hopes, dreams and expectations, in marriage and committed relationships. The companionate marriage is held in high regard, so when one or the other strays, it not only feels like betrayal but is also experienced as a personal rejection. 'How could she/he do that if they loved me?' People feel so distraught because the trust that they felt united them has been broken.

Much of our time is spent making loving relationships, searching for someone we can really put our faith in, someone we feel we can always rely on. If that trust is suddenly taken away, it can be like a house of cards blown over in the wind. If you seriously damage the foundations of a relationship by destroying trust, it makes you question the rest of the relationship. The fear is that everything you once valued will prove to be as insubstantial as the trust you once had for your partner.

Another very important element is sex. So many hopes are invested in having great sex in marriage, that if you discover the one you love is having great sex elsewhere it challenges your belief in your own sexual attractiveness. You start to ask, 'What's wrong with me?' or, 'Have I lost the ability to please my partner in bed?' A loving sexual relationship is such an essential cornerstone of modern marriage, that if one person strays it is often seen and experienced by their partner as a fatal blow. We feel forced to confront the fact that maybe we, or our relationship, are lacking a vital component. Because we think of sex as the ultimate intimacy, which we have promised to share with our partner exclusively, it makes us feel so very vulnerable when we are betrayed. When we find out that something we thought was special between ourselves has been happening with someone else, we feel one of the key rules of the marriage contract has been broken. An unfaithful partner not only makes the other person feel rejected, but can also totally devalue the whole relationship.

The disclosure of an affair is always painful. Being 'caught in the act' if you are a public figure provides the media with endless fodder for speculation on the subject. No one is protected. Royalty, politicians, bishops, footballers, rock stars, actors and film stars are all targets. Hugh Grant, Paula Yates and Michael Douglas (whose wife sent him off to be treated for Sexual Addiction because of his all-too-numerous affairs!) are just the tip of the iceberg.

Infidelity is not of course confined to the rich and famous. Thousands of people during the course of their lives are unfaithful. If they are discovered, their indiscretions may not be blazoned across the headlines in every newspaper, but they frequently have to face their own critical audience. Their private life will be exposed, whether it's to a partner, their children, their extended family, friends and neighbours, or people at work. This is usually intensely humiliating for both the person who has been unfaithful and for their partner. Although their feelings are likely to be different, they are extremely painful for both. As one woman said to me, 'The fact that he was unfaithful was unbelievably agonising. But what made it so much worse was the discovery that everyone knew, my family, my friends, my neighbours, even the people at work. Yet nobody told me.'

One of the main reasons people stray is because there are problems in the marriage. Someone who has been brought up in a family where there has been repeated unfaithfulness is more likely to repeat the pattern, rather than looking inside their marriage for a solution to their problems. He or she has learned that it's easier to opt out and find satisfaction elsewhere, rather than work at the difficulties in the current relationship. It can of course work the other way around. Those who have witnessed constant philandering in a parent may well have seen the hurt it caused and be very determined not to do that to someone they love, or marry someone who might do it to them.

Trying to have your Cake and Eat it

For the majority of people, affairs are about wanting to have the love and security of marriage, and also the illicit excitement of an extramarital temptation. Affairs frequently cushion an unhappy and disappointing marriage. It's the 'having your cake and eating it' syndrome, which is why the majority of people having affairs want to keep them a secret. Once an affair is out in the open it usually has to end, as most spouses will not tolerate their partner having an affair. Other affairs, when discovered, can mean the end of the marriage. Until it happens, you can never be entirely sure which it will be.

Many people who have affairs seem to operate under a double standard. They think it is wrong to be unfaithful, they know they would find it unbearable if their partner were behaving in the same way. But for them, it is so irresistible that they choose not to resist temptation. They embark on an affair, a brief encounter or a one-night stand, telling themselves philosophically, 'Let me be good, oh Lord but not yet!'

Moving On

The discovery of an affair is always painful. For some, it does
mean the end of a marriage. For others, their marriage gets
stuck in a time warp. They feel they are not able to, or they
don't want to, separate. Neither do they feel able to move on
and to start the process of rebuilding their marriage. This
memory of the affair hangs over them like a black cloud
of hurt, pain and resentment. This is what happens between
Brian and Erica in Alison Lurie's book *The War Between
the Tates*:

> *It is night now. Brian turns a page; its shadow flaps slowly
> across the table. Hearing another sigh, he looks up at his
> wife. She is staring into the middle distance out of eyes
> circled in muted blue.*
>
> *Now Erica turns her head. For a moment their eyes
> meet; then both look down. Erica knows that Brian knows
> what she is thinking about, and he knows she knows he
> knows. This mutual knowledge is like a series of infinitely
> disappearing, darkening, ugly reflections in two opposite
> mirrors. But if he asks what she is thinking, she will not
> admit it. She knows that he does not want to ask anyhow;
> he does not want to bring up the subject again. And she
> knows she must not bring it up.*
>
> *So they say nothing. There is nothing to say.*

It does not have to be like that. Many marriages can, and
do, survive an affair. But it is not easy picking up the pieces
and putting the marriage back together again. It does mean
taking an honest look at the marriage, and often confronting
some very uncomfortable and difficult things. Men do tend
to be more resistant than women to looking at what might
have precipitated the affair. They are more likely to blame
the woman for what has happened, and less likely to blame
themselves. Women frequently blame themselves for their man
straying, but it is necessary for both partners to be prepared to
look at what went wrong.

Chapter Six

REBUILDING A LOVING RELATIONSHIP

Love one another, but make not a bond of love:
Let it rather be a moving sea between the shores of
  your souls.
Fill each other's cup but drink not from one cup.
Give one another of your bread but eat not from the
  same loaf.
Sing and dance together and be joyous, but let each one of
  you be alone,
Even as the strings of a lute are alone though they quiver
  with the same music.

Kahlil Gibran, The Prophet

The sense of devastation that follows the aftermath of an affair is hard to imagine if you have never experienced it. In the early days the feelings are of shock, hurt and anger, and many couples find that they become stuck in their mutual misery. But it does not have to end with each of you wrapped in silent hostility, or shouting and yelling the same things a million times over. The reality is that the majority of marriages do survive, but not always easily. The problems that affairs cause are one of the main reasons people go for counselling, or write letters to agony aunts.

It is very tempting on discovering an affair to believe that marriage is finished, that you must rush to the solicitor with demands for divorce. However, that is not usually the best solution. It might be so ultimately, but taking longer-term decisions in moments of extreme crisis is usually a mistake.

Whatever you decide needs a lot of thought and discussion, particularly if there are children. This is so whether you try to rebuild the relationship, or whether you feel the marriage or relationship is over and you want to end it.

Relationships can Survive Affairs

When Joan found out about her husband's affair, she wanted to pack her bags and leave. She described discovering it as being worse than childbirth. 'The pain was excruciating,' she said. 'And there was no lovely end result as there is when giving birth, just more and more pain.' Joan had been suspicious for some time that Leonard was having an affair as he had been coming home later and later from work, and their sex life had taken a downward turn. One morning she was walking near the offices where Leonard worked, and she noticed his car parked in a side street. He was in it and he was not alone. She watched as he talked earnestly to the woman with him, then put his arms around her and kissed her for what seemed an eternity. When Leonard arrived home later that afternoon Joan confronted him, and he admitted it. He said he loved the other woman, but did not know what he wanted to do. Joan, who had met the other woman once or twice, said, 'She was just the opposite to me: small, blonde and very quiet, whereas I'm tall, dark, very outgoing and chatty.' She added with a grimace, 'She was also fifteen years younger than me.'

Most of that evening, and late into the night, Joan ranted and raved at Leonard. The more angry she became the more silent Leonard grew. The next morning Joan could not take any more. Leonard seemed uncertain whether he wanted to stay in the marriage or leave to be with the other woman. Joan felt she just had to get away to think, so she left the children with Leonard and booked herself into a hotel for the weekend. When she returned on the Sunday night, she started to pack Leonard's bags, at which point he said he did not want to go, and that he wanted to see if they could sort things out. He told her he had finished the affair.

For nearly a year it was touch and go. Every row ended in Joan telling him to get the hell out of her life. One of the conditions Joan made, if they were to try again, was for him to tell her everything that had happened: when the affair started, where they met, how often, what he felt about her, and what she had been like in bed. Leonard said that, except for the last question, he would go over it with Joan again and again. It was, he said, excruciatingly painful, not only for Joan but also for him, as each time Joan wanted to talk about it he saw how much he had hurt her. The guilt was enormous, and he was also coping with his own feelings over the sudden ending of the affair. He was missing the other woman very much. Part of her attraction had been that she was gentle, not bossy like Joan, and she only had eyes for him. He said she made him feel a million dollars, especially with his fortieth birthday looming around the corner. But Leonard also knew that Joan was aware of him missing the other woman, and that hurt her even more.

Over time both Leonard and Joan acknowledged that their marriage had been in a rut. Joan admitted that she was bored with just being a wife and mother, and Leonard told her he was fed up with his job. They had been spending less and less time with each other, and because of the frustration and dissatisfaction with herself and her life, Joan had been constantly criticising Leonard about many aspects of their life together. Leonard had reacted by going out more and more, or when he was at home just opting out of the relationship. So along with the talking, and trying to understand the reason for the affair, they also started to reconstruct their lives. Leonard changed jobs, which was important because it meant he did not see his ex-mistress any more. He also found a job that was much more up his street. After much searching Joan also got herself a job working in a clothes shop, which she really enjoyed and which made her feel much more confident and fulfilled.

Joan said that one of the things that made a real difference to her was that Leonard put up with her going over and over what had happened and why, till she herself found that she was bored with it. He was also very loving towards her. She also said, 'One of the mistakes I made was to have sex with him too soon. It was only a couple of weeks after the discovery of the affair. I was trying to rid his mind and mine of the other girl and to prove that I was great in bed. But it left me feeling dreadful, cheap and even more hurt.' It was only many months later, when trust and some closeness had been re-established, that they were able to start to enjoy lovemaking again. Three years on, the memories are still very painful but they both say that the marriage is stronger than it was for many years leading up to the affair.

You Need to Talk

There is almost always a need on the part of the person who has not had the affair to talk about it at length. Most people feel they really need to know the details of it. Just as the betrayed partner wants to talk, so the unfaithful partner rarely does and will often strongly resist questioning. However, I cannot stress enough how important it is to talk. It is part of the healing process to talk things through together. It is not fair if the unfaithful partner says; 'It's over now, let's just put it all behind us and get on with the rest of our lives.'

If the unfaithful partner refuses to talk, the marriage gets stuck, and the chance of rebuilding the relationship is far more remote. If all the questions the faithful partner wants to ask are rebuffed, nothing is resolved. The faithful spouse is then left with imaginings whirling round and round in their head until they feel they are going mad. It is just not possible for them to simply brush their thoughts and feelings aside. These imaginings do not go away but fester and grow, driving the couple even further apart. Constantly having to suppress feelings of hurt and anger can often lead to depression, or, if nothing has been resolved, the betrayed partner can become hugely resentful and demoralised until eventually, maybe several years later, the marriage hits the rocks.

When Neil discovered his wife had been having an affair, it was right in the middle of a very critical time for her at work. Although they talked, it wasn't for long. Neil's wife Libby said it was just too stressful. She insisted that she had to give all her attention to her work as there were significant changes going on in her company and she feared that she might be made redundant. As the weeks went by, she still refused to talk, and said that it had been a meaningless affair, so why couldn't Neil just forget it? Neil thought he still wanted to stay in the marriage, but he also wanted to know who her lover had been. Libby refused to tell him. Neil became quite obsessed with this, and spent hours thinking about who it could have been. Libby was asking him to trust her, and accept that the affair was over, but she would not trust him enough to tell him who the man was. There was always some excuse why it was never the right time to talk about it. The marriage became stuck, and after a year or two the couple slowly started to drift apart. For Neil and Libby there was no happy ending.

There will be times when it is better not to admit with whom you had an affair. For example, you may feel the truth will cause more damage than the secrecy. However, not admitting it makes it very difficult for the faithful partner to start to come to terms with what has happened.

Who did you Betray me With?

Almost as soon as an affair is discovered or admitted to, the first thing that the betrayed spouse wants to know is, 'Who have you been having an affair with?' When this information is not forthcoming it almost always enflames the situation even further. By withholding that secret, it feels as though the mistress or lover is being protected. Andrew did not want to tell his wife the name of his mistress because he thought she might go round to her flat and attack her. Jason's wife refused to tell her husband the name of her lover because she was afraid he would telephone her boss, spill the beans and make her lose her job. But though there may seem lots of very good reasons for not telling, withholding that information means endless anguish for the faithful partner. It prevents the really open and honest talking that is essential if the damage is going to be repaired. It also means that nearly everyone is then a suspect. Is it one of your friends, someone your partner works with, or someone they met at the gym or when away at a conference? Most deceived partners find it intolerable that the mistress or lover should know you are the betrayed husband or wife, yet you have been kept in the dark.

When it's your Best Friend

Your partner having an affair with your best friend is not just the theme of films and books, it happens every day in real life. It is a double betrayal, and is painful in the extreme. The two people you thought you could really trust have completely let you down.

As the awful realisation hits you, you remember that you have probably talked to your friend about your partner, and indeed your marriage. You might even have confided that you think your husband or wife is having an affair, while all the time it was your best friend they were being unfaithful with. Because the whole episode is so humiliating and the deceit so great, the anger and the hurt are going to be even more intense.

A close friend would be in the habit of calling round for coffee, joining you for supper, sharing picnics and even holidays with the children. So when you realise there was a hidden agenda behind all of these activities, it is hard to reconcile. Not only did your friend collude in it but, even more importantly, your partner was deceiving you in all aspects of your life. It is undoubtedly the end of a friendship, and it does make the chances of rebuilding the marriage less likely.

When it Happens in the Same Social Set

Another very difficult circumstance is if the affair has been within the immediate social circle, or at work. It might be over, but you're left with the question of who knew and who didn't. Should someone have told you? If they didn't, was there a conspiracy? It can feel pretty humiliating all round. The repercussions of an affair are like a stone thrown onto ice: it breaks the ice where it lands, and the cracks spread out in increasingly large circles. The discovery of an affair almost always affects not only the couple but also their children, the immediate family, mutual friends, and even the workplace.

Tessa's husband's main interest outside work was music. He played clarinet in a local orchestra, and when he had an affair it was with someone who played in the same orchestra. It was brief, and Ben bitterly regretted it. 'It was one of those things that just happened,' he said, crossing his arms and sinking into his chair. This is said so often, but affairs never just happen, there are always reasons, and choices to be made. Saying that the affair 'just happened' was Ben's way of not accepting responsibility for his own behaviour. He was implying that he had no power to stop it. It can also be a way of trying to diminish the impact on your partner, by playing it down and declaring it to be unimportant. If an affair is discovered, it can't be dismissed so lightly.

Tessa discovered Ben's affair after he had been away from home with the orchestra for a couple of nights. On his return, when he was unpacking his suitcase, Tessa noticed a piece of paper lying at the bottom of the case. She picked it up to ask Ben whether he wanted it, but as she handed it to him, something about the expression on his face made her look more carefully. She saw that it was a hotel bill made out for a double room with breakfast for two. She confronted him at once and he admitted to having an affair with a woman in the orchestra, but he completely refused to say who. Tessa tried to get the name out of him, but he was adamant.

The annual Christmas party was looming, and Tessa knew the other woman would be there. She could not bear the thought that the woman would know who she was, but she wouldn't know her. Everyone would be a suspect. It was at that point they came for counselling. Ben said that with the affair now over, it would only make matters worse if Tessa knew who it had been with. Why couldn't Tessa see how sorry he was, and just concentrate on getting on with their lives?

In reality, they were both stuck in entrenched positions. Neither had been prepared to look at what had led to the affair in the first place. The marriage had been drifting along for some time. Tessa resented the fact that she got little help with the children and no emotional support for herself. She could see that this was leading to constant rows. They were growing apart, spending less and less time with each other, and sex was almost non-existent.

Ben had to recognise what an impossible situation he was putting Tessa in by expecting her to go to the party, yet stay in the dark about the identity of the other woman. As he explored his reasons for this, it became clear to him why he was acting in this way. His mother had been a very emotional and demanding woman, he was an only child, and as he grew up he became more and more aware that his mother dominated his father. Every time she did not get her way, she became hysterical. His father tried to keep the peace by acquiescing, but eventually gave up on that and started to opt out of the marriage by being around as little as possible. As Ben grew older, it was left to him to be on the receiving end of his mother's constant shouting and screaming about his father.

As a result, even when Tessa made reasonable requests for his time and emotional support, he unconsciously feared that she was going to become like his demanding and hysterical mother. At the first sign of an emotional demand he became like his father and withdrew from Tessa. As they grew further apart, the affair was a way of opting out even more. Part of the counselling was helping Ben to understand why he was behaving like this, and how he could learn to trust Tessa. He had to recognise that her needs were not the same as his hysterical mother's had been. Slowly he was able to let go of his fears, and he became far more loving and supportive to Tessa.

When Ben realised there would be no hysterical outburst, he told Tessa the identity of the other woman. He also said that instead of going to the party, he would like to take Tessa to the theatre, which was something he knew she loved.

Affairs in the Workplace

The two most likely breeding grounds for affairs are among a circle of friends and neighbours, or at work. One of the reasons why more women are having affairs nowadays is because more women are out at work. They now have the same opportunities as men have always had. Another change has been in the status of those having affairs. In the past, men were more likely to have affairs with unmarried women, often in more lowly jobs – the stereotypical boss–secretary affair. Nowadays, with more women holding down jobs of equivalent status to men, affairs are just as likely to be with a married or divorced woman in a relatively equal position.

Workplace affairs are fraught with complications. The two people having the affair are inclined to think that no one has noticed. They go to endless trouble to arrive and leave separately, or to show indifference when the person they are having the affair with is being talked about, or comes into the room. But more often than not, they have been spotted together at some wine bar gazing into each other's eyes, or the sexual chemistry between them is such that their colleagues soon become suspicious, and so are on the lookout for any give-away signs.

It often causes resentment among others at work, especially if a mistress or lover is getting preferential treatment, perhaps even being promoted on the grounds of desirability in bed rather than talent for the job. The complications don't stop there because if the affair comes to an end, it can often be difficult continuing to work in the same office. If one of you has grown tired of the affair and the other one can't accept it, there is always the fear that they will tell the boss, jeopardise your job, or tell your spouse in retaliation.

Discovery throws up a different set of complications in the workplace. The person who has not had the affair finds it incredibly hard, if not impossible, to cope with the thought that their partner is seeing their ex-lover or mistress at work. It is bound to give rise to feelings of intense jealousy. Just the thought of them being together, perhaps sharing emotional intimacy or sexual attraction, is unbearable. They may also fear that it will start up all over again. Social functions can be a nightmare, particularly when everyone else knows what has been going on. It is very important that the person who has had the affair appreciates how awful all of this may feel for their partner. It does need to be talked about, not swept under the carpet.

If it is very difficult for the faithful partner to come to terms with a workplace affair, so it is important to see if it's possible for one of the involved parties to move jobs, or departments. If not, it's essential to restrict any contact with each other as much as possible. If your spouse is continually worrying about what is happening from nine to five, it will make rebuilding the marriage even more of a task. Even a drink or an occasional meal with the ex-mistress or lover for old times' sake is not really acceptable.

Playing Away from Home

Liaisons away from home territory are usually more opportunistic than deeply felt. It's rather like the way some people think of sex on holiday, 'No one here knows me, so I can get away with more.' You somehow convince yourself that you won't be found out, and frequently you are not, but there are no guarantees. You can end up scoring an own goal.

Linda discovered that her husband Chris had had an affair because the woman he had had a one-night stand with found out his address from the hotel register and wrote to him. Linda already had her suspicions and opened the letter.

Linda was a very pretty and outgoing woman in her mid-thirties She had a wide circle of friends, many of whom she had known from school and college. She had three particular friends with whom she had shared everything. They had all married but their friendships had continued, and now included their respective husbands as well as their children. When Linda discovered her husband had been unfaithful, she was totally torn apart. With all the other things that had happened in her life she had always talked to the other three, but this time she felt she couldn't.

After much talking between her and Chris, both agreed that they loved each other and did not want to end the marriage. They were very committed to their children and the life they had built around them. Linda's dilemma was that she felt incredibly humiliated by Chris's infidelity, as well as very hurt and angry. Although part of her wanted support and understanding from her friends, she also felt it was disloyal to talk to them about it. She was aware that as she and Chris were trying to sort things out, maybe it would be easier in the long run if friends did not know, but in the short term it only added to her loneliness and isolation.

Because her friends knew her so well, they could tell something was wrong, but they were also sensitive enough to realise that on this occasion she didn't want to talk about it. One of the reasons that Chris and Linda went for counselling was because they knew that an objective counsellor could help them rebuild their relationship. She was not part of their friendship network, and what was said would just be between the three of them. It also gave them a chance to talk about whether they wanted to tell their friends.

It's all Over Now – or is it?

One of the most painful situations I see in counselling is when someone who has been unfaithful swears dishonestly that the affair is over. They may have genuinely tried to finish the affair, only to start it up again. Maybe they never intended to finish it (a fact they failed to disclose to their partner) and only tried to be more careful, to avoid being caught second time around. This sort of on/off affair, or one that continues in secret, often occurs when the affair has been going on for some time, perhaps months or even years. It can be a full-blown love affair, an obsession, or just extremely sexually addictive.

* * *

When Helen discovered that her husband Larry's affair was still going on two months after he had promised he had ended it, she gave Larry an ultimatum, 'I can't share you with another woman. The affair has to end, and so does any contact with her. I just can't trust you any more.' Larry said, 'It's unreasonable of you to think I can just cut her out of my life. That is too brutal. She's a friend as well, I can't do that to her, she hasn't anyone else to turn to.' For Helen this was one of the most unkind things that Larry could have said, because he highlighted not only how important the affair was to him, but how deep a friendship he also had with the other woman.

Larry felt Helen was being unreasonable and that if he promised that there would be no sexual relationship, she should let him disengage from the friendship at a gentler pace. Yet again Larry talked Helen into giving him one more chance, promising the affair was over while secretly continuing to see his mistress. Helen found out where the mistress lived and went round to see her. She confirmed that the affair was far from over, and so Helen filed for divorce. Several months later Larry was dumped by his mistress, but Helen had had enough and refused his pleas to have him back.

It is not unusual for the person having the affair to feel that they love both their partner and their lover or mistress. They believe that loving one person does not exclude them from also loving someone else. The person not having the affair, however, is feeling that if their partner really loved them, they wouldn't be putting them through all this pain. 'If you really love me', they often ask, 'how can you continue to hurt me by trying to maintain the marriage and the affair?' It is a valid point.

Coping with the Aftermath of an Affair

Whatever sort of affair it is, it causes havoc with relationships. There are recognisable patterns to the sort of emotions people experience and have to deal with once the affair is out in the open. Just as people who lose a partner, either through death or divorce, have to try and cope with a whole range of difficult and painful emotions, so too do those caught up in the aftermath of an affair. Not everyone will experience all of the following feelings in the same way or in the same order, and some will be felt more strongly than others, but there is a general similarity in the emotions experienced. Understanding them can be the beginning of making some sort of sense of what has happened.

The Shock

Shock can vary from a sort of numb disbelief that such a thing could have happened to you, to a total inability to cope or do anything. Making a cup of tea, collecting the children from school, or taking in what is said to you just becomes impossible. This state can last for just a few hours, several days or even longer. It's a way of the body and the mind taking time out before really having to confront the awful truth. If you had no idea that your partner was being unfaithful, the discovery is quite devastating. Even if you did suspect it, having it confirmed can equally knock you for six.

The Anger

Crimes of passion, ranging from murder to grievous bodily harm, are not infrequently committed particularly by men when a spouse discovers their partner's affair. It is natural enough to experience very strong feelings at such times. It might even be said to be normal to feel murderous or violent towards your partner, or the other person involved. Most people fortunately exercise sufficient control to refrain from physical abuse, though they may do harm to their partner's property, or that of the other person. It becomes a substitute for the real thing.

Destroying or damaging something that your partner loves or values is particularly tempting if your partner is leaving, or threatening to leave, for their mistress or lover. In these circumstances the frustration and anger felt by the one abandoned can be at boiling point. If the unfaithful partner is not around for you to vent your anger on, then their property or that of the mistress or lover becomes the target. If the person you want to shout and scream at refuses to listen or is no longer there, making free with their belongings can be a very attractive form of expressing your anger. There is the infamous story of the woman who was so angry when her boyfriend dumped her for another girl that she went to his home while he was away on business. She dialled a recorded New York information service and left the phone off the hook, knowing he would be away for a whole week.

Lady Moon is another famous example. When her husband left her for another woman, she distributed the contents of her husband's expensive and considerable wine cellar to local doorsteps, just like delivering milk. She was angry and hurt because not only was she ditched for another woman, but he then set up house with her in the same village.

If the marriage is going to have a chance of survival, the person who has not had the affair must be given the opportunity to express their anger. They will want to do this for much longer than the unfaithful partner will want to hear, but that's part of the penalty for badly hurting your partner. The person who has had the affair, or been caught in the act like Hugh Grant and the prostitute Divine Brown, would prefer to put everything behind them. The last thing they want to do is talk, because experiencing all the raw emotions their partner is expressing is very distressing. They do not like seeing at first hand how much they have hurt the person they frequently still love and care about, because it reinforces their own feelings of regret or guilt about the affair.

It's important to remember, however, that talking is an essential part of the healing process, if there is to be one. Unexpressed anger does not go away. It seethes away under the surface, only to explode at a later date, often at something quite unimportant which has little to do with the real source of the anger, but is just the trigger for what has been buried beneath the surface. Unexpressed anger can also turn in on itself, and the person then becomes depressed. If the marriage is going to continue, or if you are trying to conduct a civilised divorce, anger has to be expressed, acknowledged and understood.

The Pain

Pain and anger are closely related. Anger is often used as a way of expressing the pain you are feeling. You experience excruciating pain thinking of the person you love making love to someone else. All sorts of thoughts flood into your mind. What did they do? Where did they do it? Was it better than with me? What is wrong with me? Were they prettier, better looking, younger, more interesting? Surely he could not do this if he really loved me? Maybe she will leave me for him? Is this the end of the road, and is our relationship over?

Julie discovered that her husband had been having an affair with their next-door neighbour. They used to meet when Julie went to keep-fit classes, leaving her husband to babysit. Her husband and mistress had made love in the sitting room, on the rug in front of the sofa. Every time Julie walked into the room she was confronted by the rug and a mental picture of her husband and his lover rolling around on it. One day she took the rug, cut it into little pieces and posted it bit by bit through the letterbox of the other woman's house.

One of the things I get asked most frequently is, 'How do I get rid of the pain?' The problem is that there is no magic wand. Pain can't be waved away. Logically people know that, but it still does not stop them longing for there to be an end to it, or at least some respite.

The reality is that it takes a long time for the pain to diminish, much longer than people anticipate. One woman who came for counselling because of her husband's affair said, 'I am so confused. I feel so let down and alone. I would never have believed I could have felt so bad. I keep asking myself how he could hurt me so much if he really loved me. But at the same time I feel such a weak person to let this still be affecting me so strongly three months later.' The first three months can seem interminable, but the truth is that it is unlikely that the pain will diminish much during the first month or two.

Normally, after three months things are still far from all right. Piecing the relationship together again takes a long time. The pain does eventually fade, although it often takes a year or two for life to return to normal and for you to feel good again. Eventually you find you can go for days, weeks, months and even years without thinking about it. Don't be surprised that when in future years you do recall what happened, it is usually accompanied by some pain. But the awful pain of those first few months does not last.

The Resentment

When it comes to resentment, the person who has not had the affair naturally blames the unfaithful partner for what has happened. Very often, women blame the other woman more than their husband or partner. They make excuses for his behaviour and see her as the seductress. Men invariably blame their wife or partner for being seduced more than they blame the man who has seduced her. Most men still have a fairly macho image of how they should be sexually. Men's image of themselves as always being sexually potent, always able to satisfy a woman, anytime, anywhere, anyhow, lives on. Even if a man is not all that successful sexually, he very rarely admits it. When his partner is unfaithful this image is severely knocked. To discover his partner has been unfaithful is a totally undermining experience, because the implication is that he is not satisfying her in bed. Not only does he not like that thought, he particularly does not like the thought that this is what the rest of the world will also think.

When Will, who ran a highly successful business, met his wife's lover for the first time he said, 'I just couldn't see what Annabel saw in him. The man was a down-and-out. He had hardly had a decent job in years.' Geoff, the man in question, was not nearly as successful as Will, but one of his attractions for Will's wife, who had left her husband for Geoff, was that he wanted to spend time together as a couple, something which Will had had no interest in, or time to do, for years. He was also tall, rather good looking and very much in love with Annabel, qualities totally ignored by Will. Even if he had noticed, it was not something he was going to admit.

Men rely very much on their professional or social status for personal identification and confirmation that they are worthwhile and valuable. They frequently assess themselves, as well as the other man, by what job they do. Women, on the other hand, tend to be much more concerned with how the other woman looks. Is she prettier, slimmer, younger, and how does she compare with her? There is often a great need to confront the other woman, to see what she looks like. In the early stages of the disclosure, the desire to harm the other person can also be very powerful.

When Liz discovered her husband's affair she found the address of the other woman in his diary. One evening she turned up on her doorstep and waited for her to return from work. She told me, 'I was quite amazed. I thought she would be a long-legged blonde, but in fact she looked just like a middle-aged woman returning from a long day at the office. She wasn't even particularly pretty. She was very shocked to see me there, but invited me in and gave me coffee. I thought she must have seduced my husband, but in fact she said it was the other way round. That really hurt.'

Many women cast the other woman in the role of predator. Despite feeling very angry with her husband or partner for being unfaithful, a woman frequently blames the mistress for being the seductress and throwing herself at her husband. This is because, if she can cast the other woman in the role of temptress, it is not quite as painful as acknowledging that it was her husband who was the seducer. Men, on the other hand, may be incredibly angry with the other man, but they will also rationalise it with the thought that 'men will be men'. They are much more likely to blame their wives. They feel that a woman should resist a man's approach. A man's wife behaving badly is not acceptable although, if he is the seducer, he is often happy for someone else's wife to be susceptible to his charms.

It is natural to resent a partner who has betrayed you, as well as the person with whom they have had the affair. Both are of course to blame, but it is your partner or spouse who has let you down most of all. They have broken the promises they made to you, they have hurt the person they love. As time goes by it is important to try to stop attributing blame, if you want to rebuild the relationship. Holding your partner totally responsible for what has happened can prevent you looking at why the affair happened in the first place, but it does take time to get to that stage.

The Humiliation

Every time I see another politician's wife standing by her man on the steps of her front door, smiling bravely at the rows of cameras, my heart goes out to her. For most people it is hard enough to bear the fact that your family, friends, neighbours, and maybe even work colleagues have known about an affair before you did. How much greater is the humiliation when you are in the public eye. It seems pretty cruel and undignified to be expected to show a calm, brave face of support for your husband when inwardly you are crippled with shock, anger and pain. It must make an impossible situation even worse. Nor does it end there, because you then have to face the papers the next morning, with their endless column inches on how you looked, your facial expression, the trace of recent tears, what you were wearing, and your body language. Perhaps the greatest humiliation of all is the inevitable list of comparisons drawn with the mistress. In some cases, even your past life is dragged up.

Fortunately, most of us do not have to face such public scrutiny. Nonetheless, it is not easy to face your own circle of friends and acquaintances, whether in the local supermarket, at the school gates or at your place of work. Because you are feeling so ultra-sensitive, you think that where two people are gathered together they are bound to be talking about you. You fear you have been made a fool of, that others knew, and wonder why you have been so blind. You may indeed have been the last to know, but don't blame yourself for that. You may have known but had not been able to confront them or prove it. Either way, it's not an easy situation to cope with.

If you have to walk into a room or be somewhere you feel awkward or fear you are being talked about, it's helpful to break the ice yourself. Smile and say something like, 'I guess you know things are pretty upsetting at the moment, but it's not something I want to talk about.' You can then move on to another subject.

It is always helpful if the person who has humiliated you can acknowledge just how much they have hurt you. It can't change the past, but at least you feel that they have understood how their behaviour has affected you. On the discovery of an affair, there are losses to be coped with too. The loss of sexual exclusivity, of self-esteem, of trust. If the relationship ends, there is also the loss of the hopes and dreams you shared for the future. It is necessary to acknowledge the losses before the process of rebuilding self-esteem and trust can begin.

The Loss of Sexual Exclusivity

Whether it's a brief liaison, or a full-blown affair, to discover that something you thought was special between the two of you was being shared with someone else is extremely painful and undermining. It is natural to wonder what the other person was like in bed. Even if you are pretty confident about yourself sexually, it's all too easy to imagine that they are a million times better than you. That is frequently not the case. The reality is that the attraction is usually to someone different from their normal partner. It might be reassuring to recognise that it is the novelty factor which makes it exciting, and not necessarily because the lover or mistress is particularly sensational in bed. Both men and women have said to me in counselling, 'It wasn't necessarily better sex, sometimes not as good, but it was different and variety can be quite a draw.'

'Every time he touches me,' sobbed Gemma, 'I think of him touching her, doing the same thing to her as he is doing to me, and I can't stand it. I want to make love because I want to get close again, but then when we start I cannot bear to continue.'

Neville said of his wife, when he discovered her affair, 'To begin with I just couldn't bear the thought of making love to my wife again. Then after a few months, when we tried to have sex, I wanted to go inside her, I wanted to feel close to her, to be one again. But then I thought that her lover had been there and I just felt sick, I could not go on. Eventually these feelings did go away, but it took over a year before we were really able to make love again.'

'For months after the affair was over,' Jenny said, 'when I thought about John having sex with that other woman, I felt so humiliated. I kept torturing myself thinking about him and this girl and what they must have done together. Did they do what we do? What did she have that I didn't? I know he has come back to me, but for a long time I felt like second best.'

In modern marriage, the importance and emphasis placed on sexual fidelity means it is not really surprising that when unfaithfulness occurs, most people find it very difficult to re-establish sex within their own relationship or marriage. Some try to cope with how rejected they feel by rushing in and trying to have sex with their unfaithful partner, as if by having great sex you can eradicate the fact that they have been making love to someone else.

If you try to resume a sexual relationship too soon, it is often at the expense of expressing all the hurt and anger that the affair has made you feel. You bury these feelings, hoping that having sex together will drive them away, but it doesn't. As time goes on, you discover that it is not possible to keep up this charade. Because you are still hurt and angry with your partner, your body switches off sexually and the whole experience can feel empty and cold.

It is helpful to recognise that if the affair has had some meaning for the person involved, they may be experiencing the loss of that affair. Their partner making a demand for sex will only highlight the fact that it is too soon for them.

They will either make an excuse to avoid sex, or find they are suffering temporary impotence. This then only reinforces the rejection their partner is already feeling.

For most people, it is better to build up the emotional side of the marriage before embarking on a sexual relationship. This usually works better than rushing into lovemaking, thinking that it will cement the marriage and that the emotional commitment will follow. It is almost always the other way around. There really are no satisfactory short cuts.

The intensity of the pain does not remain. What your partner did or didn't do in bed will become less and less important and, given time, be almost forgotten. It's very difficult to believe that these intensely hurtful and painful thoughts will ever fade but given time and care they do eventually drift into the background. However, do heed one word of warning. It is not appropriate to go into too much detail about the intimate sexual details of what you did in bed together. It is difficult enough for the betrayed partner to think of the person they love having sex with another person, without knowing every detail of what went on. If you give into pressure and tell them every detail of what happened, it is even more difficult for them to eradicate these thoughts from their mind, especially when making love.

The Loss of Self-esteem

One of the hardest things to cope with if your partner has had an affair is the decimation of your self-esteem. The thought that your partner has been spending time in and out of bed with someone else does feel like a big rejection. It knocks the often shaky confidence most people have in themselves. It is important not to start imagining that the other person was special, better, more intelligent or more worthwhile than you. The reality is that often they were just different.

Self-esteem, like trust, cannot be rebuilt overnight. It takes time to re-establish. It means that your partner has to give you lots of reassurance about their feelings for you. However, you cannot rely totally on your partner to build up your self-esteem. You, too, have to work on it and recognise that there are lots of areas of your life in which you do very well. Allow yourself credit for this. Self-esteem cannot be restored unless the affair ends. If someone vacillates between their spouse and their lover, it further undermines confidence.

Self-esteem takes a further dive if your partner leaves you for someone else. You can quite literally feel terror at being abandoned. Most of us carry within us unresolved childhood fears of separation. When we cried for our mother's attention it would sometimes not be possible for her to attend to us, so we would experience fears of being separated from our primary love object. If we were left alone for too long we might even feel abandoned. If, as a baby, this happened too frequently and we were left to cry for too long, it would provoke feelings of panic. These early childhood fears can be re-activated when a partner leaves us. Once again we are in touch with some very primitive childhood fears, and it's the reason why some people believe that they will be quite unable to cope on their own.

When Mattie's husband left her for a younger woman, she felt total panic and was quite unable to feel there could be life after Felix. She had several drinks, took a load of sleeping pills, then panicked and called Felix to say what she had done. He telephoned for an ambulance, and then immediately drove home at top speed. He got to the house too late to catch the ambulance, so rushed to the local hospital not knowing what he was going to find. When he got there, his wife was having her stomach pumped out. She survived, but caused a huge scare to herself and to her family. Her husband was adamant that the marriage was over. She begged him to return, but he refused even though he did call her every day for several months to see how she was.

Mattie had many good and loyal friends who also helped her through those early days, but she realised that friends cannot be there all the time, and that she needed further help. A few weeks after leaving hospital she started counselling to help her through the first difficult and painful months of being on her own. She slowly began to talk about how her father had left her and her mother when she was four. As a result, her mother had had a nervous breakdown, which meant that she had had to spend several months in hospital. During that time, Mattie never saw her and was not told where her mother was, or if she was coming back. Mattie was looked after by her grandmother whom she did not really know very well. She remembered the pain of being suddenly left as a small child by both her parents, and wandering around her grandmother's house looking for her mother and father.

This early childhood experience had left her with a fear of being left by those she loved. When her husband subsequently left her all those years later, she felt totally overwhelmed by another sudden loss, just as she had done all those years ago as a little girl. When you feel something very intensely as an adult it is often because it has touched on a painful experience in the past. It was not until Mattie had made the connection between her painful past and her present situation, that she was able to understand why she felt such panic at being left. It was only then that she was able to accept that her marriage was over.

Mattie also discovered that she could survive on her own, and she was slowly able to rebuild her life. She found that she coped on her own far better than she thought she could. Her friends stood by her, she found a part-time job that she enjoyed and did well at, much to her surprise. As the months went by there was a great improvement in her self-esteem, and a year later she was enjoying life again. She still at times missed her husband, but she did not feel the need to rush into another relationship.

Self-esteem does take time to rebuild. If the relationship is continuing, it is important that the person who has had the affair shows their partner lots of affection and tender loving care. However, you will have to do some work on your own self-esteem as well. That can mean giving yourself more time and attention, whether it's something frivolous like an expensive haircut or buying clothes, or more long-term changes, like a new job or more fulfilling social activities.

The Loss of Trust

The deception should not be underrated, as it can hurt as much as the act of infidelity. Many people who discover their partner's unfaithfulness say the fact that their partner has lied and deceived them is as painful as the unfaithfulness itself, because the trust they had in their partner has been broken. In the early days after the discovery of an affair, the web of lies and deception haunt you. Maggie, whose partner of eight years had been unfaithful, said, 'The thought of him making love to another woman is bad enough, but to know that at the same time he was also lying to me is tearing me apart. I will never be able to forget that.'

To have been lied to, deceived, cuckolded, makes you feel a fool. The lies devalue the relationship. Most people believe that if two people love and respect each other it is understood that they do not abuse that by lying. The trust you had in your partner has, for the present, been wiped out. The person you always felt you could turn to has betrayed you, so they are not there for you when you need them most. To add insult to injury, the sex that you thought was something special between the two of you, you now discover your partner has been enjoying elsewhere.

The reality is that to be able to conduct an affair, to find the time to be with someone else, involves you in a whole web of lies. You may have lied about where you were, who you were with, and why you were going to be late home. When Natalie's marriage broke up and her husband walked out, she discovered a whole network of unfaithfulness. One of her husband's favourite excuses, she now knows, was to say he was arriving home from a business trip a couple of hours, or even a day, later than he actually was, which then enabled him to spend time with his current mistress.

Along with the deception, which is agonising enough, is the realisation that it takes two to lie. To enable the unfaithful partner to be with their mistress or lover, that person was also in on the deception, perhaps planning together what they could say to the deceived husband or wife, maybe even lying on the bed next to each other while the unfaithful partner telephoned home to say they would be working late, and not to bother waiting up for them. In this case the deceit is now mixed with disloyal behaviour, and is even more painful to deal with.

If you have been betrayed and lied to, it is easy to feel that the whole of your marriage is a lie. You remember times you have shared together, and the things that you have said to each other. You become aware that during the time the affair was going on, your partner was also doing and saying things with someone else. For the person who has been lied to, it can start to negate the past. It can devalue what you thought existed between you and your partner. It is important to try and hold on to the fact that your partner's betrayal does not mean that what he or she shared with you meant less to them. Ann who was a pretty woman in her mid-forties, said of her husband's unfaithfulness, 'Even when I did get him to admit to the affair, he still maintained that he only saw her occasionally and hardly ever contacted her.' She continued, 'It was only when I had the telephone bill itemised that he was forced to concede that yet again, he had been lying. I realised my gut feelings were right. He had been calling her all the time. One of the worst things was when I realised that once, just after we had made love, and while I was drifting into sleep, he had gone downstairs and phoned his mistress. It made what had happened between us completely meaningless. I keep going over and over all the lies he told me. I just don't know what to believe any more.'

These thoughts are painful and very understandable, but the reality is that during the time the affair was going on, it does not mean the rest of your partner's life was not important to them. An affair might have coincided with a very stressful time at work, illness in the family, or a recent redundancy, and may have been used as an escape from the problem. It does not have to cancel out the rest of a person's life and marriage. The two can run concurrently, with both having meaning and value. Trust is easily broken, but not so easily mended Rebuilding it does take a lot of time and effort, and couples have to learn to trust each other again.

The Loss of Hopes and Dreams

If an affair means the end of the marriage, you are not only coping with the loss of a partner, but with the loss of your hopes and dreams. Most people go into marriage believing it to be for life. Divorce means those dreams and plans you have made come to an abrupt end. It is similar to mourning the death of a partner. The reality is, you will not end up old and grey together, go on a world cruise, or on the planned retirement trip up the Amazon. You will probably not share your grandchildren together. Family reunions may either happen without one of you being present, or will frequently be tense occasions at which you try for the sake of others to put on a good face. It is likely to be the cause of sadness for some time before you can adjust.

The Desire for Revenge

If we have been very badly hurt we usually want to hurt the person who has hurt us, demanding an eye for an eye, a tooth for a tooth. It may not be very commendable but it is very understandable. Most of us have not acquired very saintly qualities when it comes to the desire to seek revenge. An Italian woman who was taking part in a discussion on unfaithfulness, when asked what she would do if she discovered her husband was having an affair, rose from her seat, tossed her mane of long curly hair, and with eyes flashing looked straight at the questioner and said with great passion, 'I would kii-ll 'im. Simply kii-ll 'im.' The famous case of Loretta Bobbitt, who when she discovered her husband had been unfaithful cut off his penis while he slept beside her, will probably go down in history as a chilling warning to all errant men.

It is normal to feel murderous, but fortunately most people are able to draw the distinction between what they might like to do, and what they actually do. However, that is not to deny that many men, and some women, do resort to physical violence against their unfaithful partner, which can result in severe bodily harm or even death. Usually revenge is more likely to be restricted to damaging the possessions or property of the unfaithful spouse, or the other man or woman involved.

Guy and Penny had been to a New Year's Eve party at a friend's house in the village where they lived. There were quite a few tensions around in the marriage and they had both had rather a lot to drink that evening. As they walked home in the early hours of the morning, they started to argue. In Penny's opinion Guy had spent too much of the evening dancing with Nancy, another friend of theirs who lived in the same village with her husband Colin. Penny had felt over the preceding months that there was something seriously wrong with the marriage. Guy was always out, he was continually making excuses to avoid sex, and had lost interest in the house and garden. Penny was becoming more and more convinced that Guy was having an affair. She had challenged him several times, but he had always denied it.

That New Year's evening when Penny confronted Guy, he had been drinking quite heavily, lost his temper and eventually admitted that he was having an affair with Nancy. Neither of them had any sleep that night. Penny was distraught. In the morning she rang her mother and asked her to have the children for a couple of days, telling her what had happened. Guy said that he would end the affair, pleaded with Penny to forgive him and said that he wanted to save the marriage. Penny agreed he could ring Nancy, just to tell her the affair was over and they would not meet again. They struggled through the next few months with Penny wanting to believe the affair was over, but never being really sure. She increasingly felt that Guy was lying to her.

One day at the beginning of March, Penny heard him talking on the phone to Nancy. Guy had not heard her come into the room as she had told him she was going to visit her mother, so he thought he was on his own in the house. Penny heard Guy telling Nancy how much he was missing her. She picked up his car keys from the hall table and walked out to the garage. She got into Guy's Jaguar, his pride and joy. She then drove slowly down the drive, and as she came to the gates she deliberately made sure that she scraped the car all down one side against the gatepost, denting it and stripping off the shiny new paint. Guy heard the noise, looked up from the telephone and saw with horror what was happening. As he stood there transfixed, Penny reversed the car. This time she successfully aimed at the gatepost on the other side of the car, where she inflicted similar damage.

Guy ran out into the drive, screaming at her to stop. Penny got out of the car, flung the keys at him and walked back into the house, leaving Guy to take in the full impact of the damage. Penny said later, 'I wanted to hurt him because he had hurt me so much, first by the affair and then by lying to me that it was all over when clearly it wasn't. When I heard him on the phone to her, I just saw red. I knew how much his car meant to him, but he had hurt me so much I couldn't take any more.'

It is normal for the injured partner to feel and act like a hurt and rejected child, overwhelmed with feelings of hate, and concerned by the desire to hurt the person who has hurt them. Because of this, the person who is trying to cope with these overwhelming feelings often turns them into actions. They are acting out their pain, maybe by attempting suicide, becoming hysterical, resorting to violence, screaming at their rival on the telephone, or damaging their partner's belongings.

Revenge often gives the perpetrator short-term satisfaction, but it usually causes uproar in its wake. It can be very disturbing for the children, who are probably having trouble enough trying to make sense of an impossibly painful, disturbing and stressful situation. Revenge is best avoided if possible. It helps if you can talk through the ending of the marriage. Even if your partner has left you for another, it gives you an opportunity to say how you feel, and to express your anger to the person who has hurt you. If possible, it can give you some insight into why the marriage is over. This does not take away the pain, but in the long run it means it is a little easier to come to terms with the end of the relationship.

When Adultery Becomes Serial

If you both want to work at the marriage it is possible to get over one affair, but each time another affair happens it severely reduces the chances of the marriage surviving. Rebuilding a marriage after an affair takes a lot of courage. It is not easy to allow yourself to love and to trust someone again. If, yet again, you are betrayed by your partner, it is doubly hard to trust them. How can you believe that it won't happen again and again?

The more a person gets away with being unfaithful the less inclination there is to change. Consistent unfaithfulness can turn the marriage from being an equal adult-to-adult relationship into one where the unfaithful partner acts more like an irresponsible teenager. When they are caught behaving badly, they seek forgiveness from the hurt and angry parent. They say they are sorry, and promise that it won't happen again. To constantly expect your partner's forgiveness for yet another affair is cruel, self-centred behaviour. For the one who is endlessly forgiving, it is frequently an indication of little self-worth.

It may be that you are repeating a pattern learned in childhood. If you saw your parent of the opposite sex behave like that and get away with it, you may have learned that there is nothing you can do. You may think that, 'All men are like that,' or, 'You can't trust a woman, they all let you down in the end.' Each act of betrayal, however, leaves the marriage more vulnerable to breaking down. If you are in a marriage or relationship where infidelity has become a way of life and it hurts, then it is probably time to seek outside help. In these circumstances counselling can help you either to look at why you are treating your partner so badly, or why you are prepared to be treated in such a way.

It is just as damaging when people choose to turn a blind eye to their partner's frequent infidelities. That, too, usually takes its toll on the marriage in the end. The deceived partner becomes more and more down-trodden, depressed and unhappy. They are often trapped in the marriage, trying to convince themselves that the infidelity is not happening and that their partner will change. Those who choose to ignore their partner's constant affairs often do so because they're afraid their partner might leave if confronted. The thought of being on their own feels worse than having to put up with the unfaithfulness.

Having the courage to confront your partner, rather than colluding in ignoring the infidelities, is not easy. Neither is it easy to change your pattern of behaviour and mean it when you say that you are not prepared to put up with any more affairs. You must convince your partner that you mean it when you say, 'If you have another affair then that is the end of the marriage.' It is important to stick to your guns, otherwise your partner will always feel that in the end they can get away with it, or they will try once more to sweet talk you into forgiving them.

By overcoming your fear of loss and separation, and real-ising that you can separate and even divorce your unfaithful spouse and still survive, you will be taking a healthy step out of an often unhappy marriage. There is a life out there waiting to be lived. By recognising that you are worth more than the way you are being treated, you will then be more able to confront your unfaithful spouse and end the marriage if you want to. This step is often the first time the faithful spouse of a persistent adulterer feels they have had any power in the relationship, or any control over their lives.

The Impact of Affairs on Children

Affairs do not always affect the children. An affair that is kept secret, which is non-threatening to the marriage and is conducted with someone outside the family and friendship circle, may have little or no impact on the children of the family. Of course, you can never be sure the affair will not alter your behaviour, or that it will not for some quite unforeseen reason be disclosed. Then everything can change.

The worst of all situations for children is to be drawn into the crossfire when the affair is discovered. This often happens with teenage children who are old enough to understand what is going on.

Sally called in at her father's office on her way home from school, hoping for a lift home. Her father was not quite ready, so she thought she would start some homework for her approaching 'O' levels. She could not find a pen, so she opened one of the drawers of her father's desk to look for one. She could not help noticing a letter written to him which began 'Darling Harry', and it was not in her mother's writing. She knew she should not read other people's letters, but she read on. It became clear that her father was having an affair. He came into the room while she was reading the letter. At first he was furious when he saw what she was reading, but when he calmed down and his daughter confronted him, he admitted that he was having an affair. He told Sally that things were not going well between him and her mother.

Her father said that he had not made any decisions about the future, but he asked her to keep the affair a secret. Sally was very close to her father, but she was also loyal to her mother. As the weeks passed, she found it increasingly difficult not to say anything. Her mother eventually found out about the affair, through a friend who had seen Harry and the other woman at a hotel where they were having dinner and clearly staying the night. The balloon went up.

Sally's mother said that she had had no idea about the affair, and had always thought she had a happy marriage. 'How could your father behave like this? He has no respect for his marriage vows. He is an adulterer,' said her mother, weeping uncontrollably. Her mother insisted that the fact he had asked Sally to keep it a secret meant that he did not care about her feelings either. Her father's mother, Sally's grandmother, was so scandalised by her son's behaviour that she said she did not want anything to do with him. Sally was pulled in two directions. She felt her mother resented her for knowing about the affair and not telling her, and that her father wanted her sympathy because everyone else was so angry with him. On top of that she was trying to work for her 'O' levels which, as the arguments increased around the home, became increasingly difficult.

After six months of turmoil, Sally's father left home. By then the affair was over, but so was the marriage. Her mother refused to have anything to do with Sally's father, so he and Sally worked out when and where they would met. Her father said she could telephone him whenever she wanted and reverse the charges. When he tried telephoning her, if Sally's mother took the call she would just put the phone down on him and every time Sally told her mother she was going to see her father, her mother implied, 'How could you have anything to do with such a bastard?'

It is very important that the anger that is felt when an affair is out in the open does not spill over onto the children. Children, in the main, want to love both their parents and don't want to have one portrayed as the totally guilty party, or the black sheep of the family. It is also essential for parents not to offload their hurt and anger over the affair onto the children.

If an affair is discovered and causing constant rows, arguments and tears, it is important that some explanation is given to the children. If they are old enough to understand, it is usually better to tell them what the arguments are about, but they should not be used as a confidant by either of the parents. It is too much of a burden for them to carry, nor do they need to be told lots of unnecessary facts or details which are only relevant to the adults concerned. If they are very young and can't understand the concept of an affair, then an explanation about Mummy and Daddy not being very happy with each other at the moment is one way of handling it. In both situations children need to be given lots of love and reassurance that they are not causing the rows or unhappiness.

If children discover the affair, it is not fair to ask them to keep it a secret from the other parent because that unwittingly draws them into the web of deceit. Maybe the exception to this is if the other parent really has no idea, the affair is definitely over, and the unfaithful parent is committed to the marriage. However, it is not easy to decide when a child is old enough to be able to cope with such a secret. In my opinion, they would have to be approaching adulthood.

Affairs can be disconcerting even for quite young children. This is particularly so if they involve a friend of the family, a neighbour, or someone at work whom the children know and see quite a lot of. Children from nine or ten upwards often have pretty good antennae if someone is sexually interested in one of their parents. Children don't like it. Perhaps they sense the danger signs, that this could cause problems, or they feel that their other parent is being excluded from this particular friendship.

Josh, a very lively ten year old, did not know that his mother was having an affair with his games teacher, but something about their relationship was worrying him. He would watch them anxiously when his mother came to collect him at the end of the day. He complained to his grandmother that, 'Mum is so embarrassing, because she's always flirting with the teacher.' He also started to be very difficult about going to school when previously there had been no problem. The affair did not last very long, as the teacher in question started to worry that his wife might discover what he had been up to, and he ended the affair. Soon after that he moved to another school, the affair was never discovered and Josh's problems faded away.

The discovery of an affair causes enormous chaos and uncertainty, and just as the parents may be wondering if the marriage can survive it, so too will the children. The future will feel uncertain and this affects the children because they will worry that the arguments, the tears, the devastation and unhappiness will never end, or might even mean the finish of the marriage.

Children frequently overhear their parents arguing over an affair, as things do tend to get fairly heated. They may hear one parent threatening to leave, telling the unfaithful partner to go, or begging them to stay. It is not surprising that children then reflect their fears in changes in their behaviour. This can range from being very naughty, to being silent and withdrawn. It can be a refusal to go to school, or an inability to concentrate when they get there. If they are younger, they can suffer from regressive behaviour like thumb sucking or bed wetting.

All these symptoms may indicate that children are suffering

because of the turmoil caused by the affair. It is important that their fears are recognised, they are given as much reassurance as possible, are allowed to talk about how they feel, and are able to express their anger. It is quite usual for children to feel angry with the parent who has had the affair, because they see how much they have hurt their other parent, and because they are also hurt themselves by what is going on around them. It is not easy for most children to understand why parents have to behave in such a way.

Other Ways in Which Children Can Be Hurt

One thing that is particularly difficult for the child is if the parent who is having the affair vacillates between their spouse or partner and their mistress or lover.

George had been married to Gilly for fifteen years when he met and fell in love with Verity. She was divorced with two boys of twelve and ten, a similar age to George's two daughters. Over a period of about six months George had twice left Gilly to go and live with Verity, only to return home later.

For George the marriage had been fairly empty for several years. He knew that Verity was everything he wanted and his love was reciprocated. George felt very bad about leaving his wife, who insisted she still loved him but what was really finishing him off was the agony of not seeing his daughters, and the huge guilt he felt at leaving them.

He had always been a devoted father and was very close to his daughters. Their mother was trying to put on a brave face, but they saw how unhappy she was. They were also missing their father very much, and deeply resented the fact that he was living with Verity and her sons. They did not want to share their father. Their way of dealing with the pain of their father's affair and absence, was to refuse to see him or have anything to do with him while he was living with Verity. Occasionally Emma, the elder of the two, would write a brief little letter begging him to come home.

When he was with Verity, George found that he started to really resent her two boys. For a start, it did not help that he thought they were pretty ill-disciplined compared with his two children. Even if they were trying to be friendly to him, he was unable to respond and kept rejecting their approaches. He was missing his own children so much and feeling so guilty that he was taking these feelings out on Verity's two boys by criticising them and not wanting to join in any of their activities. This of course was further complicated by Verity resenting his behaviour towards them, which led to bitter arguments.

Vacillating between the two women prolonged the uncertainty for both of them, as well as for his children. In the end George did leave, but it took over two years of intense hard work, a lot of patience on George's part, and much support from Verity, before his daughters were able to accept that he could still love them and be a good father, even though he was no longer living with them full-time. It also took time for Verity's sons to accept him after his early rejection of them.

It is important if an affair is discovered that one parent does not run the other one down in front of the children. This is not easy, as emotions run very high when someone discovers their partner's infidelity. You may find it very difficult not to criticise your partner in front of the children because you are so hurt and angered by their affair and the ending of the marriage. However, drawing the children into the rows and arguments between you and your partner will only make it more difficult for them in the long run, and jeopardise their relationship with their other parent even more.

Affairs Can Be a Catalyst for Change

What happens to a marriage after the disclosure or discovery of an affair is always unpredictable. It may mean the end, and it will always rock the marriage to its very foundations. But it can also open up possibilities for change, however painful. As affairs are so frequently a symptom of problems within the marriage, once they are exposed the couple involved also has the opportunity to see if they can rebuild or reconstruct their relationship. This can be on a better and more fulfilling level than before the affair, which may not be easy but has been successfully managed by many couples. Such a crisis throws marital complacency, boredom and indifference to the four winds. It gives a couple the chance to look at the options and talk about what changes are desirable and achievable.

Malcolm was totally knocked for six when he discovered that his wife Judy had been having an affair. He was particularly outraged as he felt that he had worked so hard for her and their three daughters. How could she be so disloyal? In fact, over the last two years he had become more and more remote from her. He worked long hours, was always socialising after work with colleagues, and often drank too much. When he did get home he never made time to hear about Judy's day. He would have something to eat and then fall asleep in front of the television. Everything from looking after the children to cooking, cleaning, paying the bills, or sorting out anything that needed attention in the house and garden, was left to her. He was never too busy, however, to fit in his game of golf, or to watch sport on television. He was nearly always too preoccupied or tired for sex, but would always boast about his high libido if he was with a crowd of people.

For Judy, the final straw had been when he could not even schedule the annual family holiday into his working life. She went on her own to their cottage in France and he came over at weekends. Even then he seemed to spend half the time on the telephone. Judy said of herself, 'I was an affair waiting to happen.'

Judy's affair was with a much younger man. It was very sexual but without a great deal of emotional commitment. She knew the relationship had no future, but in the short-term he made her feel good, and was exciting and fun. She had felt so neglected by Malcolm that it was all too easy to fall for the charms of the younger and more attractive man. She was so used to Malcolm not being there that she also became careless. One day when he came home unexpectedly at lunch-time, he caught them together. They were not in bed but sharing lunch and a glass of wine, and Malcolm guessed the rest.

There were massive rows, with each giving the other the blame, but underneath they still loved each other and neither really wanted a divorce. Malcolm admitted that he had really let work and his social life take over his life. He admitted that he was drinking too much and had given Judy and the children a raw deal. But he also pointed to the lifestyle that he was supporting and said that was why he worked so hard. As he talked, he also recognised that he liked the success and power that came from the job. Malcolm was never going to be a nine-to-five man, but he was able to work out with Judy a better balance in their lives. He did not work such long hours, and when work was finished he came home at a reasonable time. He cut right back on after-hours socialising and drinking.

They now had more time together and started to go out, just the two of them, something they had not done for years. They also entertained at home, which met a lot of Malcolm's gregarious needs. Judy got herself a part-time job, which not only helped with the finances but also made her feel more confident and better about herself. She also recognised that, even before Malcolm had been working such long hours, there had been little sex in the marriage. Since the birth of their youngest child, who was just six, she had never really found the time to make love, so it was not fair to blame it all on Malcolm. It had, she admitted, through neglect on both their parts become infrequent and lacklustre. A year later their marriage was stronger, closer and more sexual than it had been for many years.

Twelve Ways to Rebuild a Relationship

In the previous chapter, I examined how and when to disclose an affair, and suggested 'the kindest ways to confess'. These can also provide the basis for rebuilding a relationship, forming twelve steps towards a happier future together.

1 **An affair is crunch time in most marriages**.
Both of you have to ask yourselves whether you want to keep the relationship. You have to talk things through even though that will be very painful. What has happened can't just be swept under the carpet, but don't make any hasty decisions while emotions are running high. It may take many weeks or months before you finally decide whether to stay together.

2 **Allow your partner to express their hurt and anger**.
If you had the affair, you have to be prepared to support your partner through a lot of hurt, pain and anger of which you are largely the cause. If they want to shout and scream and vent their feelings, it is better for them to do so, rather than be told they are being hysterical or overreacting.

3 **The 'who, where, when, and how long has it been going on?' questions**.
The person who has had the affair has to be prepared to be questioned about all of these things. It is usually necessary for the betrayed person to want to go over the facts again and again, and for the unfaithful spouse it will probably seem endless. The faithful partner needs to recognise that there comes a time when they have to move on. You have to learn to resist seizing on every opportunity to pick over the events like a terrier picking at a bone.

4 **Do not defend the mistress or lover**.
It is rarely a good idea to spring to their defence, because it then seems that you care more about their feelings or reputation than you do about your partner's. Your protection of them will only encourage your partner to attack even more.

5 **Give each other time and space**.
For the unfaithful spouse it's unrealistic to expect too much sympathy from your partner about the loss

you may be feeling over ending the affair. If it was an important affair, you may need to recognise that it will take a little time for your partner to come to terms with this.

6 There comes a time when the blaming has to stop.

You can't go on forever blaming your unfaithful partner. They might well be the one who has committed the greater crime, but if you can't move on you both end up the losers. There is a time to leave behind such thoughts as, 'I will never forgive him. I blame him for what has happened and he does not deserve my forgiveness.' It's all too easy to allow blame to hang over you like a black cloud blocking out any chance of the sunlight filtering through into the marriage. If this happens, it completely obscures anything that was good in the relationship. The more you hang on to your bitterness, the more your marriage will disintegrate.

7 Avoid a revenge affair.

Embarking on a revenge affair to show your partner how much they have hurt you is not a good idea. It only complicates the issue and delays or jeopardises the chances of recovery.

8 Why did it happen?

There comes a point when this question has to be asked. It is particularly difficult for the person whose partner has strayed to look at and accept that there might have been problems in the relationship that led to the affair. Being able to do that is a turning point on the road to recovery.

9 Ringing the changes.

It is only by looking at what went wrong that you can start to put things right. Each of you may have needs which are unmet by the other, so it's important to establish what they are. Talk about it, make a list with the most important ones at the top, and then negotiate some changes. For example, I might like your partner to: show you more affection; spend more time with you; make love more often; go out more; see more of your friends. The aim is to understand each other's needs and do your best to meet them.

10 The faithful partner can never forget about an affair, but they can learn to forgive.
To begin with, thoughts of the affair are with you every minute of the day. The pain does fade eventually, and it's important not to keep dragging up your partner's old sins to punish them every time there is an argument.

11 Take time before making love again.
It is important not to rush into having sex with your partner when an affair has been discovered. You need to know that the affair is over, and that you are both trying to rebuild the relationship. You may feel you have to prove that you are better than the ex-lover, and that your partner could have as good a time with you as they imagined they had with the other person. In reality, you cannot act your way through something as intimate as lovemaking when your heart has been broken, and your trust betrayed.

It is not uncommon for a man to suffer from impotence when he does start to have sex again with an unfaithful partner after she has ended an affair. This may continue for many months because the trust has been broken and because, in the early days after the affair, he may be unable to blot out the picture in his head of his partner making love to someone else.

12 Rome was not built in a day.
Trust cannot be rebuilt in a day, or even a week or two, but if a relationship is to survive and flourish there has to be trust. In the early days you have to be very careful to tell your partner where you are going, when you will be back and make sure that you are where you said you are going to be. If you are going to be late, telephone. It is also important to help rebuild your partner's self-esteem and trust

in you by making them feel that it is them you love and want to be with.

It is through exploring the past, understanding what has happened and why, and then deciding what your options are, that a relationship is able to move forward. Marriages really can be more loving and more fulfilling than prior to the affair, but it does take a lot of time, care and motivation on both parts.

Joan [whom I wrote about at the beginning of the chapter, on p.130] was desperately hurt by Leonard's affair, but he gave her time to express all her hurt and angry feelings, and she accepted that in many ways the affair was a reflection of all that was not well in the marriage. She could not lay all the blame at his door. Joan was very aware that both of them had not only to want the marriage to work, but also to avoid slipping back into their bad old ways. She said, 'Now if we see each other or ourselves slipping into the bad old ways, where we are not talking, or are starting to take each other for granted, we say, "Hey, look what's happening!" We listen to what the other has to say, and really care if we think that we might be on the slippery slope once more.' Leonard said, 'I really regret my affair. I wish it hadn't happened and I'm quite determined that it's never going to happen to us ever again.'

Mary, a woman in her late fifties, wrote to me about her regrets over her affair. Her husband has never found out about it, but she has found the guilt very hard to live with. She wrote:

Several times I have read of women contemplating having an affair, usually because they have become dissatisfied with their marriage. I would just love the opportunity to say, 'Please don't.' Over twenty years ago my own marriage went through a bad patch, and I succumbed to an affair that lasted several years. It solved nothing. My husband knows nothing about it. I would give anything not to have deceived him. I am filled with guilt and it gets worse each year. I am sometimes tempted to tell my husband, but

*I can't bear to hurt him. I can never forgive myself. I hope
if you use this letter it will help someone else to think long
and hard and hopefully say no to an affair. Believe me it's
not worth it.*

I hope Mary does not tell her husband, because it is all over
and it happened many years ago. Her hope would be that
if she did tell him it would relieve some of the terrible guilt
she is feeling, but she also recognises that it would cause
her husband a lot of pain and hurt. I hope even more that
she can stop feeling so guilty. Coping with the fact that you
have deceived someone is very painful, but you can't change
the past by bearing the guilt alone to protect a partner from
pain. What happened, happened. It is important now to move
on and acknowledge that, yes, you do have regrets, but you
should not inflict a 'life sentence' on yourself.

Perhaps the affair in the long run enabled Mary to see how
much she had going for her within her marriage. The very
fact that it is now loving and close may be what makes it so
difficult for her, and others like her, to forgive themselves
for their past deceits, but I hope they can.

Chapter Seven

CREATIVE ADULTERY

There is nothing in the world like the devotion of a married woman. It's a thing no married man knows anything about!

Oscar Wilde, *Lady Windermere's Fan*

It is frequently said that women are monogamous by nature. There are many more theories, such as: happily married women do not have affairs; a woman cannot enjoy sex with a man unless she loves him; for a woman, sex without love cheapens the relationship; it is not possible for a woman to love more than one man at a time; women don't fantasise about making love with anyone other than with their partner; a woman who has an affair always feels very guilty. 'It's only other people's wives who have affairs,' men say. 'Mine would not be interested.'

Even Alfred Kinsey in his analysis of his research into men and women's sexual behaviour speculated that women had fewer extramarital affairs than men because they have fewer sexual needs. It is still not uncommon for men, from anthropologists, social historians, bishops and politicians to the man (and indeed woman) in the street, to put forward the argument that men are driven by their genes to populate the world with their own offspring and that they have less control over their sexual drive than women do. They should acknowledge that this is a wonderfully convenient excuse for men behaving badly and controlling women by encouraging them to feel guilty about their sexual appetite.

From my experience, the majority of men and women who have affairs do not want to end their marriage. Of the women

I have spoken to whose infidelities have remained undetected, many have delighted in their affair. They have said that it was a creative and liberating experience for them. They did not want to be discovered, or to put their children through separation and divorce. They recognised that much of what they wanted was there within their own marriage, and were often aware that a marriage with their lover would not be more successful or happier than what they had; indeed it could be a lot less happy. They clearly realised that many of the things they liked in their present marriage would not be found with their lover. For many women, their affair provided a path to self-fulfilment. Many felt that it enhanced their marriage and enabled them to develop areas of themselves which were restricted by marriage. As they saw it, 'creative adultery' made them feel better about themselves, their lives and their marriage.

Men too can experience adultery as creative, although they are more likely than women to be sexually motivated when embarking on it. Although women, like men, are seeking sexual pleasure, there are other equally important reasons for an affair, such as the fulfilment of emotional needs, a desire for intimacy or self-affirmation. Being emotionally involved with their lover usually heightens enjoyment of the affair as well as sexual desire. For women, sex is a much more passionate experience if it is able to engage both mind and body.

A Man's Affair Versus a Woman's Affair

A man can spend an idyllic afternoon making love to his mistress. While they are together she is very important to him, but once parted he can return to work and devote himself one hundred percent to the job in hand. When he goes home at the end of the day, he will probably think about his mistress, thrill to the excitement of what they did together, but will not necessarily want to be with her. Instead he moves into the home and family segment of his life, closes the door marked 'mistress' and opens the one marked 'wife and family'. He is genuinely pleased to be with his wife and children, and enjoys all the security and comfort of family life. The mistress can be safely slotted into another compartment quite separate from his marriage.

If a woman is having an affair, she is more likely to want to merge with her lover and try to create emotional intimacy. She may want the combination of the marriage and the affair, just like many men, but when she parts from her lover, she carries thoughts of him with her more than men do. A woman is more likely than a man to go over what they did, and particularly what was said. How deep are his feelings? Did I please him? When are we meeting again? I wonder what his wife and children are like? What is he doing now? Is he with her? Can I really believe him when he says he is no longer sleeping with his wife? (This last one is a very common male lie, I'm afraid.)

The majority of men who have affairs can keep them relatively separate from their marriage or work. Admittedly, some men who have affairs do fall hopelessly in love or become totally besotted with their mistress, in which case their love affair often takes over their lives. Most men, however, are more in control of their emotions and of their relationships with their mistresses, than the majority of women are with their lovers. However, change is happening even in this area of relationships. For example, when Leo's mistress finished the relationship, he would not leave her alone. He telephoned her ten or eleven times a day, drove up and down outside her house, begged her to come out to lunch with him, and threatened to tell her husband unless she continued the affair.

The Masculinisation of Sex and the Feminisation of Love

It is important to acknowledge that there have been changes over the years in men's and women's attitudes to love, sex and affairs. Not all women are looking for deep committed relationships when they embark on affairs. Nowadays women have more understanding and appreciation of their own sexual desires and potential. They recognise that, like men, they can enjoy sex with someone they are neither committed to nor in love with. They are, in fact, more likely than previous generations to engage in more conventionally masculine forms of casual sex. An increasing number of women's affairs may well be more sexually orientated than emotionally based.

At the same time, men are also placing greater importance on a more rounded relationship or affair than a purely sexual one. As well as enjoying new sexual experiences with no commitment, they too are beginning to look for intimacy and affection, even love, in their sexual relationships and affairs. Men are finding that women make good friends as well as mistresses. A good proportion of the time they have with their mistress is now spent in talking and enjoying activities other than sex.

A woman whose husband continually denied he was having an affair, had him followed by a detective. She discovered that he did occasionally take his mistress to bed, but there were many more occasions when he took her out to dinner, to the theatre, or an art gallery.

Joe said of his mistress, 'Sex is great, but I particularly love the fact that we have the same tastes in art, music, and theatre. Enjoying these with her makes me feel really close to her, sometimes closer than to my wife.'

Although the sexes are drawing closer together in their sexual and emotional needs, there are still quite distinct differences. Men may love their wives, but they still need to retain a centre of independence in their relationship with them. They want to love and be loved, and even to be close, but too much invasion of themselves and their own personal space makes a man feel uneasy. They are the same in their affairs; they do not want too many demands made of them. If a mistress becomes too emotionally demanding in an affair, a man will often end it. After all, they have 'an emotionally demanding woman' back home, so they certainly don't want the same pressures applied to them in their affairs.

A man will often interpret really wonderful sex as emotional closeness to a woman, whether within marriage or an affair. It is extremely satisfying for him and may well have met all his emotional needs too. He has, after all, found what he is looking for. For most women, however, they too want great sex, but they are looking for more, certainly within their marriages and often in their affairs as well. If men and women could accept more easily what makes the other feel emotionally close, it might lead to far less disappointment and frustration.

Reasons to be Unfaithful

The struggle between commitment to a partner and desire for another is a hard one. Motives for adulterous relationships are complex and can range from a longing for new sexual experiences to an escape from the pressures and frustrations of everyday life. There may be a need for self-affirmation in some way, perhaps to reinforce a person's own attractiveness and ability, or there may be a desire to compensate for an unloving, difficult, frustrating, or sexless marriage. Is it realistic to think that two people can be totally and exclusively faithful to each other for forty or fifty years or more? Has Western society set up codes of behaviour that most people are going to breach?

Our greater knowledge, understanding and capacity for sexual enjoyment makes it more difficult nowadays for men and women to stay faithful. Did previous generations have an easier time resisting temptation because of the real risk of pregnancy, for example, and because the average life of a marriage was much shorter?

Women Behaving Badly?

Traditionally women have felt more guilty about their affairs than men. It has long been accepted that an unfaithful woman is not behaving as a 'good girl' should. She is judged, and she judges herself, as falling from grace. Women, after all, are still seen as the prime guardian of the family's physical and emotional well-being, so to pursue her own needs or desires goes against society's expectations. I am not suggesting that men should be given the 'good philanderers' seal of approval, but they are not saddled with the same expectations of good behaviour.

The emphasis on the male role within marriage is still as economic provider with less emotional involvement than women. The man feels freer to pursue his own individual needs, whether through an affair, a brief one-night stand, or in sport or leisure activities. During my last twenty years of counselling, however, I have been seeing changes. Women nowadays feel more entitled to pursue lifestyles that bring them greater self-fulfilment and personal satisfaction.

Olivia, a young, newly married woman of thirty, said that she was quite surprised by the conversation of the girls at work who were eight or nine years younger than her. She would hear them talking on Monday mornings about the weekend's activities. They seemed to revolve around men, so nothing new there, but it was how they were talking about them that surprised her. She said, 'They would talk about their success with men, which appeared to be measured by how many men they had "pulled" at a party that Saturday night.' She remembered her own conversation at that age being far more about how to assert yourself when the man taking you on a first date expected a meal ticket to your bed.

The question is, when the current generation of twenty year olds moves into marriage, will their boundaries on infidelity be more easily crossed than previous generations?

Dalma Heyn, author of *The Erotic Silence of the Married Woman*, interviewed hundreds of American women for her book and in so doing exposed the myth that men, by nature, play around while women are monogamous. She showed just how many women as well as men are having their cake and eating it. Women are choosing to have affairs that run parallel with their marriage. She says that some of the women may still

have felt like 'outlaws' for breaking away from the image of the
perfect wife, but they also spoke candidly about 'recovering
a capacity for pleasure' through their affairs, of recovering
'a long-missing vitality' in themselves, of 'unfreezing', and
of being released from the stiffling confines of a traditional
marriage.

Women seeking affairs for their own pleasure is not just
an American phenomenon. It is, I believe, very common in
Britain too, although we are not quite so aware of it. These
affairs are frequently kept secret, not just from partners but
from friends and family as well.

Lydia's Affair

Lydia was a very shy and beautiful girl, highly intelligent but
also deeply insecure. She had been very strictly brought up,
by a father who had little interest in her. He was constantly
unfaithful to Lydia's mother, who put up with it even though
she did not like it. Lydia's mother compensated for her
husband's unfaithfulness by enjoying a very comfortable
lifestyle, beautiful clothes and a packed social life, which
gave her little time to dwell on her husband's indiscretions.
During much of her childhood Lydia, an only child, was left
in the care of nannies, then packed off to boarding school
at the age of eight. She was quite popular and made friends,
but her shyness got in the way of establishing really close
friendships with the other girls. She looked on with envy at
those around her who were much more relaxed and outgoing.
One thing she was not short of was boyfriends. From about
twelve or thirteen upwards, there were always boys around.
At first they were the brothers of the girls at school and later,
when she moved to live and work in London, sharing a flat
with friends from school, she was always the one who could
pick and choose which man's invitation to accept.

At nineteen, Lydia fell deeply in love with Edward, who
was three years older than her. Over the next two years they
had a very passionate affair, but when she found out that

he had slept with another girl after a rather drunken party, she was quite devastated. Here was history repeating itself. She broke off the relationship, but a few weeks later Edward called her, said he loved her, and pleaded with her to get back together again. During the next year they broke up and made up several times, and in one of the periods when they were apart she started going out with Jack, who utterly adored her. She began to think she was in love with him. Edward who was stunningly good-looking, very confident, and self-assured, was sought after by every girl who met him, but he was also unreliable and, she suspected, unfaithful too. Sometimes he seemed very much in love with her, and at other times she felt she was losing him. Jack, on the other hand, seemed charming, dependable and very much the faithful type. He was not very good-looking, but he seemed fun and he wanted Lydia. After only knowing each other for a few months they got engaged, and a couple of months later they were married. Within a year she had produced their first child, and two more followed shortly after that. Edward married within the year and asked her to the wedding, but she did not go. Shortly after that, he moved to live in America with the woman his parents had always wanted him to marry and Lydia lost touch with him.

It was not long into her marriage that Lydia realised that though she loved Jack, it wasn't with that intensity of passion that she had felt for Edward. By then, however, she had two children and another on the way. She found that Jack had two sides to him. He was very charming and laid back, but he also had a vicious temper, which he would lose at the slightest provocation. As Lydia became more self-assured and mature, he felt threatened by her new found confidence, so he would frequently undermine her. It turned out he was unreliable as well. He never stayed in one job for long, and Lydia had to learn to cope with little money and constant worries about when he would next be unemployed. The more pressure Jack was under at work, the more he took it out on Lydia. In their social life Lydia was still the centre of men's attention, which added to Jack's insecurity. Unlike Lydia's father he was faithful, but Lydia was not. After five years of marriage she embarked on her first affair.

Lydia said, 'With James it really was instant attraction. We were at a party and I felt someone staring at me. When I looked up and saw him, my heart literally skipped a beat. He made it quite clear from the very beginning that he wanted to see me again, and though at first I refused, after about three months of him calling me and talking endlessly to him on the telephone we met for lunch. I think I knew we were going to end up in bed. I dressed so carefully, I knew I was looking good, and as soon as I saw him I knew how much he wanted me. He made me feel wonderful. After lunch we drove into the country, found somewhere very quiet and secluded, and made love. It was a very sexual affair, but he was good for me too. He never put me down, he was always interested in what I had to say, and what I was doing. It was because of him that I gained the confidence to do a degree, which opened doors into jobs I would not have dreamed of applying for without his encouragement.

'James was married with children a similar age to mine. He loved his wife and I, in my way, loved Jack, so we both agreed right at the beginning of the affair that neither of us would break up our marriages as too many people would get hurt. Jack was basically a loving husband and a good father to the children. I had strong beliefs that marriage was for life, as my parents had eventually split up when I was fifteen. I was determined that my children would not go through the same experience. When my father went off with one of his more persistent mistresses, I was deeply hurt. I had felt so very rejected and I didn't want to hurt others as I felt my father had hurt my mother and me. Also, I recognised that if I did marry James, he would never be faithful. For me, faithfulness in the man I married was essential.' Then she smiled ruefully, 'I'm afraid I haven't applied the same code to my own behaviour.'

Over the next twenty years Lydia had four affairs. All of them lasted two or three years or more. All the men were married, many were from the social set in which she and Jack moved, but there was always an understanding that neither of them would ever ask the other to end their marriage. With all her affairs Lydia exercised a lot of control. She did not meet her lovers very often, she was immensely careful to keep the risks down to the minimum, and she never told anyone else. Now, twenty-five years after her first affair, Lydia remembers them all with pleasure. Lydia is certain that Jack was and is unaware of her secret life.

Five years ago Lydia answered the telephone, and she recognised the voice immediately. It was Edward. He had been back in England for two years and he suggested that they meet for a drink. Lydia refused. She said, 'The children were all involved in their "A" levels and university exams. I couldn't risk meeting Edward. I couldn't be sure that I wouldn't still love him. I wasn't prepared to jeopardise my children's happiness, or Jack's. You see, with Edward I couldn't be sure, given the opportunity, that I could keep to the agreement I had with myself, that an affair must not end the marriage. It might seem very immoral to some, but for me my affairs gave me such confidence and great satisfaction, and they were wonderfully sexual. I always knew I was in control, but with Edward I never was. We might have met and found we had nothing in common, but I might have fallen in love again, and I couldn't handle that.'

What Lydia was also doing with her affairs, and it was part of their attraction, was getting the time and attention she never received from her father. His mistresses had, she felt, always competed for his time and attention, and she had always lost out. There was, she admitted, a narcissistic need within her for sexual attention, but the affairs also helped her with her confidence, as the attention had always done from the many men in her life. With none of her affairs did she allow herself to really fall in love with the man involved. She did not want to experience the rejection that she had felt from her father's lack of interest in her. She had fallen in love with a man who, like her father, was not faithful, and before he could reject her yet again she had taken control and rejected him.

Lydia married a man who loved her, who found her beautiful, and very sexually attractive. His insecurities and his temper made him difficult to live with at times, but he provided three things that were really important to Lydia: he was faithful, he was a good father, and he loved her. In return, Lydia was a good wife, an excellent hostess, she worked hard and, most of all, she adored her children. However, she set up triangular relationships over which she had a lot of control and used them to avoid getting too close to any of the men in her life. This gave her protection against being hurt, as she had been as a child. The trouble was, although Jack loved her, he was always afraid she would leave him for someone better looking, more successful, more interesting. Part of him needed to put her down in order to have control over her and keep her in the marriage. Now that the children have finally left home, it will be interesting to see what happens to the marriage.

A Fear of Intimacy

Lydia's affairs were not only about being in control, or repeating family patterns. As is so often the case, they were also about the avoidance of intimacy. A triangular relationship like an affair directly involves three people: the husband, the wife and the lover or mistress. This means that you no longer have an exclusive relationship as a couple, because there is a third person sharing your life. The frequent dilemma is that while part of you longs for a close, intimate, loving relationship, the other part of you is so afraid that if you find it, you could lose it. You may find yourself initiating action that will distance you from your partner, even though that person had no intention of withdrawing from you. Your fear that the person you love might abandon you is so terrifying, however, that your response is to withdraw from them before they jettison you. In this way, embarking on an affair reduces the intimacy in a marriage which could otherwise make you feel too vulnerable.

This fear of intimacy tends to be located either in past childhood experiences, or in an earlier loving relationship. A person who has been badly hurt by a parental divorce often feels abandoned by the absent parent. Someone they loved and trusted has left them to go and live elsewhere. They reason to themselves that if their parent really loved them, how could they then leave them? If the absent parent sets up house with someone else shortly after leaving, it further confirms the child in their fear that their parent loves someone else more than them. If as a child you were deeply hurt by this happening, and it was not dealt with or recognised, the pain of this can be carried forward into adult relationships. If the absent parent has little or no contact with the child after leaving, that child can grow up afraid that if they commit themselves wholly to one other person, that person might leave, or stop loving them. Anyone with these unresolved fears is likely to avoid too much intimacy within marriage or a committed relationship, so as not to be hurt all over again. Quite simply, they are afraid to put all their eggs in one basket.

An Erotic Escape from Everyday Life

Many married women feel submerged by the demands of juggling their lives. Husbands, children, work, shopping, cooking and cleaning are their first priorities. They are so busy meeting other people's needs that they feel there is little time left for their own. Just keeping up with the demands of those around them is a full-time job. For a woman in that position, an affair can seem very attractive. Many women I have spoken to said that having an affair was about taking something for themselves.

'It was something just for me,' said Sue, an attractive lawyer in her late thirties. 'The affair began at a time when I felt if I had one more demand made on me by Frank, my husband, or any of my four children, I would scream. The affair was exciting, I was doing something I wanted, I was fulfilling my needs instead of everyone else's. Jeff would slip away from work and book in at a nearby hotel, then he would telephone me with the room number. I would discretely join him in the hotel, just taking the lift to his room, where he would be waiting. No one really ever noticed me. It was our secret, and it was fun. We would have two or three hours together once or twice a month. Jeff would call room service to provide cool, sparkling white wine and maybe a simple salad. I would hide in the bathroom when they delivered it to our room, I felt like a twenty year old again.

'We would spend the afternoon talking and making love, then we would return to work. At the end of the day, we would both go home to our families. Neither of us made any demands on the other. We wanted the affair, but neither of us wanted it to upset our marriages. It was wonderful having the security of marriage and the excitement of an affair, an erotic escape from everyday life. Also, I felt here was one area in which I was in control. We met when I wanted to, he ordered the food and wine that I chose. Just being myself seemed to please Jeff, and sex was so great we could never get enough of each other.'

Sue discovered the pleasures of self indulgence, of doing something just to please herself rather than meeting other people's needs. It was also an area of her life which gave her control, an equal footing in a relationship. This is something which is missing in so many women's marriages.

Out of the Line of Duty

Gemma wanted some control in her life. She felt that as each year went by, more and more demands were being made upon her. She also recognised that part of her liked this. She was the eldest of five children, and had become used to caring and looking after others. Like many eldest daughters of large families, this role was what was expected of her as a child. She had fulfilled these expectations and carried them into married life. At twenty-three she fell in love with Stephen, who was a young and rather dashing curate. He totally adored her and they were very happy together. Gemma never imagined that she would ever be unfaithful, yet when she had been married seventeen years she began a passionate and intensely pleasurable affair with Robert.

At this stage, Gemma was a very busy mother of three boys aged twelve, thirteen and fifteen. Stephen was now a vicar in a very busy city parish, with Gemma his pretty, lively, and immensely popular wife. Where other women would fuss about giving a supper party for eight, she would organise a harvest supper for a hundred, do the church flowers with some of the women of the parish, and ferry her sons to football, or Scouts, as well as making sure the homework was done.

Most of her life with her husband had been spent moving with him from parish to parish, with little or no say in where they went. She and Stephen still had a good marriage, though each of them worked so hard they had all too little time together. Mealtimes were always interrupted by calls at the door, or parishioners on the telephone, and the pressures of the job did begin to take their toll. Stephen was fairly ambitious and several jobs came and went that he wanted. He became rather fed up and a little depressed. Money was increasingly tight as the boys grew older and their needs became greater. Their oldest son, Joe, started truanting from school and experimenting with drugs, and this caused more stress. It is not easy for vicars' children, particularly in their teenage years. Just as vicars and their wives are expected by their parishioners to have perfect marriages, so are their children expected to be model children.

They were moved to a new parish where Stephen worked hard, but he wasn't happy. As a vicar, he felt that he should be more accepting of the job, but he was finding it very difficult. Gemma had not wanted the move either, the children were missing all their old friends, and Gemma felt that she was having to support everyone. It was at this point that she met Robert.

At thirty-five, Robert was four years younger than Gemma. He was very successful in his job and loved all the things she was interested in, like art, music, theatre and opera. He had joined a working party to raise funds for the church as he had a lot of good and lucrative contacts in the area. His company also sponsored local good causes as well as the opera, concerts and theatre in London. He would occasionally offer Stephen and Gemma tickets to some of the concerts, or to the local playhouse. Stephen had little interest in the theatre, though he enjoyed concerts, and time was always at a premium, but they did manage to go occasionally. Gemma soon realised that she was becoming increasingly attracted to Robert, and he made it very clear this was returned. He had been divorced a couple of years before, and had a string of girlfriends but nothing very serious.

Robert was very attractive, and used to getting what he wanted in life. He pursued her relentlessly. For Gemma this was a total aphrodisiac. Stephen's increasing irritation with his lot was getting to her, as was the recent move that she had not been very happy with either. She was also feeling fed up with the years of unstinting parish work, and three demanding teenagers. Here was a man who was really interested in her. He just charmingly and persuasively brushed aside her struggles with her feelings about how vicars' wives should behave, saying that he would wait until she was ready.

One evening Stephen was unable to go to a fund raising meeting for the church roof at Robert's house, so Gemma offered to go in his place. It was a cold, wet, blustery night, and only two other people turned up. Not much could be achieved and the meeting broke up early. As Gemma rose to leave with the other two people, Robert touched her arm and asked her if she could spare a few minutes while he searched for some papers that he wanted her to give to Stephen. When they were alone he took her in his arms and kissed her, and her resistance left her. And so she began her affair with Robert. She said several years later, when the affair had long been over, 'Part of me will always know that I behaved badly, but I don't regret it. I love Stephen, but I also loved Robert. I felt alive, desirable, he was tremendous fun, and amazingly clever. Every single and divorced woman in the parish was after him, but he had chosen me.

'We had to be very careful, but we had a marvellous time. When I was with him the rest of the world was forgotten, we talked and talked, we listened to music, we drank champagne and we made love. The lovemaking was out of this world. With Stephen sex was good, but with Robert I experienced such ecstasy that I hadn't known was possible. Sometimes we would talk about going to Florence or Venice for a few days, but I knew I would never be able to find a reason to be away for as long as that. We never talked about a future together, because I think we both knew that wasn't possible.

I loved Stephen, he was a good man, and I knew I couldn't hurt him, the children or his ministry.

'After about a year Stephen started to become suspicious, and I knew that what I was doing carried a very high risk. It was a constant struggle to control my guilt about it. Then suddenly out of the blue, Stephen was called in one day by the Bishop and offered a dream job. He was over the moon. I was pleased for him, really pleased, but I also knew it would mean the affair would have to end. I felt heartbroken, and sometimes I think if Robert at that moment had tried to push me into leaving Stephen I might have succumbed, but probably not. I know I made the right decision.

'We moved to a completely different part of the country, and the affair came to an end. I was offered a very interesting job within the church, which was a great honour, and it absorbed all my time and emotional energy over the next two years. I wouldn't have another affair, the risks were too great, and as things improved for Stephen, who now had the job he wanted, they also improved between us. Our marriage is not perfect, but things between us are still reasonably good. Sometimes I see him looking at me and I think, did he know about my affair with Robert, or is that my conscience pricking? I think I may have hurt him very deeply, I hope not. But for me it will always be an important part of my life. I can't regret it.'

For Gemma, like Sue, her affair was not only very fulfilling sexually, but it also made her feel good as a woman. She had felt so submerged by the demands of the parish, her husband's disappointments over his job, and the children's discontentment, that the affair was something that she took for herself. She felt alive again, it built up her confidence, it was stimulating and fun. It also came at a time in her marriage when those things were in short supply. She was a little in love, too, and she admitted that the pain of ending the affair was excruciating. There was no one she could share it with. She would not have got the job she did if anyone in the church had known. She knew that she would be condemned for her behaviour, and she also knew that her husband loved her and relied heavily on her. If she had ever told him, he would have been devastated, so she never did.

Gemma broke out of the perfect wife mould that Dalma Heyn describes in her book, but as she was also carrying even higher expectations of herself and how she should behave as a woman and a vicar's wife, she could not handle the guilt. Running an affair alongside her marriage was too high a cost for her. She did not regret her affair, but she became extremely judgmental and very cruel to one or two of her close friends who had left their unhappy marriages and remarried someone else. They were instantly dropped by her. She condemned them for their behaviour and completely shut her mind to the reasons why they had decided to end their marriage. Ten years later this lively, sensual and sexy woman has become square, very middle-aged, and deeply immersed in church affairs, rather than adulterous ones. It seems to me the only way Gemma could cope with her erotic needs was to bury them. Sadly, she did not feel enough in control of them to channel them back into her marriage. Sex with Robert became idealised and much as she loved Stephen, he did not fulfil her sexually as Robert had.

Purely for Pleasure

Sex was not part of Lisa's marriage. She had been married to Nigel for seven years, and remembered being very attracted to him when they first met. He was very good-looking, popular and great fun. They had two children in quick succession. To start with, Nigel found the change from bachelor life to married life extremely difficult. He had been very used to doing what he liked, with whom he liked and when he liked. But he adored Lisa, and when he realised the demands that the children were making on her, he became a much more involved father and loving husband. They both described their marriage as happy. They were good friends, enjoyed each other's company, and loved their children. But there was one major difficulty, and that was that Lisa seemed to have lost all interest in sex.

The truth was not, in fact, that Lisa had lost interest, but that she had lost interest in sex with Nigel. They would make love, but only at Nigel's instigation, and Lisa put as little into sex as she felt she could get away with. She avoided kissing Nigel as much as possible, as he no longer turned her on in any way. The sexual chemistry just did not work any more for her.

Lisa's sexual frustration was eating away at her. She did not want to end the marriage, but she knew she could not live without a fulfilling sexual life. One morning in early June she was standing on the station waiting for the train to London. She noticed a man further along the platform, deeply engrossed in his paper. She thought he looked very handsome. Just at that moment the train arrived and she climbed aboard. One hour later as they approached London, Lisa got up and collected her things and walked towards the end of the carriage, ready to get off the train. As she stood by the carriage door, the train drew to a halt just a mile from Paddington station.

She sighed and looked at her watch, and when she looked up he was standing beside her. He smiled and said to her, 'Is this going to make you late for an appointment?' They started to talk. Lisa discovered he was a freelance journalist and aspiring writer, who was on his way to see his agent. She told him that she was meeting a girlfriend from her modelling days for lunch. They were, she said, now both married with several small children between them and this was one of those rare days out. A few minutes later the train pulled into the station. As she got off the train he handed her a card and said, 'My name's Daniel . . . do call me. We could perhaps have dinner together.' When she looked at the card she saw he only lived about ten miles away from her. Lisa stuffed the card into her bag and set off to meet her girlfriend. Over the next month she thought about calling him, she even got as far as picking up the telephone to dial his number, but each time she drew back at the last minute. Then one day, after another boring sexual encounter with her husband, she dialled his number. They arranged to meet for lunch in a country pub halfway between her house and his. It turned out that Daniel was also married.

They got on well. Daniel told her he had noticed her standing on the platform because she had such lovely long legs, and she admitted she had also been looking at him. A few days later he called. His wife had gone to a conference in Brussels for a couple of days, and would she like to come over for supper? She normally went to the gym once a week, so she arranged to see him that night. Lisa said, 'I don't think we ever got around to supper. The urgent need to make love was so strong we could hardly wait to get each other's clothes off.' Their affair was very sexual. During the day she looked after the children and did the shopping, but as she lay in bed at night, Lisa felt shudders run through her body when she thought of Daniel. She felt sexually reawakened, she felt great. She saw very clearly what she was doing, and she was enjoying it. She said, 'I wish I could have felt about Nigel the way I felt about Daniel, but I just didn't. I know Daniel made me more content within my marriage. Nigel did notice a difference but he never guessed why. My affair was purely for pleasure, because apart from sex we had little in common.' To Nigel, Lisa seemed more alive, more sparkling, and sex improved a little. He did not know it was because Lisa fantasised about Daniel when they made love, which she found made it more enjoyable.

Lisa supplemented the disappointing sex within her marriage with her affair with Daniel. She never felt herself to be in love with him, but she found him sexually irresistible. She did not want more than that, because she had most of what she wanted within her marriage. She realised that if she took away the wonderful lust she felt for Daniel, they had little in common. But that did not matter. She was not looking for a deep intimate relationship. Lisa had what she wanted, a sexual relationship with no strings. It was the same type of adulterous liaison that men often have. Lisa was quite determined to take what she wanted, and suffered no pangs of anguish or remorse. The gap between the sexes in this area is certainly closing.

The Missing Ingredient

Jordan set up his adulterous liaisons not only for his own enjoyment but also, 'To add spice to my marriage.' He had for some months lusted after Janey. They met occasionally through work, and sometimes when they were away at conferences. Janey was married but she always seemed to return his interest.

Jordan told his wife Lynn, in a very light-hearted, jokey sort of way, that he found Janey attractive. Lynn would from time to time tease Jordan about her, but at one conference Jordan and Janey did end up in bed together. He said, 'It was very exciting, she was wonderfully uninhibited and extremely good in bed.' They did not make any arrangements to meet again. They both agreed that it was a one-off experience, and neither wanted to do anything further that would jeopardise their marriages.

Over the next few days, when he and Lynn were talking about the conference, he told Lynn that Janey had been there. 'Did anything happen?' Lynn asked curiously. 'No,' said Jordan, but he told Lynn that he had gone to her room. He said, 'I nearly kissed her, but then I realised how much I had to lose and how hurt you would be if I had slept with Janey.' He told his wife reassuringly, 'I might fancy her. But you know I'm not going to do anything about it.' Apparently Lynn was a little doubtful at first, but she did believe him.

Jordan said he and Lynn had a particularly good sexual relationship and a very loving marriage. The use of sexual fantasy was very much part of their lovemaking. Both found it added spice and variety to sex and made it even more exciting. That night when they went to bed, he suggested to Lynn that they should act out the scene about what he would have done with Janey, if he had gone to bed with her. Lynn was turned on by this, so Jordan pretended to fantasise about what might have happened. In fact, he recounted in minute detail what had actually happened. Lynn found this exciting and she in turn imagined herself to be Janey. This soon became a regular fantasy that they enjoyed incorporating into their love life.

After a while, Jordan started to contemplate the idea of repeating the experience. He would occasionally have a one-night stand when the opportunity presented itself. He would then, with Lynn's encouragement, introduce those experiences into his and Lynn's lovemaking.

Jordan was not only meeting his own need for an occasional injection of uncomplicated sex, but he also felt that it benefited the marriage. He was quite certain that Lynn never suspected, and he said it added spice to their already good sex life. He said he was extremely careful to keep the risks of being found out to a minimum. 'Anyway,' he added, 'my policy is, never admit to an affair. Once you do that, you're lost. A woman will never let you forget, and then you don't have a leg to stand on. If you don't admit to an affair, there is always an element of doubt. With my occasional affairs there was never any emotional involvement. They were, in the main, just one-off occasions, and I always practised safe sex.'

Maybe Lynn did not suspect the truth or maybe, for her own reasons, she chose to ignore it. Jordan would argue that his adultery made his marriage happier and more alive, it benefited both of them. Affairs may well be creative, self-fulfilling, wonderfully exciting, and immensely pleasurable for the person involved, but they are still a little one-sided. The advantages perhaps depend on which side of the fence you sit, whether you view the affair as the betrayer or the betrayed. If one person is putting a lot of their time, thoughts and emotions into another relationship, then this may also be at the expense of the marriage.

In Compensation

Judith, who is married to a very clever, charming, but rather remote computer expert, said, 'I have been having an affair with Martin for fifteen years. Because of my affair with Martin I feel more content and more confident generally. I can really talk to him about anything, and I know he is interested. Much as my husband Tom loves me, he has a very short attention span. Whenever I want to talk to him, I can feel him reluctantly dragging himself out of the book he is reading, or impatiently wondering how soon he can decently get away and immerse himself in his work or his computers. In the early days of my marriage, I would scream and shout at him, but all to no avail. He would just wait until I had finished, pat me on the shoulder and carry on in the same old way. I now make far fewer emotional demands on Tom, and that suits him very well.

'He wanted a more independent and self-contained wife, and that's what he's got. That's now what I am. I feel my affair, in a way, enables me to have a better marriage than I would have without it. I would never leave Tom. I know he'd be devastated. In so many ways he is a very good husband. He has been a caring father when he has been there, he is a very interesting man, he is very successful in his work, and I love him.'

As Judith saw it, she was being realistic in admitting that Tom was not going to fulfil many of her emotional needs. Her lover did, he suited her emotionally and sexually. It has been a loving and enduring affair. They both acknowledge that neither of them can leave their partners. They also have an understanding that if they outlive their partners, they will spend their old age together.

The reality is that no two people can completely fulfil each other's needs. It's whether they can meet enough of them that determines whether the marriage or relationship is happy and fulfilling.

There has been much debate and discussion about why some people in unsatisfactory or vulnerable marriages have affairs and others, given similar circumstances, resist. The majority may well be looking outside marriage for things they are not, at that particular time, finding within the partnership. But for many others this may be only part of the motivation. For some, the main reason is fulfilment of their own needs, their own individual pursuit of pleasure, rather than major dissatisfactions within their marriage.

Home Alone

Anthony, a slim, tall and attractive man in his early fifties, who recently remarried, spent fifteen years as a happy divorcee between marriages. He has lost count of the number of affairs he had, but he does admit that they were all with very good-looking women, many of whom were married, and that he thoroughly enjoyed all of them.

Anthony owns a smart antiques shop in an affluent part of

the Oxfordshire countryside, a perfect meeting ground for women with time and money on their hands. He identified something I frequently see in counselling, 'the lonely, married woman syndrome'. His first affair was with a beautiful blonde who played a lot of sport. 'She had a great figure,' he said with enthusiasm. 'Her husband was constantly working abroad for long periods of time. She was "home alone" with three young children. She started coming to the shop quite frequently, and as she was very pretty and seemed interested in antiques I asked her one day if she would like to come to some antique sales with me. So that's how it started. We'd have a nice day, go to the sales, have lunch together in a country pub well away from where she lived, and we got on well.

'One thing led to another, and we began an affair. When her husband was away, she'd telephone me and ask me round. We'd spend the evening in bed together, drinking wine and making love, with no fear of her husband returning. One evening, though, we were nearly caught out. A close friend of her husband's and his wife called round unexpectedly. She couldn't pretend to be out because of the children. Not wanting to give the game away, it took her about two hours before she could decently ask them to leave. I had to stay upstairs in the darkened bedroom. At one point, one of the children woke up and wandered into her bedroom. I hid behind the bed, and the boy went off downstairs when he heard voices.

'I also had several affairs with the lonely wives of men who worked in the City. Their husbands didn't want them to work, they wanted them at home looking after the children, being a successful hostess and making sure everything ticked over smoothly. What else are they supposed to do? You can't spend all your day playing tennis and bridge. For some of these women it can be a lonely life when their husband is working a twelve- to fourteen-hour day.

'One of my mistresses, who was married to a financier, had a huge row with him. He was so utterly immersed in his work that he wanted to install a ticker tape machine in the bedroom to keep him constantly in touch with the latest stock market prices. In the end, she told him he could have her in the bedroom or the machine. He chose her.'

Another of his conquests was a woman he had seen in his

shop on several occasions. 'She was very fanciable,' Anthony said. 'I had been wondering whether I was in with a chance, but thought I probably wasn't. Then one evening there was a ring on my front-door bell, and there she was. She said her husband was away and, as she was just passing, she thought she'd call in.' 'What did you do?' I asked. 'What the lady wanted,' he replied, 'I took her to bed.'

Anthony is now happily remarried, and faithful. Let's hope that his new wife is neither a bored or lonely wife, but I imagine he knows not to leave her home on her own too much.

None of the married woman Anthony had affairs with wanted to leave their marriages. Neither were they, according to Anthony, unhappy. A lot of the time they had a good life, but they also spent a lot of time apart from their husbands, and were only too pleased to have a 'no strings' affair. 'Good uncomplicated sex,' was how Anthony described it. 'It's always best,' he said, 'to lay down the ground rules right at the beginning. If any one of them had suggested leaving their marriages, I'd have been off like a shot. The arrangement suited us both.'

A Romantic Interlude

'I had a wonderfully passionate affair which started one hot sunny afternoon in Africa,' said Justine, a very beautiful woman in her seventies. 'I was thirty-six when I met Charles, and he was just a few years older than me. The affair was so amazing I can hardly believe it really happened, but it did quite unexpectedly. I was living with my husband in Africa, where he was a military attaché, and we had been with a group of friends to watch a football match. I noticed Charles because he was a new white face in the middle of Nigeria where everyone knew everyone. He was extremely good-looking, I could hardly take my eyes off him. He had been serving in Ghana and had come to visit friends for the weekend.

'We talked, and I don't think we had exchanged more than ten sentences when he said, "I must see you again." I said,

"I'd like that, too. But it's not possible because you live so far away." As he was leaving to spend the weekend with his friends, he came over to me again and said, "Let's meet again." I said, "Where?" He replied, "I'll be on holiday in Europe in one year's time." "Where? I'll be there," I said. "Eleven o'clock on the twentieth of May, at the Sacher Hotel in Vienna."

'During that year, we never exchanged a letter or a phone call, we had no contact at all. But we did meet. What he told his wife, or how he arranged to be in Vienna, I don't know, but he managed it. When I walked into the hotel in Vienna, he was sitting there at the bar. I was completely bowled over. I don't think I really expected him to be there. I think I went to the hotel out of sheer curiosity, but when I saw him there it was unbelievable.

'This happened nine years after my marriage, and it was my first affair. We had a long lunch and then I returned to my hotel and changed. In the evening we went to the opera, then we went back to the little inn where he was staying and made love. It was fantastic and sexually it was perfect. I was staying with friends. We met every afternoon and made love for two or three hours, and then I took a taxi back to my friends' house. They never suspected that I was having an affair. After a week I had to leave to go and stay with my mother in our house in the country. Charles followed me hot foot and stayed in the next village in a hotel, and the affair continued for another week. I saw him every day. We made love all the time. Once, we made love under a magnolia tree, but we were never able to spend the night together. At the end of the week he had to return to Africa.

'When I think back on it, it was really such a romantic story. We had only spoken briefly on that previous meeting. The chance of meeting up again, halfway across the world, seemed impossible, but it was too good a story to miss. My two children and I stayed on with my mother for another two months. We must have kept in touch, because on the evening of my departure on the four-day journey to Rome followed by a flight to Nigeria with my children, a hundred red roses were delivered to my mother's house. My mother said, "What does this man do?" I said, "He was just a friend from Africa."

'I never saw him again. We didn't try to keep in touch. We both knew it was something special, and I really didn't want it to go on. It was just a mad chapter, a romantic interlude. But it was also very special for him, because ten years later he wrote me a love letter which, sadly, I dared not keep in case my husband found it. He said the two weeks we had spent together were, for him, "The Jewel in the Crown". I've never forgotten him, or the affair either.

'When I met Charles I had been married nine years. It was my first affair. I did have another affair several years later, but when my husband discovered it he told me it must end, and that he wanted to know nothing more about it. I discovered many years later that he had several affairs during that time as well.' Justine clearly had no intention of letting her affair disrupt her marriage. She had absolutely no regrets, 'I loved my husband, and he loved me. He was so discreet about his affairs, that though there were one or two occasions when I thought he might have been unfaithful, I never confronted him, and, anyway I'm sure he would have denied it. Much later, I did discover that he had occasionally been unfaithful. It was so long ago and we had such a good marriage that I don't think I really minded. Anyway, I hadn't been a totally loyal wife, had I?'

Justine had been brought up in a marriage where her father had several long-term affairs with her mother's friends. Her aristocratic mother seemed to tolerate this, and was herself always surrounded by many admirers, some of whom may also have been her mother's lovers.

Justine adored her husband, and she always felt they had a very happy marriage. He was, she said, such an intelligent, amusing, witty, good-looking and successful man, how could she not be in love with him? She felt sure during their marriage that he had also had affairs, but they were both very discreet. They never lied about them to each other, but they never acknowledged their affairs either. Justine did not feel that they threatened the marriage. Even now, many years after the death of her husband in a tragic skiing accident, she still feels she had a very happy, loving and wonderfully sexually alive marriage. She said, 'I was as much in love with my husband after twenty years of marriage as when I first met him, and I believe he was with me.'

Nearly all the women I spoke to about their affairs felt they loved their husbands, and many also loved their lovers. They did not doubt that it was possible to love two men at the same time. They may have loved them in different ways, with a different intensity of feelings, but they had no doubt that they loved them both. Others admitted freely that though their affair was not a love affair, they still valued it, and had few regrets.

Living Life on the Edge

Richard, a slim, good-looking man in his mid-thirties, has few regrets about his affairs. He is, he says, happily married. He loves his wife, and they get on well together. He said, 'I expected to be faithful when I married, but I haven't been.' He seems to have little inclination to be faithful and enjoys both his marriage and his affairs.

'In my view,' said Richard, 'the reason you have affairs is insecurity. They feed your ego.' Richard married his wife Ann four years ago, when he was thirty. They have a four-year-old son. 'We're trying right now to have another child. I had to be persuaded to have two, anything more would require the third degree. I'd never thought about having children. I'm very bad at forward planning.

'I had several relationships before marriage, but only two which were very serious. I was faithful during the first, but unfaithful in the second with the woman who is now my present wife. When I met my wife for the first time I fell for her in a really big way and continue to have a very high opinion of her. My relationship with my wife has gone through a number of phases. We had a steady relationship including living together for a number of years. We then split up for eighteen months, got back together again, and we got married in a registry office when she was four months pregnant.

'I was always more keen to get married than she was as she had always regarded it purely as a technicality. But the fact that she was pregnant made her change her mind. I intended to keep up a steady one hundred percent relationship, which would have been unusual for me as my track record has not been very good. I thought I had changed my attitude. I really believed that, but I've since discovered that I haven't really changed.

'The fact that affairs are illicit excites me. I think that represents a substantial part of the reason why anyone goes into an affair. It's a bit like taking drugs, I get a buzz. I don't have strong religious feelings. I think that it's a bit like those people who get turned on by having sex in a place where they can get discovered, only it's a cerebral version of that. I don't think affairs are romantic. I think they're sordid if the truth be told, but not all of them. It's the risk-taking element. Byron said that you should always live your life at the edge of danger, and I know what he means. It makes it more interesting. I was married less than three years when I embarked on my first affair. I went through a lot of anxiety. It's difficult to decide how much of that is fear of being discovered, and how much is guilt-related.

'I met Susanna through work. I was on secondment to a commercial organisation and met her because she had come in to pitch for some business. The personal chemistry was very good, and I thought there was a bit of interest there. I was involved with organising an opera, and dished out some tickets to an advertising contact. When I turned up she was there and the vibes were just so strong. I could have just stopped there, but I was flattered and interested and intrigued. It was three years since I'd been in that kind of situation. It wouldn't be too much of an exaggeration to say that Susanna almost threw herself at me. It was very powerful stuff, a bit like not smoking or having a drink for six months. When you do, it hits you very hard, you're on the ceiling straight away.

'I suppose it began in the interval of the opera. In the first half I was at one end of the row and in the second I moved under some pretext. I arranged for everyone to change seats to network. We sat next to each other and held hands. After the opera I phoned her, and we made a date for a week later. We went out together in the evening to a bar. She was divorced. She said she was thirty-eight but later I discovered she was really forty-one. She'd been married twice and had a four-year-old daughter. On the first evening we were quite frank in discussing that we had quite strong feelings for one another, but we didn't sleep together that evening. From when we first went out, there was never any question that this was simply a casual social meeting. It was accepted by both of us that it was the precursor to something more serious.

'When I think about it, I was a complete amateur in what I told my wife. I know better now what to say and do. It was a Monday evening. As well as my job I also teach at an evening class. When I got home late that Monday night, my wife asked me where I'd been and I said I'd been teaching. She said, 'No you weren't, because it's half term.' I then had to backtrack rather hastily. I said I'd been out drinking with colleagues. And funnily enough, because I had something to hide, I then invented some story that I'd been out with them and not told her because we'd all got a bit drunk and I'd had a snog with some girl or other. It's like pleading guilty to shoplifting when you're guilty of murder, and taking the lesser rap. She believed me.

'The biggest drawback of adultery is that it involves someone with whom you ought to have an open and trusting relationship, and that does worry me. Deceiving someone is bad, because as soon as you start you feel sorry for them, because you know something they don't. I've always felt that pity and contempt are very closely related emotions. When you start feeling sorry for someone you can also start to despise them, and when you start to despise them the relationship is finished. But I don't think that about my wife. Perhaps that's because I love and admire her, and because I think we have a good relationship.

'I've had three affairs in the last four years. My second affair was important to me, but the one with Susanna wasn't. It was fun in some ways. Susanna had quite a glamorous lifestyle, and she knew people I knew, but she very quickly made no bones about being quite emotionally dependent on the relationship. My worst nightmare was a sort of *Fatal Attraction* scenario developing. I thought, any minute now she'd turn up on the doorstep and tell my wife that I was really in love with her.

'I did tell her that I'd never leave my wife. I don't know how much effect that kind of moral contraceptive has on people. The affair lasted about six months. We both got sick of it because she kept on about how much she liked me and I kept on saying, "You can't say that because it's not in the script." She stopped returning my phone calls or she just blew me out on a date. After a while I got bored. Sexually it was very good, but in the end that's all it was. I don't really go into it for that kind of thing. I get into affairs out of insecurity and the need to boost my ego. The insecurity stems from my childhood in ways I can't really define or explain.

'I find it difficult to show my emotions. I'm too detached. I rarely lose my temper, I don't cry, I don't have outbursts. I'm too much of a control freak. As a child I was always terribly bookish and never very exuberant. I'm never badly depressed and never really flying. It's the control that keeps me like that.

'My affair with Susanna finished last year. Two months later I had started another affair. Rosalind was one of my students. She is quite the most beautiful girl I've seen, with the exception of my wife who is the most beautiful person in the world. I can still see her sitting in my class with her gorgeous red hair. She is heart-stoppingly attractive. I was in love with her, and I think I still am. I've always made a habit of encouraging my students to come down the pub afterwards, to get to know them better. She came with several others. At the end of the evening I said, "Shall I walk you home?" As we were walking I took her hand. She responded, we kissed and made a date for the following week, and that was how the affair began.

'She's twenty-nine and for the last five years had had an affair with a married man with children. It didn't seem to put her off that I was married. She never asked me to leave my wife directly, and I'm not a hundred percent sure she wanted me to. I was so wrapped up in her, but she was very careful about the level of emotional commitment she gave me. She told me soon after the affair started that the affair was quite frankly "a sexual disaster, of epic proportions".

'Most of the time I didn't get an erection and she continually told me how bad it made her feel that I wasn't performing, which wasn't what I needed to hear. Our relationship in terms of sleeping together lasted just three months. We only managed to have penetrative sex three times. I just couldn't get it up. She saw it as rejection. She said, "this is the first time it's ever happened to me." And since she's had something like thirty-two sexual relationships it seemed kind of right.

'I thought, it's not working in bed with her because I'm married. I can't either offer her or receive in return the kind of commitment that I need in order to make it a success. On this occasion I did get very depressed. I went a bit haywire. I was short tempered at home and quite aggressive, which isn't like me in a relationship. I was still able to make love to my wife, so that wasn't a problem.

'Rosalind was quite hurt by the fact that it didn't work out in bed. But having seen it in reverse, being in bed and not having enjoyed it that much, then the last thing you say to somebody is, "It wasn't really very good, was it?" because it's not a very constructive comment. If you want it to get better you have to say, "Why don't we try this?" It's better to be positive because people's sexual egos are so easily bruised. It's so important to your self-esteem. I never said this to Rosalind, but I could see it wasn't going to work out unless I was a free agent, unmarried. I love my wife and I couldn't abandon my child.

'I don't know if my wife suspected anything. During the course of my relationship with Rosalind I didn't come home on three separate nights, without warning, which is a ludicrously stupid thing to do. I gave a variety of excuses. I have a close friend who leads a very riotous lifestyle and I said I went there one night. Another time when she knew I was in a funny mood, I said I was going drinking with a friend from work and I just didn't turn up at home. When I got back the next day she didn't question me. She's extremely self-confident and self-reliant and wouldn't bother to give me the third degree. She's not going to get a private detective.

'Sometimes I think the solution would have been for Rosalind to agree to be my mistress, so we could be totally committed to each other, but she won't. Of all the relationships I've ever had, the people I consider I've been the most head over heels in love with are my wife and Rosalind. She's the only person who, looking back into the past or at the present, I could think of usurping my wife in my affections.

'The fact that I can fall in love with someone I had an affair with doesn't stop me having more affairs. It's a chance in a million, bad luck for me. All it's succeeded in doing is making me unhappy, and that's not what you want out of an affair. As a rule of thumb, if I don't care very much emotionally for the girl it's very much easier for me sexually and I don't have any problems, which must be a rather cruel paradox to inflict on oneself. So my affair with Rosalind ended because sexually it was just not working. I still see her, it's a bit painful but I enjoy her company.

'My third affair started a couple of months ago. It's with someone I met through work, and she's married. That they succeeded one another so rapidly does suggest to me that I've gone for a compensatory second best. Amanda is the first married woman I've been out with. She doesn't have a good marriage. She wants a good sexual relationship. She's twenty-eight, tall, with a nice, full figure and rather Sloany, which isn't my type usually. Her husband is much older than her, he's fifty-seven. She's attracted to me because I lead a bit more of a disreputable lifestyle than her husband will allow.

'We met a couple of times for lunch and then I suggested that we had dinner together. I started liking her more, and we agreed to spend the night together in a little hotel in a quiet side street on the far side of town. Sexually it's working out with Amanda, in fact it's brilliant. No problems. Once I'm in a sexual relationship and it starts to work, then I'm very uninhibited with no hang-ups about virtually anything.

'Before my relationship with Rosalind, what always happened was it took me a little while to get used to someone new, then after some ego stroking, and having been to bed with them three or four times, as if by magic the self-consciousness vanished. I was able to get an erection, no worries. With Amanda there was no problem at all. Amanda likes me to stimulate her without any involvement on my part other than purely physical. That's great because that's what I like. Later on she does it to me. I find it easier to concentrate on the other person, because if they're turned on they aren't going to be judging me. And also you can say that's good, it's working, and your confidence comes flooding back and that makes you feel desired. My affair with Amanda may be quite long term.

'I would never advance the argument myself, but I can see that in some circumstances, if your marriage isn't in serious trouble, an affair could be a positive force if you're careful. If you have friction because of an incompatible sex drive, it takes care of that as well. If one of your difficulties is, like me, having a fragile ego, then it makes you feel good and better about all aspects of your life including your marriage.

It has self-interest written all over itself, though. Show me a bloke who says he started an affair to improve his marriage, I'll show you a liar.

'I've always liked relationships that are very touching, constantly embracing and kissing and saying, "I love you," and that's just not how Ann, my wife, is at all. That's alien to my wife and I do find that quite difficult. I look up to her a great deal. She's a stronger person than me, more commonsensical and equally intelligent. But I'm never absolutely sure that she really loves me. I'm quite certain I love her more than she loves me. Ann's feelings for me are more practical. When we first knew each other we went out together for quite some time. Then she ended our relationship, by which stage it had become an open relationship and we were sleeping with other people. She went round the world for fifteen months and had another relationship during that time. When she got back to this country I told her I'd very much like to get back with her, and she said yes.

'Becoming my wife was a kind of considered view, and I've never been able to free myself of the thought that she sat down with a blank sheet of paper and said to herself, "Who is the most likely kind of solid, stable character who can offer me a good income, a good future, home, and loving relationship? On the scores it must be him, so let's get married!" It's always struck me as being a very practical sort of decision. Whereas I was always passionate about her she is merely appreciative of me.

'So maybe I'm searching for something that isn't quite within my marriage, even though I like my marriage. In my other relationships sexuality was being used as a kind of metaphor for affection. I have a sort of good sexual relationship with my wife. It's what I call OK and is better now than it has been in the past, but routine in some respect, and certainly far less experimental than relationships I've had in the past which I've enjoyed more. Why? I think it's her fault. But you feel such a rat saying that about someone. She likes the way we have sex and that's fine by her. It's conventional, but not much variety. I don't want to swing from the chandeliers or go about in rubber or leather, but I do like a change and she doesn't particularly. We used to argue a lot about the frequency, but she's made a conscious effort to vary the routine. There's a mismatch of desire. I'd like to make love about fourteen times a week, maybe in the mornings and evenings. She'd be happy once a week. But she knows it means a lot to me, and that's not only for the physical release. So we make love about three or four times a week.

'I see my marriage continuing. I don't know about continuing with affairs. Sensibly I should say no, because the law of averages says you'll get caught eventually. You can't keep on. I've already come very close to being found out with Rosalind because it was an affair of the heart and it altered my behaviour to my wife, which is the big give away. So I don't know what will happen. I've always enjoyed relationships with clever people more than with those who aren't. My mistresses have been attractive in different ways, but they've always been interesting people. Susanna had an interesting lifestyle. Rosalind is one of my most promising students, and Amanda has a strong interest in politics. She was involved in demos and squats and drug taking. I've been incredibly dull. I like the contrast between us. I don't like getting old. I'm a civil servant living in Hertfordshire with one child. That's got to be boring with a capital B.'

On the surface Richard is confident, articulate and in control, but underneath he is deeply insecure. He never felt his father particularly loved him. He was closer to his mother, who was more loving. His father was an intellectual but critical parent. A critical parent frequently undermines a child's confidence and damages its sense of identity. If someone you love and look up to puts you down and continually finds fault, it makes you feel very insecure. You frequently grow up not feeling loveable or valued for yourself, but only valued for your achievements. It also creates a fear of failure, because that could mean the loss of parental love or approval. All of these insecurities are carried forward into adult life.

Richard looked to his affairs to bolster his ego. They made him feel more desirable, and therefore less insecure. With Rosalind sex was a disaster because he had fallen in love with her. Loving her made it too important to him that sex should be perfect. If you set up expectations that are too high, the chances are that you will fail. Anxiety makes you step outside yourself and evaluate your own performance. You're dissociated from your feelings and, instead, start judging your performance. This can prevent you from going with the feelings. Your body reacts by not giving you what you most desire. What made it even worse for Richard was that Rosalind's own insecurity was so high, so when Richard failed to get an erection she felt rejected, and immediately criticised him and put him down. She became like the critical parent his father used to be, and that further undermined him and reinforced his performance anxiety, or fear of failing.

By falling in love with Rosalind, Richard also felt he had broken his own code of behaviour, which was only to have affairs that were fun or interesting and made him feel better about himself. Loving Rosalind made him feel guilty about being unfaithful to Ann. The result was that he continually failed to get an erection, even though he desired her enormously. This happens to so many men who have affairs. Guilt really does, much to a man's frustration, and often the humiliation of the ardent lover, renders a man impotent with his mistress. Richard's affair also increased his insecurity, because for someone who needed to be in control, falling in love made him lose it. He also feared losing the wife and son he loved, and at the same time he was uncertain about the depth of Rosalind's feelings for him.

Richard was the first of his generation to go to university, but his parents were grudging about the cost and refused to pay their parental contribution. Richard said, 'For the first two years I had to live in grinding poverty, which really hacked me off because I'd made a real effort to get to university. When I decided not to complete my PhD my father said, "Well that's two-and-a-half years wasted." I thought, "You bastard!" But I didn't show my anger, and since then I've come to appreciate what my parents did for me.'

Richard's way of dealing with anger or painful emotions, is to cut himself off from them and intellectualise the situation. This is reflected in his relationship with his wife. He chooses someone he loves very much, but who is seemingly independent and self-contained like his father. Part of him is afraid of committing himself too much to her. He is not sure how much she loves him, so he supplements his need for love and approval by having affairs. Having affairs also creates a distance between them because of the deceit. It's his way of unconsciously trying to minimise the risk of getting hurt or rejected by her. She is similar to his distant and emotionally cool father, so family patterns are repeating themselves. Richard defends himself from the pain of not being loved enough by boosting his ego through his affairs and listing his achievements as a way of being what Ann wanted: someone who would be loving, safe and secure, a good provider, and who would give her a good life. A passionate marriage was not on her agenda.

A Passionate Affair

> *What constitutes adultery is not the hour which a woman gives her lover, but the night which she afterwards spends with her husband.*

> George Sand

Anais Nin, the diarist, poet, and erotic writer, had a very passionate love affair with the American writer Henry Miller. She had an affair with him while married to Hugh Guiler. Here she writes with passion to Henry Miller. The letter shows the depths of her feelings and, in the last line, the conflicting loyalties of conducting an intense affair and a marriage.

Louveciennes
September 6, 1932

Henry,
You have just left. I told Hugh I had something to add to my work. I had to come upstairs [to] my room again, and be alone. I was so filled with you I was afraid to show my face. Henry, no departure of yours has ever left me so shattered. I don't know what it was tonight, which drew me to you, to hold you . . . It was a great pain to me that you should

*be leaving. When you are thoughtful and moving, I lose
my mind. To stay with you one night I would throw away
my whole life, sacrifice a hundred persons, I would burn
Louveciennes, be capable of anything. This is not to worry
you, Henry, it is just that I can't keep from saying it, that
I am overflowing, desperately in love with you as I never
was with anyone. Even if you had left tomorrow morning
the idea that you were sleeping in the same house would
have been a very sweet relief from the torment I endure
tonight, the torment of being cut in two pieces when you
closed the gate behind you. Henry, Henry, Henry, I love
you, love you, love you. I was jealous of [Jean] Renaud
who has you all these days, who sleeps in Clichy. Tonight
everything hurts, not only the separation, but this terrible
hunger of body and mind for you which every day you are
increasing, stirring more and more. I don't know what I
am writing. Feel me holding you as I have never held you
before, more deeply, more sadly, more desperately, more
passionately. I kneel before you, I give you myself and it
is not enough, not enough. I adore you. Your body, your
face, your voice, your human self, oh Henry, I can't go
now and sleep in Hugh's arms – I can't. I want to run
away just to be alone with my feelings for you.*

The intensity of Anais Nin's feelings for Henry Miller is very
clear in her letter to him. Her marriage did in fact eventually
break up, but that was not until the late forties, nearly twenty
years after the affair began. By then the affair had cooled.

In this chapter I have been looking at how women and men
have combined marriage and an affair. Many of the women
have been captivated, devotedly in lust or in love, with their
lovers. Even so, they were not looking to the affair as an
alternative to the marriage. They wanted their marriages and
their affairs. In their opinion their marriages were fairly good,
they were very happy. They did not look to their marriages to
provide everything, which of course no marriage can. But
neither did they want to leave their marriages to spend their
life with their lovers, nor on their own.

I am not advocating affairs. I have seen all too frequently

how much hurt and devastation they can cause. But there are men and women who genuinely feel that there are times in their marriage when they can handle both the marriage and the affair, when they feel the affair will not detract from the marriage, and might possibly even improve it.

I think most of the men and women described in this chapter would admit that rightly or wrongly their affairs were something they were taking for themselves. It gave many the opportunity to develop a part of themselves that they felt unable to in the marriage. This ranged from brief, but sexually very exciting, affairs to deep and more committed love affairs. Some of the women did feel guilty about finding love or taking sexual pleasure, or both, outside marriage, though far from all. Justine, for example, felt absolutely no guilt at all.

Women more than men are struggling emotionally with the fact that they have stepped out of the good wife mould. Men appear not to have to struggle quite so hard with their consciences. This is partly because they tend to be better than women at separating their affairs from their marriage, and also because they still do not take equal responsibility with women for looking after the nurturing side of the marriage. Men in the main still see their primary role as providers and protectors of the family. They are freer to opt out emotionally.

However much men and women may justify their affairs, there is no getting away from the fact that they are deceiving their partner. The very fact that they have their own secret world that their partner knows nothing about means that intimacy in the marriage is eroded. An affair does mean that part of you is being intimately shared with someone other than your spouse.

In the next chapter I will be exploring how the unmarried mistress fares in this eternal triangle. If a woman is single or divorced and is having an affair with a married man, she often finds that it is the man who has the control, unlike married women who feel they have a lot of control over their affairs. One of the deep frustrations, and often one of the great areas of hurt, is that she feels relatively powerless. The married man usually calls the shots.

Chapter Eight

MISTRESSES AND LOVERS

> *By the time you swear you're his,*
> *Shivering and sighing,*
> *And he vows his passion, is*
> *Infinite, undying—*
> *Lady, make a note of this:*
> *One of you is lying.*

> Dorothy Parker, *Unfortunate Coincidence*

Just as affairs are increasing, so is the kept mistress a dying breed. She is being replaced in greater numbers by a more independent woman. The modern mistress is far less likely than her mother or her grandmother to be set up and constantly waiting for her lover. In the past the mistress was often provided with a little flat, paid for by her married lover. He would buy her clothes and jewellery and give her an allowance. In return she had to be available when her lover chose to visit her. Her job was to provide him with a diversion from the ordinariness of his marriage. She had to be welcoming and fun, to look lovely, be sexually passionate, and make him feel he was a good lover.

Nowadays a single, divorced, or widowed woman who is having an affair with a married man is a much more independent woman, both emotionally and economically. She has a life of her own. She will be financially independent. She will probably be working, which is of course where so many of these affairs begin. She will have her own flat or house, which she rents or owns. She will have her own group of friends and social life. She may also occasionally be unfaithful to her lover, which is a constant worry for the majority of married men who are having affairs with single women. The modern mistress may also be having more than one affair at a time.

The French are jealous of their mistresses, but never their wives.

Jacques Casanova, *Memoirs*

The Independent Mistress

Some women choose to have an affair with a married man, because they see that as a way of keeping their independence. They do not want him full time, they would frankly find it boring to settle down with just one man. They thrive on the excitement of their limited time together, and enjoy conducting the relationship on high-octane adrenalin. They like the unpredictability and uncertainty of when and where they will meet. They feel they see the man at his best, always attentive, ready to talk and to listen, with eyes only for them when they are together. For them, this far outweighs the security of a marriage or a committed live-in relationship.

Liz, a glamorous and very successful woman in her early thirties, said, 'My affair suits me perfectly. I spend my time commuting between London and Italy. I don't want the hassle of remembering to stock the fridge, or having to say when I am going to be back and keeping to it. This way I've got almost total freedom. My lover lives in Florence so we meet up when I go over there. Perhaps a romantic lunch in some out-of-the-way restaurant, or an afternoon spent together in his flat with no fears of his wife interrupting us as she is neatly tucked away somewhere in the country. If he comes to London we paint the town red, or spend hours making love in my home. I know if we were together all the time that feeling wouldn't last. But it's not just about sex. He's a fantastic person, tremendous fun, and very wise. I can always test out my latest work ideas on him, and on top of that he adores me. At the moment I'm not ready to settle down, and I don't want children. I know he would never leave his wife and children. For me that's real security, because I don't want him to. This relationship suits me just the way it is.'

For men, what is the attraction of an unmarried mistress? Jacqueline, a pretty woman in her thirties, was having an affair with Bill, a married man who says he is happily married and that he loves his wife and children. On the BBC programme *Mistresses* she said, 'When a married man is looking for another woman he is looking for sex, not a housekeeper. Sex is the glue that binds this relationship together.' Journalist Sally Morris took an even more pragmatic view when she said, 'For most men the driving force behind taking a mistress is simple: sex. The truth is that no matter how many books are written on how to spice up your marital love life, what most men crave is not wild imaginative sex with their wives, it's sex with someone else. Usually somebody young, attractive and, most importantly, available.'

In my work as a counsellor I know I am not going to see many happy, ecstatic lovers or blissfully contented and satisfied mistresses like Liz. Of course I am not denying that they exist. In the early days of an affair most people do feel it is blissful and, because it is such a heady experience, it usually masks the fears and the guilt and the worries about what the future holds. However, many of those who embark on an affair with a married man or woman find that the loveliness of the affair fades as time goes by, and the relationship is beset with agony.

Another Woman's Husband

A mistress should be like a little country retreat near a town, not to dwell in constantly, but only for a night away.

William Wycherley, *The Country Wife*

As a mistress you are sharing the man in your life with another woman, even if she doesn't know it. You are also sharing him with his children, his job, his friends, his parents, his in-laws, his hobbies, his golf, his squash, indeed his other life. So proportionately he is likely to be spending much more of his time involved with these other people and things than he is with you.

The excitement of the secret meetings, the heady sense of how much you are desired, the afternoons of total passion begin to seem less exquisite, if for much of the rest of the time he is with someone else rather than with you. Some men are able to work out their lives so that a reasonable amount of time is spent with their mistresses, but it does not feel so good if you are constantly finding that a planned meeting you had been looking forward to is yet again cancelled as they hurry home to their spouse

Some of the hardest times that the unmarried mistress has to cope with are the weekends alone, or thinking of him at Christmas gathered around the tree opening presents with his wife and children. Meanwhile, you are with your parents, who never stop asking why you don't get yourself a nice boyfriend. Then there's the family holiday when you hope he can find some way of calling you, or the times you lie awake in the middle of the night wondering whether you can really believe him when he tells you that sexually his marriage is dead. Perhaps the most difficult of all are the hours you spend willing and waiting for that telephone to ring, so poignantly and painfully described by Dorothy Parker:

Please, God, let him telephone me now. Dear God, let him call me now. I won't ask anything else of You, truly I won't. It isn't very much to ask. It would be so little to You, God, such a little, little thing. Only let him telephone now. Please, God. Please, please, please . . . This is the last time I'll look at the clock. I will not look at it again. It's ten minutes past seven. He said he would telephone at five o'clock . . . Please let me see him again, God. Please, I want him so much. I want him so much. I'll be good, God I will try to be better, I will, if You will let me see him again. If You will let him telephone me.

Oh, let him telephone me now . . . I won't telephone him. I'll never telephone him again as long as I live. He'll rot in hell, before I'll call him up . . . It would be so easy to telephone him. Then I'd know. Maybe it wouldn't be a foolish thing to do. Maybe he wouldn't mind. Maybe he'd like it. Maybe he has been trying to get me. Sometimes people try and try to get you on the telephone, and they say the number doesn't answer. I'm not just saying that to help myself; that really happens. You know that really happens. God. Oh, God, keep me away from that telephone. Keep me away. Let me still have just a little bit of pride. I think I'm going to need it, God. I think it will be all I'll have.

Dorothy Parker, *A Telephone Call*

Beware of the Compulsive Philanderer

Many women who get involved with married men get their fingers burnt. The married man who has an affair with a single woman is often looking for the fun and excitement of illicit love, but he is not necessarily searching for more than that. It is not a relationship for which he is going to leave his wife, children and comfortable lifestyle. Jane Clark, the wife of the promiscuous former cabinet minister Alan Clark, seems very well aware of this when she talks about her husband's many affairs. The women who get entangled with such men frequently don't appreciate that they are the 'love them and leave them' type, so they end up getting very hurt.

Alan Clark married his wife Jane when she was sixteen and he was twenty-eight, and he has been unfaithful to her all his life. Jane Clark does not like it, but she puts up with his philandering because she loves him and because he's mad about her. She says, 'The fact he has affairs is part of being married to him and I always knew what he was like. If I want to remain with the man I love, I just have to put up with the affairs. But I happen to know that he's mad about me. There is no point making a fuss, it will only ruin our relationship. A lot of married couples don't talk at all. We have a very strong marriage. But I'm always upset when he is having an affair. Time is so precious, it is such a waste when it is frittered away. It's incessantly boring when it's going on but I know it will blow over.'

She admits she usually knows when he is having an affair, 'He always looks sheepish and I just have ways of knowing.' She does not collude with him totally by turning a blind eye and not acknowledging that he has affairs, as many wives of philanderers do. On this aspect of her husband's affairs she says, 'I usually confront him, sometimes I throw china. Many years ago I threw an axe which fortunately missed. But china is better, it tends to make more noise. It's better to throw things and get it out of your system.' Jane does now appear to have moved on from the very intense murderous feelings, which are quite normal on the discovery of an affair, to a rather more suppressed, world-weary acceptance that whatever she does, other than actually leaving him, he is not going to change his ways.

I spoke to one philandering husband recently who had affairs throughout both his marriages, and was now approaching his seventieth birthday. Ralph said with a regretful smile, 'In the last five years I have really slowed down. I think you can say I'm now a faithful husband.' So perhaps that's some consolation to Jane Clark, if not to her sixty-six-year-old husband.

Like so many men, Alan Clark would not tolerate it if the boot was on the other foot and it was Jane who was having the affairs. She says, 'Alan would mind very much if I had an affair, but I don't need to. There's no one else for me besides him. We have been married for thirty-five years so there must be something to be said for it.' Jane Clark's dismissive views about mistresses appear to be her way of trying to accept what she patently finds very hurtful. She says cuttingly of his flings, 'They are irritating little diversions which are incessantly boring. I am lucky that I have the inner strength to cope with it, although I find it immensely tiresome. It's not a taboo subject. Sometimes I question him about the other women, it depends on the mood I'm in. His girlfriends would be worried if they realised how much I knew.' The desire to show off is frequently the case with philandering husbands. They really cannot resist the desire to brag about their conquests to their wives.

When consistently unfaithful men are caught yet again in the act, I have noticed a distinct change in their relationship with their wives. When they are up against the ropes and worried about losing their marriage, they use all their very considerable charm and persuasion to talk their wives out of filing for divorce. However, there is more going on here than meets the eye, and it seems that there is a pattern of behaviour between the philanderer and his long-suffering wife.

At times of disclosure and of confession, their relationship changes from an adult-to-adult relationship to a parent-to-child relationship. Instead of relating to each other on equal terms as adults, the woman adopts the mother role, and the man changes from husband to child. Put simply, the man is the 'misbehaving teenager' appealing to his wife/mother to forgive him. He acknowledges that he has been a bad boy, he has indeed misbehaved, and he is very sorry, but she will have him back, won't she? This is frequently accompanied by promises, just like the errant teenage boy in trouble with his mother, that it won't happen again. He is hoping for the all-accepting, unconditional love of his childhood days. He confesses, he is really sorry, and he promises it won't happen again, even though they both know that he has been down this particular road umpteen times before. After the hurt and the rage is expressed on the part of his wife, she then colludes with him and adopts the mothering role towards the errant, misbehaving husband/teenager, and once more forgives him.

Jane Clark illustrates this when she says of her husband Alan's behaviour, 'Women are infinitely superior to men, who from the age of eighteen undergo a mid-life crisis. They are all so infantile.' She adds, 'I'm sure a lot of women would like to be mistresses. But a lot of us take our vows rather more seriously and I certainly take my marriage vows slightly more seriously than my husband does.' She obviously also has a wry sense of humour, and she uses it to cope with the pain that his affairs cause her.

If a man is consistently unfaithful, and if his wife keeps forgiving him, often in the increasingly vain hope that it won't happen again, then the message he is receiving is one of acceptance. He says to himself, 'I know she doesn't like it, I know it hurts her, but I've got away with it before so I can probably get away with it again.'

The other women, the mistresses caught up with men who are constantly having affairs, rarely appreciate until too late just how many have gone before. Promiscuous men repeatedly set up eternal triangles, but the women involved repeatedly fail to realise that for someone who is compulsively unfaithful, the person they are unfaithful with is frequently just a transitional object. He might make her feel like the love of his life, but she is often just one of many loves in his life. The philanderer is more intent on having his own needs met than meeting the needs of his mistress, except perhaps sexually. The mistress generally does not realise what an unimportant role she is really playing in the life of her lover. By the time she does discover this, her lover is thinking of finishing the relationship, so he casts her aside and returns to the security of home and hearth before setting out on pastures new.

The Thrill of the Chase

Most mistresses, when talking about their affairs, whether they are in the past or currently going on, say that at the beginning of the affair they were usually pursued very avidly. The married man spent a great deal of time, attention, and often money in the chase. I think there is nothing quite so ardent as the married man in pursuit of a mistress, rather like the spider who is very intent on catching his fly. The woman on the receiving end of this is made to feel very desired, sexy, sensual, wonderful, beautiful, the only person in the world for him. It is very powerful and heady stuff, if someone is showing that amount of interest in you. It feeds into most people's longing to be adored, loved and desired.

Many married men have really perfected the art of sweet-talking a woman into an affair by making her feel totally desirable. One woman talking about her affair with a married man said, 'He made me feel like a princess. How could I resist?' Resistance is particularly hard if the man happens to catch the woman when she is at her most vulnerable, when a previous relationship has perhaps come to grief, or if there has been a bitter and painful divorce.

The World is Full of Married Men

Vanessa had been divorced for three years when she met Tim. 'Having been in a bad marriage for ten years,' she said, 'I desperately needed to be told I was needed, wanted, and sexually desirable. Tim was a very successful, amusing and powerful man, and that was part of the attraction for me. He made it very clear that it was me he desired and said he was determined to get what he wanted. That was how he approached life. At the time I found that quite an aphrodisiac.

'I didn't set out to have an affair with a married man, it's just that none of the men I fancied were free. It didn't really matter to me that he was married. I didn't know his wife so it didn't worry me. I always knew there was no question of him leaving his marriage, and anyway I didn't want him to, but it was important that I mattered to him. I don't think it was a very good marriage but we never really discussed it. Eventually I did meet her a few times, and I realised that she was very jealous of his success. Yet that was one of the things I really liked about him. I'm very successful in my work and I like others who are also achievers.

'In the end I was very hurt by him. I thought he cared for me, then I realised he was very much a man's man. He couldn't talk about feelings, or show much affection. I was a status symbol. For him the affair was mainly based on the sex side of the relationship. When I realised this I felt very hurt. But by then I was already working with him and trapped by the fact that I was making a lot of money out of his company. I could have said "get lost" an awful lot earlier, which is what I would have liked to do. But at that stage I couldn't afford to lose the work. Eventually, once the contract came to an end, I finished the affair.

'I was fairly angry and felt used by this stage. So when he telephoned and suggested we had lunch together, which we used to do about once a week, I accepted. The day before we were to meet, I telephoned him and told him that lunch was off. I said we'd had a wonderful time but the affair had run its course and it was over. He was absolute charm itself. He said he didn't agree with me, but just accepted the fact. I was so angry by now, especially as at the beginning he had made such a play for me. I thought I meant more to him than I obviously had. So that's the way we left it, and I haven't seen him since. When I think about it now, I realise it was something that perhaps suited us both at the time.

'Not long after that affair finished I fell head over heels in love with another man. We both love each other very deeply, but sadly he is also married. He doesn't love his wife but he is a very devoted father and absolutely adores his children. I don't know what will happen. I would never pressurise him to leave his wife. It just seems to me that the world is full of married men.'

What Vanessa was describing was how very determined Tim was to have an affair. It was only when she became involved with him that she realised that having used all his considerable charm to persuade her into an affair, she was ripe for the picking.

An Affair is Just an Affair – Or Is It?

When women get involved with married men, they frequently do not realise quite how deeply they are going to fall in love. An affair often starts with mutual attraction, romantic dinners, illicit meetings. It is fun, sexy and exciting. At that stage a woman usually feels in control, but that lasts only until her feelings deepen and she falls in love. Sometimes a woman knows from the very beginning that it is an important relationship, but she takes a gamble. If she is struck by this thing called love, the feeling can be so compelling that she starts an affair with her eyes open, but with the hope that the affair will turn into a permanent relationship. A woman may also deny to herself the true extent of her feelings when she embarks on an affair with a married man.

Penny, a very lively and striking woman in her early forties, said, 'When I first met Nicholas I had no idea what an important part of my life he was going to become. We first met at a friend's wedding, and then again a few months later at a dinner party. He was so easy to talk to, and he was most impressed because I had remembered everything we had talked about the first time we met. A few days later there was a message on the answerphone and my daughter said, "Wait till you hear this Mummy." It was just to say hello and that he'd like to see me some time, but it was the intonation of the voice. I left it about a week before I returned the call, and he invited me out to lunch. It was lovely, I was terribly attracted to him straight away and I know he was to me. He was due to go abroad for a week on some work trip, but we arranged to have dinner together on his return. When we met he told me he was on his own for the next four days, and that was how the affair started.

'His wife was away so we went back to his house. He didn't say much about his wife, but I knew from other people that he had quite a lot of girlfriends, so I rather assumed that the marriage was not particularly good. At that point I didn't think about how it was going to progress and I don't think he did either. He was very attractive, I had been divorced for seven years and it was lovely having someone new. It was very exciting. I think that even then I was bowled over by him. Then, as we saw more and more of each other, I realised how much. I'd fallen in love with him. I thought he was lovely, but I'm not sure I quite knew at the beginning that it was going to become as serious as it has.'

Penny, like many women who embark on an affair with a married man, had not thought about the future. She had felt very attracted to Nicholas and thought that she could handle an affair, even reminding herself that he'd had several other girlfriends, so why not? But fairly early on in the affair she realised it was already much deeper than she had anticipated. By then, for her, there was no going back. For Nicholas it was also more than just an affair. Penny said, 'It's easy to say you love someone, but the actions have to be right too. It wasn't only what he said, which was always lovely, but because right from the beginning he was so caring. He showed this by being really interested in me and worrying about things that happened to me. He would do things like lend me a mobile phone if I was driving a long way to collect my daughter from boarding school, so I could call him in case I broke down. He was just always so very caring. It was so different from anything I had experienced in my first marriage, or subsequently.

'Even though we were very much in love, Nicholas said at the beginning that he would not and could not leave his wife. He said they were very much a family, and even though the children were virtually grown up, they would come home with their friends at weekends and he and his wife would go on holiday with their youngest and their friends. I think he was afraid that if he left his wife it would alienate his children, and he didn't want that to happen. I completely accepted this, I didn't want to break up his marriage. But as the relationship deepened he began to change his mind. He was very jealous of me because my work involves me meeting lots of men, and because I was free I suppose. I found that difficult to cope with. You have to trust people and he finds that hard to do. He judges me by himself, and he shouldn't. I've never looked at anyone else while he's been around. Sometimes when I've been in his office, he has old girlfriends ringing him up. One does it all the time, which I get a bit annoyed about, but nothing more.

'We had been having an affair for a couple of years, and I think his wife was beginning to feel suspicious. Nicholas and

I had been out to lunch and he dropped me off at work, then went home to collect some papers to take into the office. His wife Pat came out to the car and asked him whether she could borrow it for the afternoon. It's a lot bigger than hers and she had a lot of stuff she wanted to take to a charity fund raising ball she was organising. As she opened the door she saw an earring lying on the car seat. It had come out of my ear without me realising, and she immediately knew it was mine. I wear those earrings an awful lot and she has always admired them. There was a tremendous scene in which she accused him of having an affair with me. He denied it, but eventually admitted that he had taken me out to lunch. She told him that he must have nothing more to do with me, but he told her that he was going to continue seeing me and that there was nothing she could do about it. He's told her since that he can't live without me.

'She says now she can pinpoint the exact day it happened. She can't really, as she's not a sensitive person. I'm sure Pat knows that Nicholas wants to leave her and marry me, but now there's an added complication. A couple of years ago Nicholas discovered he had got MS. He hadn't told me because he thought it would make a difference to us, but I'd already worked out what the problem was. By then we were talking about our future together, and this came as a terrible blow. He is not very well off, his wife has all the money and I haven't any, so there is a terrible shortage of cash between us. And if you're going to be ill you do need that sort of financial help. It sounds very mercenary but it could kill the relationship at the end of the day. I'm not prepared to have just five lovely years and then wish we'd never met each other.

'I also have my children to think of. They both know Nicholas and like him, but my daughter is dead against anything else happening. To begin with she said, "Why don't you just get married and save this mucking around?" but since she's realised he's ill, she says my golden years would be ruined, and she's right. I would like us to be together but Nicholas's illness makes it very difficult. We see each other nearly every day, he phones me all the time, and as we both live in the same village we always meet socially, either at the tennis club or at parties. Most people in the village know about Nicholas and me because Pat has told her friends and they have in turn talked about it. Friends who know are supportive. Once Pat came to my house to tell me that I'd ruined her marriage, but I didn't say anything. She is frequently really awful to Nicholas, threatening, shouting and screaming at him. He arrives to see me, incredibly stressed, which of course is what you are meant to avoid when you have MS. Of course she's hurt, but I don't feel guilty about her, no, not at all. I have this awful feeling it's because I'm not wild about the woman that I don't have any guilt. If I liked her enormously I would feel guilty.

'Also, I don't think she loves him, she just wants him there as a husband, a convenient social asset. He always says how capable she is. I think he'd prefer she wasn't quite so capable. Personally, I think she is very bossy and suffocating and I don't know how he puts up with it. When I first met him, his feelings for her weren't too bad. But, sadly, I think I've killed those because he's seen what sort of life we could have if we were together. It's sad if I've done that damage. But who knows, if the marriage had been good the affair would not have started in the first place, would it? I don't know what will happen. I couldn't spend the rest of my life in the situation we're in now, but I love him and I don't want to lose him. He's a lovely optimist so perhaps things will work out.

'At the moment I don't feel like doing anything about it. I just don't know. I see him every day, sometimes all day and sometimes for just half an hour. If he wasn't ill, I'd like to spend the rest of my life with him. But if he became very ill there's no way I could look after him and work. It feels very sad. I keep thinking I've been through that worry and come to terms with him not being well, but I haven't really. My feelings about the future are unknown. They have to be. The big barrier is the lack of money. When you're well you can do things, but when you're not you don't know how things are going to last. But it's been wonderful that we've had time together rather than no time at all. So as far as that's concerned, I have no regrets.'

Neither Liz, Vanessa or Penny felt guilty about their lovers' wives. This was true for the majority of mistresses I spoke to.

Many started off by not really thinking about their lover's wife, and ended up really resenting her. This was particularly so if they felt that she was the obstacle preventing them from having a full-time relationship with their lover. If a woman does feel guilty, she frequently pushes these thoughts to the back of her mind because she does not believe that the man she is in love with loves his wife, or that his wife loves him. This may well be true. She may also be hoping that her lover will leave his wife for her, so she does not want to complicate this by allowing herself to feel guilty.

Can you Trust a Married Man who Cheats on his Wife?

If a man can betray his wife, can he not also betray his mistress? Many men in pursuit of a mistress are not very honest about the state of their marriage, or indeed their future intentions toward their mistress. Sara Keays found this out when she told her lover Cecil Parkinson, a senior Tory cabinet minister, that she was pregnant. He returned to his wife, and she was the discarded woman. The disclosure of the affair, her pregnancy and his broken promise to marry Miss Keays cost Cecil Parkinson his job as a minister. He said in a statement in the run-up to the 1983 Conservative party conference, 'During our relationship I told Miss Keays of my wish to marry her. Despite my having given Miss Keays my assurance, my wife, who has been a source of great strength, and I have decided to stay together and to keep our family together.' At the conference, Cecil Parkinson and his wife Ann were given tremendous applause as they mounted the platform accompanied by Mrs Thatcher. In his speech Cecil Parkinson referred rather dismissively to his affair, and thanked his wife for her support. He made no comment about Sara Keays, who felt badly betrayed by him.

That night, a hurt and outraged Miss Keays issued a statement to *The Times* which said that her baby had been conceived in 'a long-standing, loving relationship which I had allowed to continue because I believed in our eventual marriage'. She added that he had first asked her to marry him in 1979, but in May 1983 when she told him she was pregnant, he had changed his mind and said that the marriage was off. He then, according to Miss Keays (and many mistresses will identify with this), vacillated between her and his wife, once more offering her marriage. In August, according to Miss Keays, Cecil Parkinson went abroad with his wife and children, reassuring her that he still wanted to marry her. But when he returned from the holiday on 1st September he told her that he had changed his mind again.

It was not so much the affair that brought about his downfall, but the question of whether a man who behaves dishonourably and breaks promises can be a suitable cabinet minster. Unfortunately for the mistress, vacillation is a frequently recurring pattern in affairs, and many women who become mistresses do get badly hurt.

Anna, a single and successful business woman of thirty-six, said, 'Why is it that when people talk about the victims of an affair, they are automatically referring to the husband or wife as being the betrayed party, never thinking of the mistress?' She began an affair with a married man, who told her the marriage was over and that he was going to file for a divorce. They moved in together, and she thought they were very happy. But his wife caused havoc, making it increasingly difficult for him to see his children, whom he adored. When she was eight months pregnant, he left her and returned to his wife, saying he had to for the children's sake while still telling Anna he loved her. Anna said despairingly, 'Where does that leave me? I had a good life, a job I really enjoyed, and lots of confidence and now I feel I've lost the lot.'

'Don't Go Breaking my Heart!'

When Emily and Clive began their affair he made promises that he did not keep. 'I was twenty-seven when I first met Clive,' said Emily. 'He was working for a large advertising company and I went in to do a freelance job. It was instant attraction on both sides. He came into the room where I was working to see one of the directors, who happened to be asking me out at the time. Then a few minutes later he came back. He told me later that he just had to have another look. The director, who noticed this going on and whose invitation I had refused said, extremely irritatedly, nodding in Clive's direction, "He's married." As far as I was concerned he was out of bounds, but I couldn't stop thinking about him.

'Three months later I was called in again to do some more work. During that week Clive kept leaving notes on my desk, but I didn't respond. I kept reminding myself he was married. One evening that week I went to meet a date in a pub and he was late. But Clive was there, and he started talking to me. My date did eventually turn up but I wasn't interested by then and I never saw him again. Then the next day Clive and I went out for a drink. It was Grand National day. We were fooling around a bit and decided to put a bet on the horses for luck. We kissed in the betting shop, then a few days later we went out for the evening and that was the start of our affair.

'He took me out to dinner and we went back to my flat. My flatmate was out and we went to bed. It was unbelievably lovely. I was eleven years younger than him and I had never had an affair with a married man before. I believed him when he said the marriage was over and it was just a matter of sorting out the red tape and that would be it. He said he was getting a divorce, and I thought that this was it, this was the rest of my life. When I first met him, I thought, "At last I've found you." It was a real love affair for me, and for him too.

'He had to go away on a job and I went with him. We had a couple of nights in a hotel and he said, "We're inextricably bound for ever." And he was right. You see, we now have a daughter. He said the marriage was over. I chose to believe it though I know I was exceedingly anxious a lot of the time, and much of that was about denying things that I didn't want to recognise. He was telling me we were going to be together and live happily ever after, and that is what I wanted to hear. I was totally in love with him.

'I felt guilty about having an affair with someone who was

married. It offended my religious beliefs and I knew it was immoral and that you don't do this sort of thing. But he had said that his marriage was over. We had this terribly passionate, intense time and then he suddenly dumped me after three months. I was distraught and did the unforgivable thing and rang him at home. I spoke to his wife and I told her how guilty I felt and that I would give him up. And I tried to, but the next morning he telephoned me and begged me to come back, and I did. I went through two years of him breaking up and then making up. It was always him who did the dumping. He said he couldn't cope with the double life one moment, and then the next he'd say the marriage was over. I was distraught. After dumping me, he would be on the telephone the next morning begging me to come back to him.

'I ended up having a nervous breakdown. I couldn't function any more. One moment he wanted me, the next he wasn't there for me. I met him once during this breakdown. I used to get dolled up to see him, but not this time. I was too ill. We met in a restaurant and I said I felt absolutely awful. I didn't see him again for months. That was his reaction when I needed him. The breakdown was as a result of this cat-and-mouse game he played. I couldn't work. I couldn't sleep. I had let my career go so I could accompany him around the country. Eventually I pulled myself together and went back to him at his request. We'd been apart nine months. Once I'd got myself back on my feet again, he wanted me back. I felt that he didn't want me with a breakdown. It makes me angry when I think about it.

'Once again when I was desperate, I rang his home, but he wasn't there. His wife must have guessed it was me and she rang me back the next morning. We talked for ninety minutes and she said I wasn't his first affair. She said the previous one was five years before and lasted a year and she had rung up threatening suicide. I said to his wife, "I'll give Clive up if that's what you want." She said, "Don't bother on my account. Give him up for your own sake because he's a bastard." So I felt I had permission. All the time he told me he was going to leave the marriage.

'We had been having an affair for five-and-a-half years

when we had our daughter. We were going to San Francisco where he had a week's work. Even up to the last minute I wondered whether he wouldn't turn up. But he did. It was a relief when I saw him at the airport. During the whole of the flight he kept talking about us having a baby. I said, "Don't say this unless you really mean it, because I adore you, I love you. But don't muck about with my emotions on this one. It's far too important." He said, "No; I really mean it, I want you to have my child. It will enable me to get out of my marriage." He said he was a lousy father the first time round and wanted the opportunity to make good this time, and I believed him. I loved him desperately. When we got to San Francisco we went to our hotel straight from the airport. I was using a cap at the time and he hurled it across the room, so we made love without contraception. It was September. The next time we made love I said we must use the cap. Sometimes we did and sometimes we didn't. We were playing Russian roulette with contraception and I got pregnant two months later. I was thirty-two.

'I was thrilled to be pregnant, I was so excited. At the beginning I was about to tell him that I was pregnant, but my mother got in first. Clive and I had arranged to meet and my mother was with me. I was going to tell him on my own but she blurted it out. He froze, he looked terrified, and that was how it was. Throughout the pregnancy he swung between being lovely and being horrible. He never dumped me, but at one point he did say that I should have an abortion. I had an abortion when I was twenty-two and to this day it causes me such distress, and he knew about that. He implied something disgusting like you've done it before, have it again. Then he said, "What would you say if I asked you to choose between me and the baby?" I said, "Fuck off. It's not fair to play around with someone's emotions in such a cavalier fashion." I was heartbroken. I remember him looking at me with hatred in his eyes, and fear because I wouldn't do what he wanted.

'After fourteen weeks I had this bleeding and nearly lost my daughter. One day I stood up and there was this rush of blood and I was absolutely petrified. I couldn't bear the thought of losing the baby. I got an ambulance and I was taken to hospital. I was so frightened. She was such a wanted baby. I got to hospital and they put a heart monitor on and I could hear her heart and it was one of the best sounds I'd ever heard in my life. Clive came to see me and he was so sweet. He kissed my stomach. He assured me that if anything happened we'd have another one. But I wanted this one! I can't help feeling that he was secretly wishing that I would miscarry the baby. Our relationship continued throughout my pregnancy. The plan was for him to be with me. He always said he would bring the green wellies and the gown, champagne and cigars.

'The baby was late, and I'm convinced that I was so terrified of losing it I just didn't let go. It was fifteen days late, so eventually the baby had to be induced. It couldn't have been on a better day for him. I went into the hospital on Monday. He rang the hospital to say he was on his way but he didn't turn up that day. The induction wasn't doing a lot and on the Tuesday afternoon they took me into the delivery room. There was a cot in there with a pink cover. Is it going to be a girl, I thought. Again he rang to say he was on his way, but again he never arrived. I kept hoping that he was coming. Then at midnight I thought, perhaps he's panicking and he has gone out drinking. It was heartbreaking. I couldn't understand what was happening. I thought, he'll be here in the morning.

'Then there was a problem. The baby's heartbeat dropped and they were talking about doing an emergency caesarean. I was petrified. I didn't want to have a caesarean. They told me in the hospital that it was a difficult labour because of him promising to come and then not turning up, as if I was hanging on to her, waiting for him to be there. She was born on Wednesday morning and they had to use forceps to get her out.

'And then my baby was there. I didn't dare look at her at first. I couldn't believe that there wouldn't be anything wrong. They had to peel my face round to look. I couldn't believe I could produce something that wasn't wrong. When I saw her I was so delirious about her. But Clive never turned up. I realised he had abandoned me when I was in labour. There were no flowers, no card. On the Thursday afternoon he rang. Sister said I couldn't speak to him as I was breastfeeding. She said to me, "He's rung from the pub and would you ring him." I didn't ring him. I was too hurt. I got home on Sunday and expected a hundred apologies. But there were no calls, no apologies, no messages, cards or flowers. I was all alone with my baby. My mother would have been with me but my stepfather was dying of cancer. But despite all that I was over the moon because I had my daughter.

'I didn't hear from Clive, so I sent him a solicitor's letter and he denied paternity so I took him to court for maintenance. Paternity was proved conclusively. I was desperate for him to see our daughter. When she was seven months old he had seen her in the court waiting room from a distance only. Denial of paternity was worse than him not turning up at the birth. I couldn't believe he would do that. The birth, almost, I could understand. But the court case was cold-blooded. It was all about money. Yet I thought he wanted the baby. I asked him why he had changed his mind and he said, "I was telling you what I thought you wanted to hear." I was stunned. He said, "That'll teach me to tell lies."

'I still desperately wanted him to see his daughter. He had to see my prize. When she was two, I went back for a rise in maintenance which was granted. He met his daughter for the first time in court. He knelt down to speak to his daughter and I told her, "This is your daddy." She took to him like a duck to water and vice versa. He said, "Can we go for a drink, I really need to talk." My mother took my daughter home. He said that the reason he hadn't asked to see her was to punish me for taking him to court. But he then said that he would like to start seeing her. To start with he saw her spasmodically, but now he sees her more regularly. She adores him and has a lovely time when she's with him. The affair restarted after being "just good friends" for two years. I said, "I'll come back if you leave," which I did, but he didn't. The affair continued for another four years during which I had a couple of attempts at breaking away from him. Then, as my fortieth birthday approached I ended it. I thought, if I don't make a change now it will carry on for the rest of my life. But two years later the affair started again.

'He's still promising to leave the marriage. I still love him, but if he did leave his marriage I don't know now if I would go back to him. I just don't know if I could trust him. I'd have to see. There would be conditions. I'd have to see an absolute commitment to change. He'd have to be in counselling or therapy. I've known him fourteen years. I doubt if he's been completely faithful to me. I don't think he's had a real affair. He was never an affair man, more a one-night stand man. I've tried endlessly to understand why he has never got out of his marriage. He still says he doesn't love his wife, and the children are grown up now. He seems to be so terrified of change, which must be rooted in his childhood. But I can't find out what went on.'

Emily absolutely adores her daughter, has no regrets about having had a baby, and says she does not regret the affair. But she has been in and out of this relationship for fourteen years, and because she has been so enmeshed with Clive during that time, she has not met another man with whom she could fall in love, marry and have another child. All of which she now longs for.

It is easy for those on the outside looking in, or for those who have never been there, to say, 'How foolish, why did she get involved in the first place? She deserves what she gets.' They can even question why she did not get out when Clive first let her down all those years ago. But for women who fall in love with married men and stay in the relationships hoping against hope that they will leave their wives, there is usually a pattern in their family background that is being replayed in their relationship with the married men. Given the same opportunity another woman would not have got involved in the first place or, if she had, when she saw the way things were going, would have terminated the relationship much sooner.

The endless waiting that many women do for the man to leave his wife is not uncommon. Most of us, if we look around at our family, friends, work colleagues or acquaintances know someone who is having an affair with a married man. Frequently the unmarried woman (though sometimes the unmarried man) is hoping against hope that some day he will leave his wife for her.

In many ways Emily's background was a classic case of

women who frequently end up in this position. Her father left her mother for another woman when Emily was two years old, which is at the height of the oedipal stage, when the little girl is competing with her mother for the attention of her father. Not only did she not get his attention, but at that point he left for another woman. Her mother was pregnant at the time with her younger brother. He quickly married the other woman, and shortly after the birth of her brother, her father's new wife had a daughter by that marriage. Her father and his new wife had four daughters in four years. Emily had not only to cope with a lot of jealous feelings when her brother was born, but was then further displaced by the birth of four half-sisters.

Her mother meanwhile had a series of broken relationships, and so Emily learned that men cannot be trusted. In her relationship with Clive there was a lot about trying to reclaim the father who had abandoned her. With Clive she was trying to get him for herself, and lay to rest some of those painful feelings so deeply felt all those years ago. Her only experience of men was ones who betrayed you and let you down.

Her relationship with Clive was repeating patterns from childhood. Clive could be hugely loving and very demonstrative, but he also had a rejecting and neglectful side just like her father. Her childhood experience of her mother was also one of love and rejection. Her mother gave her periods of intense love, but she also had to endure periods of separation from her. When she was seven she and her brother went to live with her father for a year as her mother was too ill to look after them. She was then sent to boarding school as a weekly boarder for a further two years. She grew up experiencing being loved followed by periods of rejection and neglect. In Clive, the pattern was repeating itself. He was so utterly what she was used to, which is why she said with a smile, 'When I saw him across a crowded room it was so familiar. He's also a very charismatic man, with a wicked sense of humour, very sexy and talented.'

I am not suggesting that she knowingly wanted to repeat the destructive, neglectful elements of her childhood relationship with her parents. She didn't, but that was all she knew. What was so familiar to her was that she perceived Clive as hugely loving. He used all his charm and charismatic personality to make her feel this way. In the early days of their relationship he used this to his full advantage to woo her and win her, and then reject her just like her father before him.

He made her feel like the only woman in the world for him. He told her romantically that they would be inextricably bound. He told her all the things she wanted to hear. Emily interpreted this as never again having to experience those feelings of abandonment and neglect that had so dogged her childhood. Then when she did experience Clive's behaviour as being like that of her father, loving one moment and rejecting the next, because she was emotionally damaged and so vulnerable in that area, instead of saying 'get lost' she kept hoping he would change. She was the little child desperately wanting her father's love. She was trying to recapture the love, time and attention that her father deprived her of as he left her to pursue countless other women and marriages throughout her childhood years.

Emily said that when Clive was loving he was incredibly so, 'I adored being with him, and when he withdrew and said he was going back to his wife, the pain was awful. I just longed to have him back. There was also an overpowering sexual attraction. I only had to look at him to want to go to bed with him. I do regret the pain it must have caused his wife, although I'm not responsible for that marriage. I don't think the marriage was right when we met, but I understand it's now in deep trouble. I don't regret it because I've learned such a lot. I see him once a month when he comes to see our daughter. I've forgiven him now and feel a sense of sadness that it can't be what I would have liked it to be. It's OK, but sad. I can't lose contact for my daughter's sake. I hope I'll be able to trust a man in the future.'

The affair is still going on, and Emily is still waiting for him to leave his wife. She has now told him that she cannot take much more, she has set a deadline. If he hasn't left his wife by then, their relationship, she insists, will be finally over. She will not see him again. But she also says if he doesn't leave, she doesn't know how she is going to survive. So many women who embark on affairs with married men have no idea how much they are going to get hurt.

The Serial Mistress

At the age of thirty-two, Flora had already had four affairs with married men. A friend of Flora's said of her, laughingly, 'She should have a government health warning tied around her pretty little neck, saying "This woman is dangerous to your marriage".' When asked about her many affairs with married men Flora insists that it was pure chance, no more than a coincidence. Flora said, 'It's just that all the men I fall for happen to be married.' But there is a pattern to her affairs. Each of the men have been at least ten to fifteen years older than her. Each man has been very highly thought of and extremely successful in their chosen career. And all of them adored her. Unconsciously she was trying to reinvent her relationship with her father with each of them.

Flora is an actress, one of those women who, though not strictly speaking beautiful, seems to have men falling at her feet. At the beginning of all her affairs the men in question have, she said, been quite besotted with her. For Flora this was a total aphrodisiac. They made her feel like the love of their life, despite the fact that they were married. They in turn were very attractive, successful and well-known in their profession, and much sought after by other women.

Her current affair has been going on for four years and she is deeply in love with Michael, who is fifteen years her senior and married with four children. Throughout the last fifteen years of his twenty-year marriage Michael has had affairs, though none of them had been very serious for him, and most were of quite short duration. But this affair with Flora was important to him. He said, 'It's a love affair,' but he was totally torn between his longing to be with Flora and his love-hate relationship with his wife. At the beginning of the affair Flora was happy that it should be an affair and no more, but one year into the affair she was feeling quite differently. She wanted Michael full-time. For the last three years that they had been together, he had been promising to leave his wife, but somehow he never quite managed it. They would meet two or three times a week, either for lunch, or dinner, or to spend an afternoon or night together, and when they were not together they would spend hours talking on the telephone.

Flora first met Michael when he was producing a play in which she had a small part. Right from the beginning Michael seemed to take an interest in her, and Flora admitted she was very flattered by his attention. After several weeks he asked her out to dinner, and without hesitation she went. Over the next few months they frequently had dinner or lunch together. Michael's wife lived in the country and although he returned home most nights, he occasionally also stayed in London. It was on one of those nights, when he suggested that they meet in his hotel before going out, that the affair started. Flora said, 'Even before I arrived, I think I knew we weren't going to make it to the restaurant. He was rather nervous, which surprised me. I thought I was the one who would feel unsure of myself, not him. He suggested that we had a meal sent up to the room, so that we could just be alone together. He was just so easy to talk to, I felt totally relaxed with him. We ate a light super, drank wine and talked and talked. He very tentatively asked me if I would like to stay the night. I simply said yes. It just felt so right. He was a superb lover and afterwards, as he held me in his arms, I just felt this man was lovely.

'He has always talked to me about his wife. Even when I first met him they seemed to be at each other's throats a lot of the time. He seems to have a very volatile marriage. She's a musician, and comes from a large, artistic family where everyone was encouraged to express their emotions at full volume and at great length. In no time at all discussions were spilling over into arguments, with everyone shouting at everyone else. This was in complete contrast to Michael's family. He was an only child, of rather elderly, though very indulgent parents. They worshipped the ground he walked on, and in their eyes he could do no wrong. He was the first one of his generation to go to university, and they were worried when he went into acting after leaving university. They had wanted him to be something respectable, like a doctor or lawyer, but they supported him and are now terribly proud of his success.

'He was a much longed-for child and his mother adored

him. She looked after his every need, he never had to lift a finger. His father looked to his clever son to achieve everything that he felt he had failed to do. Also, as an only child he had quite a lonely childhood. He was quite determined when he married that what he wanted were lots of children, and a house full of hustle and bustle, with the busyness of family life. So initially, his wife's family seemed very attractive to him. But the demands of family life were not something he had much experience of, and like most children who are judged on their achievements, he was very determined to prove how successful he could be. As the children came along his wife needed more and more help and support, and this clashed with Michael's need to achieve in his chosen career. His wife, unlike his mother, also had her own career, and increasingly resented the fact that she felt Michael didn't pull his weight. So she constantly criticised him, put him down and told him that he was entirely self-centred. He responded by telling her that if he wasn't single-tracked in his ambition, he wouldn't have achieved what he had, and they wouldn't have the comfortable lifestyle from which they all benefited.'

For Michael, the attraction of his affairs was that the women gave him the attention and admiration he felt was missing in his marriage, and which he had been used to receiving from his mother. The attraction for Flora was that in Michael she saw what she had at times experienced with her father, whom she adored and who adored her. He had always made her feel very special and very loved. Her mother had been a more distant figure, and Flora discovered after her father's death that she had had several affairs during her marriage. But the down side of Flora's relationship with her father was that, much as he loved her, he was unreliable largely due to the fact that he was an alcoholic. He died when she was eighteen of cirrhosis of the liver and Flora was devastated. Shortly after his death she began her first affair, with a married man.

Her father, unlike Michael, had not been successful. He was talented and gifted, but because of his drink problem he had great difficulty holding down a job, so her mother had to work very hard to look after Flora and her elder sister. Much of Flora's childhood had been spent listening to all her father was planning to achieve and how much of a failure he felt, but she learned that, to her father, success was what men must strive for above all else. As a result, she was attracted to men who had already achieved success so she did not have to live with the failure that had haunted her father's life. She was also attracted to men who, like her father, adored her. In each of her relationships with married men the need for the man to be the success her father had failed to be, was being re-enacted.

The problem for children of alcoholics is frequently that they are living with inconsistency. One moment Flora was the apple of her father's eye, and the next he was drunk or depressed and hardly had any time for her. So when Michael started to vacillate between her and his wife, she was back in old familiar territory. She stayed because she kept telling herself that this time he really meant it and would keep his promises.

On many occasions she felt Michael was on the point of leaving his marriage when something stopped him. One of the children would be ill, or he felt that they needed him around. He wanted Flora but he did not want to lose the family life he had, or his house and good circle of friends. There were also times in his stormy relationship with his wife when things seemed tolerable. It was at those times that his sexual relationship with his wife would re-emerge, much to Flora's fury. Flora suspected that Michael's wife had an occasional lover and she frequently drew this to Michael's attention. This enraged him, and then Flora felt even more jealous that he minded so much.

Michael's wife did not want a divorce. Even though she complained about him never being around enough, she knew the children would miss him. When he was there he was a good father, especially now they were past the baby stage and he felt he could do more with them. She also liked being married and enjoyed the lifestyle and good social life that went with it. But Flora wanted marriage and children of her own, and with the mid-thirties just around the corner she did not want to wait for much longer. Flora was finding the whole situation increasingly painful, and started counselling because everything was getting on top of her. It soon became clear to the counsellor that however much she tried to help Flora look at what was happening in her life and why, she really did not want to acknowledge that Michael would probably not leave his wife. That was not what Flora wanted to hear, so after a few months she terminated counselling.

It seems yet again that the most common justification for not feeling guilty is that the lover and his mistress collude with each other in the belief that the marriage is not a good one. This may indeed be so, but it is also what the mistress wants to believe, and what the husband wants her to believe so he can keep both the marriage and the affair.

If a woman is battling for the man she loves, the very fact that she loves him seems in her eyes to mitigate her own behaviour. She casts aside the facts staring her in the face, that he is another woman's husband. She frequently justifies her behaviour by asking herself why her lover should stay in this dead marriage. What is the point of staying with a woman he does not love and who may not love him? Why should he sacrifice his life for the sake of the children? How can he tolerate a sexless marriage? Or whatever else she has been told or wants to believe. How, she asks herself and her lover, 'Can you settle for so little when I can give you so much love?'

The Profit and Loss Account

The mistress often feels, and maybe correctly so, that she loves or can be more loving than the woman he is with, and that if only the man leaves, she can give him so much more happiness than his wife. Maybe she can, but the end of a marriage is not just about changing one woman and replacing her with another. There is a whole network of needs that underpin a marriage and that also have to be served if a man is going to leave the marriage for his mistress. There are the hopes and dreams he had when he went into the marriage, the children, the lifestyle they have built up together, the fear of losing friends who may take sides, or may find it difficult to see him with a new woman by his side. He may have to take on her children when he is losing daily contact with his own. Then there is the cost of a divorce, and fear about his ability to finance a new relationship as well as paying maintenance to his children and possibly his discarded wife. The list is usually a long one.

A man torn between his wife and children and his mistress will often have a long hard look at the balance in what I call 'The Emotional and Financial Profit and Loss Account'. He looks at all the things I have mentioned above, and more, and weighs up whether leaving for his mistress is going to involve too much in the loss column and too little in the profit column. That is why so many men promise to leave and then don't, or vacillate between their wife and their mistress, or try to have both. Sir James Goldsmith, the financier and father-in-law of Imran Khan, maintained a wife in London and a mistress in Paris for many years and has been quoted as saying, 'If you marry your mistress you create a vacancy.' This may sound very cruel or cynical, or both, but the papers frequently report the affairs of rich and famous men who leave their second wife for another woman, with gleeful interviews from the first wife who was dumped for the wife he is now also abandoning.

For mistresses who marry their newly divorced lover, perhaps past behaviour should be taken into account. If a man comes with a string of affairs and broken marriages to his name, once the novelty of the current marriage has worn off, will he be faithful or will he be off to pastures new? Will the new wife be the one at home, waiting for him to return from another conference or working late at the office? Will she be seeing those tell-tale signs of an affair, which are all too familiar to her, becoming part of her life. The golfer Nick Faldo left his first wife to marry his mistress, only to abandon her a few years and a few children later for a twenty-year-old who was prepared to follow him everywhere and put him and his needs at the centre of her universe.

It is not only the wife and children of the unfaithful spouse who can end up getting hurt. As this chapter has shown, the mistress can also be deeply hurt. Just because the love affair is illicit does not mean the feelings are any less involved, the love second rate, or not as valid. If and when the affair ends, it is frankly devastating when the other person in this triangular relationship was seeing it as a lifetime's commitment. So often that loss has to be coped with virtually on your own because only a few trusted friends may have known about the affair. What was conducted in secret has also to end in secret.

Secrets Can Become Very Public

Sadly, an increasing number of men and women who have affairs with well-known people 'kiss and tell'. Journalist Mary Ellen Synon (known unkindly as 'the bonk of England' since her exploits on the Bank's dressing-room carpet), the ex-mistress of the Deputy Governor of the Bank of England Rupert Pennant Rae, did just this. She felt she had been unceremoniously dumped and so she spoke out about her affair. Often, if an affair is ended swiftly, or very much against the wishes of the other person concerned, there is so much unresolved hurt and rage that there is a desire to get back at the person who has caused you so much pain.

Selling your story to the press can backfire, however, with the mistress coming off worse than the man with whom she has had the affair. Jane Nottage, who had an affair with Scotland football manager Andy Roxburgh, discovered this when she sold her story to *The Sun*. She said, 'At about seven a.m., when *The Sun* was slipped under my door, I looked at the front page and thought, "My God, ten million people are going to see me looking a complete berk." At eight a.m. my parents had a serious sense of humour failure, and at nine a.m. I thought, "I don't think I made the right decision."'

Retaliation also takes place in relationships which are not in the public eye, where the mistress or lover who has been rejected then decides to spill the beans and tell the spouse. Emily had on one or two occasions rung the family home, and as a result of this Clive's wife had found out about the affair. She had broken one of the cardinal rules that mistresses are meant to comply with, and that is never to telephone the marital home.

The Well-Behaved Mistress

Experienced women stress that there are several golden rules by which the mistress should abide:

- She should have as much to lose as her lover, should the affair become public.

- She should not want to change the status quo. She should be either happily married or happily single, and quite sure that she does not want to leave her marriage or give up her single status for her lover.

- She should be restrained when asking about the state of her lover's marriage, unless he wants to unburden himself.

- Other than cooking him the occasional delicious meal, she should definitely not make any other attempts at domesticity, because that could indicate she might be thinking of changing her status from mistress to wife.

- She must be as happy with her situation as the lover.

The trouble is that human emotions are just not as neatly packaged as that. As a woman, you may embark on an affair with a married man with just these intentions, only to find you fall very much in love and want to spend the rest of your life with him. Or he may have deceived you, and indeed himself, by saying he no longer loves his wife and that his marriage is virtually over, only to find he goes back on his word. It is not only the mistress who can get very hurt, as Emily and Flora undoubtedly were, but the wife, and frequently, the children, of both the mistress and the wife can also suffer hugely.

Chapter Nine

NEW BEGINNINGS

> *Come, let us now resolve at last*
> *To live and love in quiet;*
> *We'll tie the knot so very fast*
> *That time shall ne'er untie it.*
>
> *The truest joys they seldom prove*
> *Who free from quarrels live:*
> *'Tis the most tender part of love*
> *Each other to forgive.*

John Sheffield, Duke of Buckinghamshire, *The Reconcilement*

There is Life after an Affair

An affair can mean a new beginning because it throws into sharp focus the shortcomings within the marriage. This can help the couple to try and create a better relationship than they had before. Alternatively, it might mean the end of the marriage with the affair leading to a new marriage or committed relationship. At other times the marriage might end with one or both of the couple starting an independent life on their own.

I have dealt with rebuilding your marriage or relationship after an affair in Chapter Six, but it is important to underline the fact that when a couple are trying to continue in the marriage, they usually underrate quite how much time and effort it takes to get back onto a stable footing. The person who has had the affair has to acknowledge that they have deeply hurt their partner and that they regret the pain they have caused. They have also to accept that they cannot just sweep the affair under the carpet as being unimportant and irrelevant and that, painful though it is for both, part of the recovery process is allowing the faithful partner go over and over what has happened, and why. The faithful partner also needs to accept that this interrogation cannot go on for ever. There comes a time when you have to move away from blaming your partner and look at the painful fact that there were probably reasons why the affair happened. The most common reason is because there were problems in the marriage.

The betrayed person will find their self-esteem and confidence is at an all-time low. They cannot restore that on their own. They need to hear from their partner that they are loved, and that their partner still wants to be with them. They need to be told that their partner finds them attractive and desirable.

It is natural for the betrayed partner to imagine every time their unfaithful spouse leaves the house, is late from work, or is not where they say they are going to be, that they are stealing off to see their ex-lover or their ex-mistress. Plenty of reassurance is necessary. For the first few months it will be necessary to give your partner an accurate itinerary of what your exact movements are, and to let them know if you are going to alter them. The chances are they will be checking up on you and any indication that you are not where you say you are will lead to arguments and recriminations. It's all too easy to break trust, but extremely hard to re-establish it.

If the marriage is going to survive and flourish it is essential to allow time for all of this, and particularly for trust, to come back into the relationship. It really can take a year or two. Sometimes the honeymoon period when you are so pleased that the affair has not meant the end of the marriage is followed by an unexpected period of depression. You feel, 'Surely I should be getting over this?' but it still haunts your every thought. Something may be said or done and the full weight of the unhappiness it caused returns and suddenly hits you out of the blue, but as time goes by the pain does lessen, and normal life returns.

In counselling I have seen many men and women whose marriages ended when an affair was discovered because their partner gave them no choice and announced they were leaving. At the time they were totally distraught, many even suicidal, and the counselling was trying to help them come to terms with the loss of the marriage or relationship, and the need to rebuild their shattered life. Most of these men and woman whom I have heard from or seen again a year or two later, have found that their lives became good, happy and fulfilled. Most have also gone on to make good new relationships, or are enjoying their independence. If I had tried to tell them that life would be very good again they probably wouldn't have believed me.

Irene's husband left her for a younger woman after twenty years of marriage. She thought her life had come to an end. Three years later she said to me, about her new relationship, 'Ted is just so companionable and we do so much together. It's lovely we have so much in common. It wasn't until I met Ted that I realised how little I had settled for in my first marriage. My first husband was always at work. He had no interest in our home and left me to do everything from the decorating to the gardening, and he said all our friends were boring, and went to sleep at parties.' What Irene discovered is not unusual. To stay in a bad marriage where your partner does not love you or really want to be with you is very soul-destroying.

Some people choose to stay in a bad marriage for the sake of the children, saying, 'He may be unfaithful but he is still a good father.' He may have betrayed you but divorce means losing day-to-day contact with your children. Men and women also choose to stay in unsatisfactory marriages for material reasons. She does not want to lose the lifestyle and he does not want to lose half of everything. At other times there is so little money around that splitting up would mean even greater poverty. The fear of being on your own again after so many years of being part of a couple is why some marriages that would, perhaps, be better off apart, grind unhappily on. There are often a number of reasons, but it is frequently at a high cost to an individual's health and happiness.

Starting again with Someone New

If you are starting a new life with the man or woman who has been involved in the breakup of your marriage then the chances are you will be planning to live together. Though there may be a lot of positive reasons why that seems a good idea, such as enjoying being together all the time, there are also disadvantages. The chances are that you are carrying a lot of the problems from the last relationship into the next one. You may not have allowed yourself time to grieve for the end of the last relationship. Even though you wanted it to end, that does not mean that you do not feel a sense of loss. It could be because you don't have your children with you all the time, the result of rejection by your friends as the so-called 'guilty party', losing your home and the familiar life you knew, as well as the hopes and dreams you shared. All these feelings can't be ignored. It takes time to come to terms with these losses. If you are feeling sad your new partner may not understand, and say, 'You've got me, so why are you so miserable?' But it's necessary for you both to accept that it's unrealistic to think you can just put on a cheerful face. This is a time when you both need to support each other through a difficult time of adjustment and loss.

If there are children, moving in together straight away causes even more problems, because it really does not give them time to adjust to the new situation, let alone mourn for what they have lost. It is difficult enough for them to accept that the marriage is over and that the family unit has broken up, without having to contend with someone new, as they see it, stepping into their mother or father's shoes. It is even more difficult if that person was involved in the divorce. They are likely to blame them, even if that is in reality only half the story. They have seen the hurt the affair with that person has caused their other parent, and therefore they are likely to feel hostile towards your new partner. More often than not this feeling is encouraged, especially in the early days, by your ex saying, 'I'm not having my children living under the same roof as that man,' or, 'The children can't come and visit if that woman is going to be there.'

Guilt can also badly knock 'the affair turned relationship'

for six. If you have left a distraught wife and children against their will, or forced someone into accepting that the marriage is over, it's pretty easy to feel bad about yourself and your behaviour. If you go round in sackcloth and ashes blaming yourself all the time, it's going to make you very difficult to live with, and your new partner may resent it. It may be appropriate to remind yourself that you both tried hard to make the marriage work, and what happened is not all your fault. When Conrad left his wife and child he felt so guilty that he gave his ex-wife everything. The house, the contents, the lot, and he even continued to hand over virtually all his salary to her. At the same time he expected his mistress, who was now his wife, to pay for everything in their new life together.

The road from an affair to a permanent relationship is not an easy one. It's a time when you discover whether your relationship has the resources to make this transition successfully. Sometimes the sad fact is that the affair is no more than a transitional relationship. As an affair you only had a limited time together, which meant it was very special. The very secrecy made it illicit, exciting and often very romantic. Affairs, by their very nature, are in many ways an escape from the routines of everyday life. Affairs are usually quality time, when you have eyes only for each other. If you are planning to turn an affair into a long-term relationship, the tendency is to make lots of plans and to dream about how things will be when you are eventually together. The reality is that many of those dreams may fade or die when the affair becomes a marriage. It is, of course, for all these reasons and more that the majority of people opt out of the affair once it becomes discovered, or keep it a secret, because they do not want the affair on a full-time basis. They already have a marriage that fulfils their needs really quite well.

Don't Be in a Hurry

Starting again with new relationships is not easy. Some people feel they have been so damaged and emotionally bruised by the breakup of their marriage or relationship that they feel they never want to embark on another one. Others are determined to paint the town red in an attempt to eradicate the pain of their partner's affair and the subsequent end of the marriage. So they embark on as many sexual relationships as possible, seeing this as a way of restoring their confidence and coping with their feelings of rejection. If those relationships are very good and enjoyable, that might work. But if, as is often the case, they lead to further disappointments or even rejection, it only makes things worse. A man may get pleasure and variety from a string of casual encounters, but he may also find that he has rushed into new relationships too soon, only to find that he is temporarily impotent. A woman may find leaping into bed with man after man extremely exciting. However, in the cold light of day, if the man treats her as just 'an easy lay' she feels even more rejected. Finding the balance somewhere between rushing things and excluding all possibilities of a new relationship is usually what works best. It is normal in those early days to feel, 'How can I ever learn to love and trust someone ever again?' but, in time, it does happen.

Falling in love again is about taking risks. Although some people are very contented with their single life and want to stay that way, most people after a little while hope that they will meet someone new and fall in love again. Embarking on another relationship opens up the possibility of recreating love and intimacy.

Happily Single

We are a couple-orientated society and so often people feel they are not worthwhile or do not have a life unless they are part of a couple, but that is not true. Learning to live on your own or with the children, but no partner, is scary at first. But learning to be independent, taking control of your life, adjusting to a new and different life for yourself and those around you is also a challenge. As you find yourself doing it increasingly successfully, it restores your self-esteem. When you have to fall back on your own resources you frequently fear you will be found wanting, but in fact the reverse is true. It is a huge achievement and people discover they have an inner strength they had not used before, or even known was there. It is this inner strength that enables you to build a new and different life for yourself and those around you.

Many people do not realise that true happiness comes from within and is under their control. We tend to feel that other people or events 'make us happy', which means we are far too reliant on how others treat us, or that we wait for other people to make good things happen. True happiness comes from being in control of our lives. Of course, falling in love, having a job that suits you and at which you do well, seeing your children flourish, and making new friends all contribute to the sum of that happiness. It is also important to recognise that happiness is like relationships. It has its ups and downs, highs and lows. If it didn't it would be a little too predictable and therefore perhaps even a little bit boring.

Happy Ever After?

Affairs can be a catalyst for new beginnings. Clouds do have silver linings and there are a considerable number of people who find that, given time, their marriage or relationship is genuinely much better after an affair than it was for months or years before it. Affairs can shake up relationships so that those involved realise how they have allowed their marriage to slide into a boring routine. Affairs do help people to recognise that they have been taking each other too much for granted for far too long.

The cynical say that they can always identify the married couple because they are the ones in the restaurant staring into space with nothing to say to each other, and that it's the people who only have eyes for each other who are having the affair. But it does not have to be that way. There are many couples who are married and in committed relationships where you can tell at a glance that they are in love. You can see that they are friends and lovers, that their relationship is sexually alive and extremely well, and that they are two people who are together because that's how they want to be.

I am not recommending an affair as a way of bringing about change in a marriage. There are far better and less painful ways of doing that. But they can make you realise how much you put at risk and how much you might have lost, so that this new awareness makes you value each other much more. The realisation that something very precious was perhaps so nearly destroyed makes you extra careful not to tread that path again.

I have attempted in this book to look at affairs and why they happen, to show how for some they are a wonderfully exciting and fulfilling experience, and how for others they can cause such hurt and devastation. I have tried not to judge or take a moral stance. I only hope that whatever your role is in an affair, that this book has helped. In the final analysis it is, of course, up to each individual to choose whether they will be faithful to their partner, or whether to love, honour and betray.

Side by side, their faces blurred,
The earl and countess lie in stone,
Their proper habits vaguely shown
As jointed armour, stiffened pleat,
And that faint hint of the absurd—
The little dogs under their feet.

Such plainness of the pre-baroque
Hardly involves the eye, until
It meets his left-hand gauntlet, still
Clasped empty in the other; and
One sees, with a sharp tender shock,
His hand withdrawn, holding her hand . . .

Philip Larkin, *An Arundel Tomb*

BIBLIOGRAPHY

William Acton 1857 'The Functions of Disorders of the Reproductive Organs' in *Myths of Sexuality* Basil Blackwell, Oxford, 1988

Simone de Beauvoir 1991 *Letters to Sartre* London, Radius

Betty Friedan 1952 *The Feminine Mystique* USA, W. W. Norton & Co

Dalma Heyn 1992 *The Erotic Silence of the Married Woman* London, Bloomsbury

Shere Hite 1988 *The New Hite Report: Woman and Love* London, Viking

Alfred Kinsey 1953 *Sexual Behaviour in the Human Female* Philadelphia, W. B. Saunders & Co

Alison Lurie 1974 *The War Between the Tates* London, Heinemann and Random House

Annette Lawson 1988 *Adultery, An Analysis of Love and Betrayal* Oxford, Basil Blackwell

Lynda Nead 1988 *Myths of Sexuality* Oxford, Basil Blackwell

Anais Nin 1988 *Letters from Anais Nin from a Literate Passion* London, Allison and Busby

Dorothy Parker 1937 'A Telephone Call' in *The Collected Dorothy Parker* London, Gerald Duckworth & Co.

Ronald Pearsall 1969 *The Worm in the Bud* Pimlico, Random House

Dr Bonnie Eaker Weil 1993 *Adultery* USA, Carol Publishing Group

Robert Wright 1994 *The Moral Animal* USA, Pantheon

POETRY

Dannie Abse 1981 'In My Fashion' London, Hutchinson
Lord Byron 'Don Juan'
A. H. Clough 'The Latest Decaloque'
Kahlil Gibran 1923 'The Prophet' in *Love one and Another* New York, Alfred A. Knopf Inc.
Philip Larkin 1964 'An Arundel Tomb' in *The Whitsun Wedding* London, Faber & Faber
Philip Larkin 1974 'Annus Mirabilis' in *High Windows* London, Faber & Faber
Andrew Marvell 'To his Coy Mistress'
Dorothy Parker 1937 'General Review of the Sex Situation' and 'Unfortunate Coincidence' in *The Collected Dorothy Parker* London, Gerald Duckworth & Co.
John Sheffield 'The Reconcilement'
Judith Viorst 1976 *Nothing but the Truth* New York, Simon and Schuster

REPORTS/SURVEYS

ICM Poll, September 1995
Dr Peter Howlett 'Fighting with Figures' London, Central Statistical Office, April 1995
Woman Magazine 'Letter to an agony aunt' 1994

INDEX

THE TROUBLE WITH YOU

It's easier for a man to take off his clothes in front of a woman than to lay bare his soul to her. Women, on the other hand, seek intimacy when they fall in love, but too often assume they know men's thoughts and feelings.

With such different approaches is it any wonder that the two sexes frequently end up frustrated, confused and disappointed in each other? In this book top relationship counsellor Zelda West-Meads reveals:

- why men and women speak almost different languages
- how to handle the differences between you positively
- the secrets of making love last

Zelda West-Meads has been a counsellor and psycho-sexual -therapist for Relate for more than twenty years. As Relate's former spokeswoman she put counselling on the map, making it accessible and acceptable instead of an embarrassment to admit to. She broadcasts frequently and has a regular weekly advice column in YOU magazine.

HODDER AND STOUGHTON PAPERBACKS

END THE STRUGGLE AND DANCE WITH LIFE

From the author of the bestselling classic FEEL THE FEAR
AND DO IT ANYWAY comes a book of inspirational advice
to heal the spirit and lift the weight of the world.

We live in a difficult world. No doubt about it. But life does
not have to be a struggle. We can move into the flow of our
experiences – good or bad – with a feeling of harmony, trust,
gratitude and love. This is the message contained in END
THE STRUGGLE AND DANCE WITH LIFE.

Dr Susan Jeffers, whose previous books have touched millions
throughout the world, provides the tools and concepts that
show us how to feel calmer, more in control, and excited
about life. With wisdom, humour and clarity, she opens our
eyes to what pulls us down and what lifts us up. END THE
STRUGGLE AND DANCE WITH LIFE is an invaluable
source of insight and practical guidance that inspires us to
create a life filled with peace, joy and abundance.

> '*I highly recommend this book.*'
> Deepak Chopra

> '*Susan Jeffers is a master of healing and this new books is a
> gem. Her way of looking at life is an inspiration to us all.*'
> Louise Hay, author of *The Power is Within You*

> '*A must read book! Susan Jeffers' advice is wise
> and wonderful.*'
> Marianne Williamson, author of *Illuminata*

HODDER AND STOUGHTON PAPERBACKS